Normative Transformation and the War on Terrorism

Pratt investigates the potential erosion of prohibiting assassination, torture, and mercenarism during the US War on Terrorism. In examining the emergence and history of the US targeted killing programme, detention and interrogation programme, and employment of armed contractors in war zones, he proposes that a 'normative transformation' has occurred that has changed the meaning and content of these prohibitions, even though they still exist. Drawing on pragmatist philosophy, practice theory, and relational sociology, this book develops a new theory of normativity and institutional change and offers new data about the decisions and activities of security practitioners. It is both a critical and a constructive addition to the current literature on norm change, and it addresses enduring debates about the role of culture and ethical judgement in the use of force. It will appeal to students and scholars of foreign and defence policy, international relations theory, international security, social theory, and American politics.

SIMON FRANKEL PRATT is a Lecturer in Political Science in the School of Social and Political Sciences at the University of Melbourne. His recent articles have appeared in journals including *International Theory*, *International Studies Quarterly*, *European Journal of International Relations*, *International Studies Review*, and *Terrorism and Political Violence*.

T0384765

Normative Transformation and the War on Terrorism

The Evolution of Targeted Killing, Torture, and Private Military Contracting

SIMON FRANKEL PRATT
University of Melbourne

CAMBRIDGE
UNIVERSITY PRESS

CAMBRIDGE
UNIVERSITY PRESS

Shaftesbury Road, Cambridge CB2 8EA, United Kingdom

One Liberty Plaza, 20th Floor, New York, NY 10006, USA

477 Williamstown Road, Port Melbourne, VIC 3207, Australia

314–321, 3rd Floor, Plot 3, Splendor Forum, Jasola District Centre, New Delhi – 110025, India

103 Penang Road, #05–06/07, Visioncrest Commercial, Singapore 238467

Cambridge University Press is part of Cambridge University Press & Assessment, a department of the University of Cambridge.

We share the University's mission to contribute to society through the pursuit of education, learning and research at the highest international levels of excellence.

www.cambridge.org
Information on this title: www.cambridge.org/9781009096461

DOI: 10.1017/9781009092326

First published 2022
First paperback edition 2023

A catalogue record for this publication is available from the British Library

Library of Congress Cataloging-in-Publication data
Names: Pratt, Simon Frankel, author.
Title: Normative transformation and the War on Terrorism : the evolution of targeted killing, torture, and private military contracting / Simon Frankel Pratt, University of Bristol.
Description: Cambridge, United Kingdom ; New York, NY : Cambridge University Press, 2022. | Includes bibliographical references and index.
Identifiers: LCCN 2021045489 (print) | LCCN 2021045490 (ebook) | ISBN 9781316515174 (hardback) | ISBN 9781009096461 (paperback) | ISBN 9781009092326 (ebook)
Subjects: LCSH: Security, International – Moral and ethical aspects. | War on Terrorism, 2001–2009. |Normativity (Ethics) | Soft law. | Social norms. | Terrorism– Prevention – Moral and ethical aspects. | United States – Foreign relations – 21st century. | United States – Military policy. | BISAC: POLITICAL SCIENCE / International Relations / General
Classification: LCC JZ5588 .P73 2022 (print) | LCC JZ5588 (ebook) | DDC 355.033–dc23
LC record available at https://lccn.loc.gov/2021045489
LC ebook record available at https://lccn.loc.gov/2021045490

ISBN   978-1-316-51517-4   Hardback
ISBN   978-1-009-09646-1   Paperback

Contents

Figures and Tables

Figures

Tables

Preface

Normative change is an undeniably important part of international politics, but international relations theory has long struck me as disconnected from the experience of those whose actions produce it. For practitioners, ethical concerns are interwoven with instrumental ones in ways that sometimes don't lend themselves to the distinction between acting based on 'norms' and acting based on 'rational calculations'. All too often, commentators have presented the dilemmas of security and state violence as ones of *either* moral *or* strategic decisions, where the choice available is to either be good or be effective. In political philosophy, this has produced a long discourse over the virtues of restraint in war through the establishment of prohibitions – on technologies such as gas, nuclear weapons, or landmines and on targets such as prisoners, the injured, or the very young. In social science, it has led to a binaristic debate amongst those studying such prohibitions, between those who claim the social world is built out of plastic, historically situated cultural standards and those who think it is a reflection of material exigencies. Restraint: is it a value we hold, or cynical adherence to laws to avoid the consequences of violating them? We all know it's more complicated than that, but finding a conceptually useful way to articulate how is a challenge. I think one way of doing so can be found in pragmatist philosophy, relational sociology, and theories of practice.

The 'Global War on Terror' the United States waged in the aftermath of the 9/11 terrorist attacks represented, for many, a complete abandonment of principles of restraint and respect for human rights in the conduct of war. Journalistic investigations and government disclosures revealed a system of targeted killing, torture, and privatised military violence, outrageous not just to many of the Americans in whose defence these activities were supposedly committed but to many in the world as a whole. Scholars and activists have sought to clarify what happened and how, as part of the critical project of holding perpetrators accountable and supporting future methods of pursuing security without causing undue harm. This problem – of managing the 'monster' of the state and its security apparatus – is what gives us the concrete need for helpful ways of understanding what normativity is and how it conditions political violence.

My book is part of this intellectual and political project. It is not an exercise in abstraction, and I am not dogmatically committed to the metatheoretical claims I make here, even though I hope to establish pragmatism as a valuable school of explanatory and normative thought in the field. I do not claim to know what is *really true* about the nature of reality and the shape of society. My goal is to provide a conceptual and analytical basis for explaining changes in practices of security and war so that, if we want them to change for the better, we understand the process by which that could happen.

So, many people helped me write this book. It began as a PhD dissertation at the University of Toronto, and my greatest debt is to my doctoral supervisor, mentor, and friend, Emanuel Adler. I walked into his office in my second year of grad school, asked if he would be interested in supervising a project that studied normative change from a pragmatist perspective, and he agreed. I do not know what kind of scholar I'd be if he'd declined, but I am sure it would be a less thoughtful one. I am also greatly indebted to my other doctoral supervisors, Matthew Hoffmann and Robert Brym. Both had formative influences on this project and were everything I could hope for from committee members: patient, open-minded, kind yet critical, and, most importantly, fast with feedback.

During and after my PhD, other scholars have also generously supported me, offering advice, feedback on my work, and friendship within the field. From the start of my doctoral studies all the way to strategic questions about publishers and impact, Patrick Thaddeus Jackson has been an especially active source of these things. Without any institutional obligation or formal supervisory relationship, he read much of my work and joined me in many conference panels where I refined it. Several peers have also had a pivotal role in the writing of this book. First and foremost among them is Joseph Mackay, who read every chapter twice (at least) and gave endless advice and support with revisions throughout the writing process. Everyone should be blessed with such a colleague. Christopher David LaRoche is another steadfast friend and colleague whose intellectual influence has been tremendous. Through our collaborations and our many long discussions over drinks, I developed the perspectives on normativity, security, and theory that now fill these pages. I also am so grateful to Christian Büger, Steven Bernstein, Laura Sjoberg, Daniel Nexon, David Welch, Lucas Dolan, Sebastian Schmidt, and Maika Sondarjee for the ways they have helped me clarify my ideas.

I also am grateful to John Haslam and the rest of the editorial and publishing team at Cambridge University Press, who have not once shown any frustration or hesitation in the face of my ignorance of the academic publishing process, and who ensured I survived this process with the desire to go through it again. I also owe significant debts to two anonymous reviewers, whose advice and constructive criticism are now reflected in every page. I also thank the editors and publishers of *International Theory* (Cambridge University Press) and the *European Journal of International Relations* (Sage) for allowing me to reproduce and expand on work I previously published with them. Chapters 3 and 4 contain material from my 2019 article 'Norm Transformation and the Institutionalisation of Targeted Killing in the United States', *European Journal of International Relation* 25(3): 723–47; Chapters 2 and 3 contain material from my 2020 article 'From Norms to Normative Configurations: A Pragmatist and Relational Approach to Theorising Normativity in IR', *International Theory* 12(1): 59–82.

Several academic institutions enabled my research through funding and hosting. I am grateful to the Social Sciences and Humanities Research Council of Canada, to the School of International Service at American University, and to the University of Toronto's School of Graduate Studies and Department of Political Science.

Lastly, I am grateful to my field: there is a lot about the study of international politics that I find frustrating, some that I find upsetting, but even more that I find important, meaningful, and stimulating. I am grateful to the many unnamed colleagues who have invested countless years of frustration and thought to the problems I take up here, whose writing has influenced me, who have engaged me in conversation, joined me in conference panels and seminar rooms, and welcomed me to their academic community. It is my honour and privilege to join them, and I hope to help them make a difference in the world.

I dedicate the book to my mother, Naomi Frankel, who taught me how to ask questions, how to write, and how to stand in solidarity.

1 | Introduction

Normative Transformation, Prohibitions, and International Politics

The corporate view inside CIA was 'We don't want to do covert action. And if we do covert action, we want it to be neat and clean. We don't want to be involved in killing people. Because we're not like that. We're not Mossad.'

Richard Clarke[1]

We tortured some folks.

Barack Obama[2]

1.1 Introduction to the Introduction

This is a book about norms: how they change and how they work; how they shape who does what, to whom, and how. It is also a book about innovation: creative attempts by practitioners to surmount strategic and ethical obstacles, in the process developing new ways of acting and being. Finally, it is a book about institutions and organisations and about how institutional culture and authority shapes practice and is, in turn, reshaped by it. It is about all these things because they are all parts of the huge, deeply contentious transformation that has taken place in US foreign and defence policy since 2001 as part of its global 'war on terrorism'. This book is devoted to explaining why and how a state can radically change its practices surrounding the use of violence in pursuit of national security objectives, in ways that at first glance imply counternormative, transgressive violations of established international and domestic prohibitions. It offers an account of the evolution of the US

---

[1] Quoted in Mazzetti (2013).
[2] See https://obamawhitehouse.archives.gov/the-press-office/2014/08/01/press-conference-president.

security apparatus to encompass new understandings of what counts as ethical, professional, proportional, and appropriate counterterrorism.

From the start of the millennium, the United States has engaged in counterterrorism and military activities that many observers consider to be prohibited, illegitimate, or otherwise contrary to prevailing international norms. Using unmanned aircraft, the CIA began targeting and killing specific persons as part of a massive, and still ongoing, paramilitarisation of their duties as the country's primary foreign intelligence service. Concurrently, the CIA also began a smaller, but no less significant, programme to detain and interrogate suspected members of terrorist groups, in ways that many observers, including President Barack Obama, have explicitly referred to as torture. Finally, private military and security contractors have increasingly taken on combatant duties that previously would have only been performed by uniformed and official military personnel, in ways that appear to many to be mercenarism. All this has been despite prohibitions on assassination, torture, and the use of mercenaries having been enshrined in domestic law, international convention, and institutional culture.

This change was not merely a matter of strategic need or instrumental re-evaluation of what was most efficient or effective counterterrorism. Significant actors involved in these practices pushed back against them or expressed scepticism towards them on normative grounds, articulating concerns over what was right or proper. They did so by referring not just to laws but to embedded institutional norms, organisational history, and past experience of scandal, professionalism, and other dynamics warranting focused sociological investigation. These cases – targeted killing, torture, and the employment of armed private contractors – thus raise an important and interesting question: how did the prohibited so quickly become the permissible?

I argue that previously prohibited practices emerge as a result of the situated problem-solving attempts of practitioners whose existing practices do not allow them to surmount pressing strategic and ethical obstacles. To do this, practitioners weave together ethical and strategic reasoning, in ways that cannot be explained through theories of decision-making that isolate one single logic of action. The outcome is that new practices become *institutionalised*: they became ongoing components of formal and informal social arrangements, gaining legitimacy from their position within broader authority structures and becoming part of the expected and reproduced array of activities associated with a particular role or profession. This process of institutionalisation is the concrete manifestation of normative transformation – whether or not it revolves around any single 'norm'.

Drawing on insights from relational sociology and pragmatist social theory, I show that practices – and prohibitions – transform as a result of three linked processes. The first is the redefinition of actions so that they are repositioned or displaced within existing conventional social arrangements, termed *convention reorientation*. The second is the employment of new technologies in ways that reconstitute users and change the choices available to them, termed *technological revision*. The third is the production of new authorities in existing institutional networks through the formation of new bureaucratic relationships, termed *network synthesis*.

I also argue that prohibitions range across whole constellations of institutionally embedded norms – what I term 'normative configurations' – and that they exist *in practice*. That is, *prohibitions are not ontologically distinct from the activities they regulate*, and, rather than being defined as discrete social objects ('norms'), they should be conceptualised as part of the normative dimension of action itself. This perspective clarifies the causal processes underlying how norms influence, and are influenced by, the conduct of war and policymaking. It reveals the way those three mechanisms of change transform the normative commitments of practitioners, linking macro-level cultural and ethical imperatives to the specific activities of bureaucrats, legal experts, politicians, and security personnel.

In this book I use a pragmatist approach to explain how targeted killing, torture (euphemistically termed 'enhanced interrogation'), and the employment of armed private military and security contractors all became institutionalised practices within the security apparatus of the United States, despite international prohibitions on assassination, torture, and mercenarism. I argue that the nature of post-9/11 security threats and the executive preferences of the Bush and Obama administrations generated new 'problem situations' for the US security apparatus. Executive support for bellicose counterterrorism, the rise of a military, legal, and operational logic to counterterrorist policy, and the development of sophisticated armed unmanned aerial vehicles led to the development of an extensive targeted killing programme within the CIA and, to a lesser degree, the military. The willingness of the Bush administration to approve aggressive intelligence-gathering measures and provide legal cover for them, along with the development of a new psychological science of interrogation through inducing 'learned helplessness' in detainees, led to the development of a detention and interrogation programme within the CIA, with some of its practices further diffusing into military interrogations as well. The needs of US administrators and government departments in the war zones of Afghanistan and Iraq, permissive post-invasion legal environments, and developments in communications and organisational technologies led to the extensive use of private contractors to perform security duties that would otherwise be performed by uniformed military personnel.

In all cases, apparent and applicable norms were reinterpreted and revised in the process of transformations in practice. This is in large part what makes them confusing. For scholars of international politics, it is usually not surprising when states respond to escalating threats with escalating violence or adopt less restrained foreign and defence policies to navigate more dangerous environments. This is consistent with rationalist and realist views about strategy and security. Yet thirty years of constructivist scholarship has established that there are notable exceptions to this expectation, in cases where principled restraint supersedes the choice to employ greater force. Given the prior existence of established prohibitions, formal and informal, against assassination, torture, and mercenarism, all three of the cases I examine in this book are, so to speak, exceptions to the exception; they involve a shift from principled restraint to something more permissive, and the puzzle lies in how that was possible.

A second puzzle lies in the fact that the present-day trajectory of these three cases indicates different degrees of transformation, in practice and in prohibition. Targeted killing seems to now be not only an established, normal feature of the US security apparatus but also a relatively routine practice for the United Kingdom – and while it has long been so for Israel, it has become more common since the United States ceased to disapprove of it. In other words, a transformation of practice that began primarily within the United States has since been replicated in other countries. On the other end of the spectrum, 'enhanced interrogation' has been largely eschewed by practitioners within the US security apparatus, with its associated practices and claims to normative legitimacy undermined and rolled back by internal bureaucratic and legislative opposition. Moreover, other countries allied with the United States have not set up similar programmes of violent interrogation – either they already had such programmes or they lacked the bureaucratic and normative impetus to establish them. Private military and security contractors are deployed in much smaller numbers now that the US military expeditions in Afghanistan and Iraq have largely ended, while industry-led self-regulation has by and large ended the prevalence of private combatants, but their employment in armed security duties is nevertheless now an established fixture of US government operations in a wide range of locales. Other countries also began to employ armed contractors in increasingly greater numbers during the 'Global War on Terror' years, but none in such numbers or with such integration with government agencies and forces as the United States. There is, therefore, a sense in which the United States both led the way and led the pack in these practices. And overall, while the pattern of transformation was thus the same in all three cases – an interaction of the mechanisms of convention reorientation, technological revision, and network synthesis – they vary in the extent to which the transformations are robust, institutionalised, and uncontested.

1.2 Norm Transformation and the Puzzle of Apparent Prohibition Demise

The standard narrative of the US war on terrorism is one of progressive erosion of legal and moral restraint, as military commitments intensified and security interests crystallised into a bellicose unilateralism of boundless geographic scope. On this account, the United States was shocked to the core by the attacks of 11 September 2001. Facing unprecedent domestic casualties and a public in need of reassurance, the Bush administration quickly launched a major military campaign in Afghanistan, on the grounds that the Taliban regime bore partial responsibility for al-Qa'ida's actions since it was harbouring the group and was unwilling to expel it. Simultaneous to this military operation, the United States unleashed a rapidly expanding CIA to find and unravel, anywhere in the world, al-Qa'ida's networks. Grappling with the difficulty of this task both inside Afghanistan and in unfamiliar locales across South Asia and the Middle East, the US security apparatus, under direction from the Bush administration, resorted to increasingly brutal and counter-normative means, employing torture, extraordinary rendition, and assassination. The 2003 invasion of Iraq constituted a major escalation in this process and appeared to many to indicate a kind of crusade, with the menace of terrorism, the religion of Islam, and the region of the Middle East collectively forming a new battleground in which the standards of Just War Theory were unrealistic or inapplicable (Crawford 2003). Fighting two difficult wars, the US security apparatus began, intellectually, to draw upon colonial and Cold War–era theories of counterinsurgency, while it bureaucratically came to rely heavily on proxies, in the form of armed private military contractors and allied regimes, which together offered the additional manpower and local presence that the US lacked. As these processes accelerated and then solidified, the outcome was a new normative environment and a new arrangement of security, military, and regulatory institutions.

In this account, certain moments or manifestations became emblematic of the new realities of the war on terrorism: the CIA's 'black sites' and use of waterboarding, along with detention sites at Guantanamo Bay and, after 2003, Abu Ghraib; the spectre of remote-controlled aircraft ('drones') dropping bombs on unsuspecting targets, selected in secret procedures, not just in Iraq but also in the undeclared warzones of north-western Pakistan and Yemen – and later, north and north-eastern Africa; armed mercenaries firing into crowds of unarmed protestors in Baghdad; and, throughout this process, the increasing digitisation of the US intelligence apparatus, with expanding surveillance capacities threatening civil liberties at home and filling the sky abroad with cameras and missiles. Together, these images, and the account that gives them context, imply a major shift in what right and wrong uses of force look like – and what is acceptable for a 'liberal' country to do in the name of national security.

Given the evident normative dimension to the development of the US war on terrorism, and in particular the apparent erosion or demise of prohibitions that once were extensive and strong, the literature on 'norm change' seems like an obvious place to look for an explanation. One helpful way of understanding the history and direction of this research programme is to conceive of it in terms of waves. The first wave, mainly spanning the 1990s and early 2000s (see, among others, Kratochwil and Ruggie 1986; Kratochwil 1989; Nadelmann 1990; Barkin and Cronin 1994; Finnemore 1996a; 1996b; Katzenstein 1996), sought mainly to establish the salience of a normative dimension to the conduct of international politics. By the end of the 1990s, scholars were developing complex models of the 'life cycles' of norms (Finnemore and Sikkink 1998) and of the reasons why some norms endure while others disappear or fail to become prominent in the first place (see, among others, Klotz 1995; Keck and Sikkink 1998). Beginning in the early 2000s, a second wave of norms scholarship studied how existing norms manifest in varying ways and how norm-compliance differs across contexts (Hoffmann 2010; for examples, see, among others, Shannon 2000; Acharya 2004; Cortell and Davis 2005; Sandholtz 2008; Wiener 2004; 2008; Krook and True 2012). The most recent scholarship on norms continues this trend of further excavating the role of local agency (Bucher 2014) and reaches for increasingly sophisticated sociological perspectives on the dynamics of contestation and creativity within disputes over norms (Kornprobst 2007; Wiener 2008; 2014; Schmidt 2014) – the first moves towards an emerging third wave of scholarship on the causal role of norms in IR.

Despite their diversity, most norms scholars agree on some basic things. Early work varied somewhat on the definition of a norm but converged on a view best (and popularly) summarised by the definition of norms as 'standard[s] of appropriate behavior for actors with a given identity' (Keck and Sikkink 1998, 891), with both a subjective and intersubjective dimension (Hoffmann 2010), shaping actors' moral opinions and featuring in processes of socialisation and social regulation, respectively. According to this view, norms are features of the social world that guide people in how to live and make up the context for much of their life in the first place. A consequence of this definition is that norms are treated as discrete, causally efficacious objects – as 'things' (cf. Krook and True 2012). That is, norms – however subject to contestation and transformation – exert themselves upon the world; they possess an influence as independent or irreducible objects in our social ontology and thus can play a role in claims of cause and effect. Moreover, while some second-wave norms scholarship assigns a local and fluid existence to norms-as-objects, many scholars still grant norms a great deal of autonomy across social time and space. In other words, norms exist as travelling units of moral information, embodied in social and psychological form, influencing the course of things.

Yet this understanding of norms is problematic for understanding the apparent erosion or rollback of prohibitions. Norms research has theorised the emergence and spread of prohibitions, such as on nuclear weapons (Tannenwald 1999), chemical weapons (Price 1995), and slavery (Keck and Sikkink 1998), but this work is preoccupied mainly with when states *restrain themselves* from particular forms of violence, rather than the reverse. The small number of scholars who have considered this phenomenon have mainly framed it as the 'death' of norms – for it follows that if norms have a life cycle, then they can die – suggesting that actions in apparent violation of prohibitions have occurred because those prohibitions ceased to exist. However, as an empirical fact, those responsible for targeted killing, coercive interrogation, and the use of private military and security contractors all aver the continued existence and legitimacy of prohibitions on assassination, torture, and mercenarism. They have not argued that the relevant norms are improper or wrong; they have instead claimed that their actions do not actually fall under the prohibitions. In other words, normative contestation in these cases has not been over whether assassination, torture, and mercenarism should be permissible or prohibited but rather over what these activities actually are in practice.[3] This shows evolution in the normative scope of these prohibitions: a change in the reference-relation between the articulatable principles or values associated with a given prohibition and the situational ways in which it informs right, virtuous, and appropriate conduct.

To propose that 'norm death' has occurred in these cases is therefore to take a side in an interpretive dispute that the relevant actors themselves have not yet settled, because their dispute is over what the relevant norm means, with one 'side' claiming that it continues to exist more or less unchanged. Scholars claiming otherwise are imposing their evaluative judgements on social processes as though they are objective categories, reifying analytical distinctions into supposedly independent states of affairs. This also does not accord with the evidence, which shows that involved actors raised continued normative objections and

---

[3] For example, some claim that the CIA's interrogation practices indicate the demise of the norm prohibiting torture (McKeown 2009; Panke and Petersohn 2011). More recent claims by both President Obama (2014) and prominent legislators (see Dianne Feinstein in *The Committee Study of the Central Intelligence Agency's Detention and Interrogation Program* [2014]) that such practices were both torture and wrong suggest that rumours of 'norm-death' were in this case greatly exaggerated. Yet, many of those responsible for the CIA's interrogation programme contend both charges – denying that interrogations were ineffective and that they were torture – while affirming the illegitimacy of torture as such (Harlow 2015).

justifications throughout, implying the continued existence of meaningful norms with regulative force. In other words, normative *transformation* is also, here, normative *evolution*. Extant theories of norm dynamics, even those that directly tackle the issue of 'norm deterioration' (see, for example, McKeown 2009; Panke and Petersohn 2011), along with attempts to tackle the interpretive and pragmatic evolution of *norms as such* (Schmidt 2014; Hofferberth and Weber 2015), therefore also lack the apparatus for explaining the institutional changes that have taken place in the three cases I study in this book. This means scholars must remain methodologically agnostic as to whether old norms have 'died' and been replaced by new ones and instead must trace how norms have changed.

The primary approach IR scholars have taken to norms makes this task difficult. This approach has tended to be oriented around one specific conception of 'norms' – namely, as discrete social entities, sometimes called 'ideational' in contrast with 'material', which have the ability to influence behaviour as such. Here lies a problem: this view has facilitated a progressive theoretical research programme in the field, but it is focused on the genesis of major new regulative or normative regimes, rather than more specific changes in how those regimes are institutionalised. These nevertheless can have significant consequences, as shown by the contentious counterterrorism activities I am discussing. Recent and ambitious contributions challenge these horizons but are still held within them. They are unable to escape the constraints of theorising *norms as an assumed theoretical category* and are oriented more towards outlining methods of analysis rather than proposing substantive explanatory mechanisms.

Another way to say this is that 'norms' are reifications. Reification is a discursive move that denotes institutions as objects rather than periods, places, or episodes of stability in an unfolding arrangement of relationships and practices. Lukács, in his 1923 essay on reification, defined this as when 'a relation between people takes on the character of a thing and thus acquires a "phantom objectivity"' (1971, 83). Giddens (1984) cautioned against it as well: '[Reification] refers to the 'facticity' with which social phenomena confront individual actors in such as way as to ignore how they are produced and reproduced through human agency' (180). This does not necessary make 'norms' worthless concepts, as theories are built from abstractions that simplify and summarise the world for the sake of explanatory efficiency. But it does suggest that normativity can matter in ways not captured by the concept of 'norms' as such. For example, there are settings where actors themselves do not orient their actions around norms, or they do so in ways that nevertheless are more fruitfully understood with a more processual and less substantivist vocabulary for talking about normativity than as the force exerted by unit norms. In other words, theories oriented around changes in 'norms' may be unable to offer the conceptual architecture to properly describe the kind of change that has occurred, nor how it happened.

The solution I advance here *de-reifies* 'norms' into the configurations of institutionalised relationships and practices that constitute them. By 'de-reify', I mean the redescription of 'norms' as granular arrangements of conventions, values, and routines of action spanning multiple legal, bureaucratic, and legislative fields.[4] It is a reversal of reification: instead of objectifying and concretising processes of institutional evolution, imagining them to be sociocultural 'things' with independent properties, I redefine the object in terms of sets of ongoing practices and relations that generate normativity. To do this, I develop the alternative concept of 'normative configuration', and, by using it to account for the ways valuation, disciplining, and contestation proceed in practice, I find a way of re-accounting for putative norms in non-objectified and non-concretised terms. I focus on the ways practices are structured and restructured around internal normativity and thus how innovation in practice is not only strategic or ends-oriented but also an attempt to navigate ethical dilemmas as well. I connect shifts in the forms of violence that are internationally permitted and prohibited to *concrete, problem-driven transformations* in how those within the US security apparatus defined and carried out their roles, dealt with contestation

---

[4] By 'routines' I mean actions that are standardised, normalised, often partially habituated so that they are performed without active reflection or conscious intent, and associated with a practice or position rather than personal idiosyncrasy. The closest alternative term might be 'repertoire', which conveys some of these traits but carries a greater connotation of choice and instrumentality. I have preferred 'routines' for two reasons. One is simply that 'repertoires' has a particular meaning within the voluminous literature on social movements (see McAdam et al. 2001), and I do not want to digress into this literature to ensure readers do not confuse my use of the term with how it is used there. The second is that 'routines' capture the enacted and processual nature of normativity in action. They are not bodies of knowledge, sometimes drawn on and sometimes held in store, but unfolding operations in, and on, the world.

from internal and external opponents, and oriented themselves within their institutional environments.

1.3 Plan of the Book

This book seeks to show that transformations of prohibitions on particular kinds of state violence are best explained through theories oriented around practitioner-driven innovation and contestation. In the first part of the book, I develop a theoretical and methodological approach for conceptualising the normativity of practice and for specifying the mechanisms by which it changes in form. In the second part, I examine the cases of targeted killing, interrogation, and use of private military and security contractors as cases of normative transformation through linked moral and strategic problem-solving.

Chapter 2 presents a theory of normativity. I begin by examining what theories of normativity (and norms) are supposed to explain, arguing that, in these theories, 'norms' are reified conceptual abstractions separating out the ethical dimensions of action and assigning them independent causal capacities. Drawing on pragmatist and relational social theory, I develop the alternative concept of 'normative configurations' as a way to understand how normativity operates and changes. I rest the concept of normative configurations on four premises: that normativity is embedded in action (rather than being distinct from it); that normativity provides both ends and means for action (rather than providing only ends); that normativity links ends and means recursively (rather than ends influencing means but not vice versa); and that normativity crystallises into institutional arrangements through the stabilisation of practices (rather than through discursive or formal constitutive processes independent from practice). Together these premises can orient investigations of normative changes without referencing the movements or life cycles of norms. In other words, in this chapter I explain what is involved in conceptualising prohibitions as 'normative configurations' rather than as 'norms' and when this makes for more satisfying theories of practice and action.

Chapter 3 lays out three specific mechanisms denoting the causal processes of normative transformation in the three cases I investigate, as well as a three-step methodology for analysing them. My proposal is that what may appear from the outside to be 'norm death' is the outcome of practitioners engaging in problem-solving through attempts at reframing contentious issues and actions, finding new technological aides, and navigating bureaucratic politics. These attempts drive the operation of the mechanisms of convention reorientation, technological revision, and network synthesis. I then outline how to structure case-specific data to map out a given normative configuration, identify where its potential for transformation lies – essentially, where actors are most likely to need to innovate upon it – and trace, over time, how a transformation was brought about. Finally, I discuss the types of data that may be employed for this form of analysis and how the particular challenges of data collection in the study of often-covert security institutions has led me to prefer some kinds of data over others.

Chapter 4 examines the case of targeted killing and the prohibition on assassination. I find that the (international) prohibition on assassination was institutionalised within the US security apparatus primarily through executive orders and informal standards of professionalism within the CIA, revolving around civil–military relations and the separation of military functions from the intelligence services. The prohibition also rested on military laws and ethical standards defining assassination as perfidious or dishonourable. Following the 11 September 2001 terrorist attacks, the executive and legislative environment for counterterrorism changed, establishing both pressures and permissions for the CIA, by way of its internal counterterrorism unit, to develop the capacity to target and kill specific individuals, primarily outside of areas where broader expeditions of US forces were deployed. By redefining its counterterrorism function as (para) military rather than civilian, by employing (and pushing for the further development of) armed unmanned aerial vehicles (UAVs), and by forging new alliances with friendly officials in the Bush administration, the CIA developed a robust targeted killing programme, undergoing a bureaucratic transformation in the process. Under the Obama administration, this transformation intensified, even as by this time targeted killing operations were also being performed by uniformed military units. During this second phase, targeted killing underwent additional legal and organisational formalisation, institutionalising it within the structure of the US security apparatus. As a result, both the practices of targeting and the prohibition on assassination changed.

Chapter 5 examines the case of the CIA's detention and interrogation activities and their relationship to the prohibition on torture.

This prohibition was affirmed in a broad array of domestic and international legal commitments, as well as in the institutional culture of the FBI, which until then had been the USA's primary agency responsible for conducting counterterrorism interrogations. With both pressure and permission from the Bush administration to step up its human intelligence-gathering capabilities and to take the lead on a more bellicose, global approach to counterterrorism, the CIA began experimenting with methods that would previously have been normatively proscribed. I find that in addition to executive facilitation, a key technological process drove this transformation: the establishment of a new 'science' of interrogation based around 'learned helplessness'. This in turn allowed proponents of coercive or violent interrogation to frame what they were doing as something other than torture, thereby continuing to affirm the torture prohibition while engaging in actions that would previously have been prohibited under it. Unlike in the case of targeted killing, however, the Obama administration sought to reverse this change in practice and reassert the torture prohibition. Assisted by negative publicity and mounting evidence of inefficacy and scientific illegitimacy, the mechanisms of normative transformation at work in this case, I find, did not result in robust institutionalisation, and thus the normative configuration establishing the prohibition largely reverted to its status quo ante.

Chapter 6 examines the case of the USA's extensive employment of armed private military and security contractors to perform 'combat-like' duties in the war zones of Afghanistan and Iraq, despite international prohibitions on mercenarism. This change in practice is not just particular to the United States, but the United States has nevertheless been, by a considerable margin, the most enthusiastic employer (and provider) of such contractors. I find that this normative transformation began with the urgent need for manpower in the occupation and reconstruction phases of the wars in Afghanistan and Iraq – and in particular the need for armed protection details to guard buildings and offer protection to convoys. As contractors flooded the two war zones, military and government officials restructured their chains of command and communication, improving flows of information, learning to coordinate operations, and developing professional standards to regulate the industry. The current global state of affairs does not feature many private military and security contractors deployed in identical ways to uniformed soldiers, and thus the prohibition on mercenarism has clearly not gone. However, both within the United States and elsewhere, armed contractors are now a normal part of stability operations, and thus a clear change in practice and in prohibition has nevertheless occurred.

Finally, Chapter 7 offers some conclusions about normative transformations, prohibitions, and the study of practices – not only with respect to the state and violence but also beyond both. First, I compare my case-specific findings to develop some meta-level analytical and methodological observations. I also connect my findings, which are generally focused on changes specific to the US defence and foreign policy apparatuses, to the broader issue of the normative status of assassination, torture, and mercenarism in international perspective. I argue that there are some insights about the current state of international prohibitions that can be drawn from an examination of their role and status in the US security apparatus, even without examining the contemporary policies and practices of other states. Second, I discuss how my approach to conceptualising and tracing normative transformations can be used to study transnational communities and global non-state governance, which are two significant areas of study in the field that lie outside the usual category of norms scholarship. Third and lastly, I discuss two normative implications of my findings, pertaining to the ethics of counterterrorism as a matter of practical ethics and to the relationship between facts and values as a matter of meta-ethics. Ultimately, I claim that a practice-centric, pragmatist, and relational approach to normativity promises to open up a wider range of social processes for analysis, and this is of value to scholars, practitioners, and activists in a number of areas.

2 | A Theory of Normativity

2.1 Introduction

The value of a pragmatist and relational view of normativity lies in two contributions. The first is that it escapes the 'co-constitutionalist' binary that is ontologically embedded in most existing IR theories of norms. Co-constitutionalist theories envision a world where norms are discrete social structures that are reflexively or recursively linked to the agency of individual actors. In other words, norms shape what people do and then in turn are shaped by those doings. This approach makes a great deal of sense in considering major revisions in how states conduct themselves, such as the emergence of movements for total bans on particular kinds of weapons or for an end to institutionalised practices such as slavery.[1] It makes less sense, however, when actors deny that a new norm has emerged, even when they have embraced new practices that would previously have been widely considered counter-normative. It also makes less sense when it is unclear to scholarly observers whether a norm is being violated, whether it has disappeared entirely, or whether it has changed in referent even if not in name. For cases such as these, clarity and analytical purchase is best found in breaking 'norms' down into their component social parts.

The second contribution is that it revises the vocabulary of IR theories about norms in ways that connect with cutting-edge constructivist research on practices and relations. This comes from a thorough overhaul in how to conceive of normativity, agency, and change, shifting the analytical focus away from the socially embedded individual and towards social arrangements or 'figurations'.[2] Growing bodies

---

[1] On these, see Price (1995); Tannenwald (1999); Keck and Sikkink (1998).
[2] Norbert Elias' concept of 'figuration' (1994; see also 1978) situates normativity within a wide span of processes and relations, from the psychology of face-to-face interaction to the workings of national bureaucracies and international affairs.

of scholarship employ terms such as 'practices', 'performances', 'fields', and related ontological terms that locate drivers of transformation not in the sensibilities or dispositions of decision-makers socialised to want or feel certain culturally appropriate things but in how ways of life and ways of knowing cohere in action – and where *action* does not resolve neatly into *actors*.[3] The existing terms of the norms research programme contain assumptions – again traceable to a co-constitutionalist ontology – that are in tension with these other approaches, and the introduction of new terms sustains the existing insights of norms research while allowing for the more diverse production of novel ones.

In this chapter, I lay out the concept of the *normative configuration* as one such alternative, defined as an arrangement of ongoing, interacting practices establishing action-specific regulation, value-orientation, and avenues of contestation. All 'norms' are normative configurations, and while analytical benefits can and have accrued from their 'arrestation' (Jackson and Nexon 1999) into a social object, these benefits are contingent upon historically particular case features. In other words, only in some situations is arrestation a reasonable and helpful analytical move. Scholars should also be able to break norms down into their constituent, moving relations – de-reified – and explore their normativity itself as the outcome of particular kinds of practices and processes that may be rearranged in a wide range of ways. My goal is to provide a new analytical architecture for theorising normative transformations in cases where the status and content of norms appear to change in ways that are hard to understand in terms of old norms, new norms, norm emergence, norm cascades, and other such norms-talk familiar to the field.

I present this alternative in three sections. First, I discuss the state of IR literature on norms and how it is unable to adequately account for the normative dynamics that are evident in the cases I examine in this book. Second, I draw on pragmatist and relational social theory to propose as a new alternative the concept of the normative arrangement and situate it within broader IR discussions of order, normativity, and change. This should provide a meta-theoretical framework specifically designed for analysing normative transformations within institutions

---

[3] Indeed, this is why Actor–Network Theories have advanced the alternative term 'actant' (Latour 2005).

of government.[4] Third, I position the alternative I propose within existing social theoretical literature on the explanatory and ontological role of norms (and cognate concepts) and the IR scholarship that literature has informed, connecting the critique and revision of norms scholarship I propose to broader shifts within the field, mainly in the study of practices.

2.2 Theoretical Approaches to Norm Change in International Relations

Normativity interests scholars across the fields of the social sciences and humanities. The term 'norm', in various forms, enjoys widespread currency not just in sociology and political science but in philosophy, psychology, economics, and anthropology, carrying a range of overlapping meanings both within and across these fields. Broadly, 'norms' may refer to values, mores, conventions, identities, classificatory schema, shared expectations of behaviour, and associated practices (Cancian 1975; Moore 1993; Bicchieri 2005; Elster 2008), shaping actors' moral opinions and featuring in processes of socialisation and social regulation. As a concept, it clearly can serve a wide range of possible research agendas and ways of apprehending the world.

The study of norms has also preoccupied constructivist IR scholars seeking answers to the question 'what do values, principles, and rules *do* in international politics?' The history and direction of this research programme can be understood in terms of waves. The first wave, mainly spanning the 1990s and early 2000s, used the concept of norms to talk about normativity, introducing it to a discipline otherwise consumed by rationalist debates over the comparable merits of neorealism and neoliberalism (Hoffmann 2010). The earliest of this literature (see, among others, Kratochwil and Ruggie 1986; Kratochwil 1989; Nadelmann 1990; Barkin and Cronin 1994; Finnemore 1996a; 1996b; Katzenstein 1996) sought mainly to establish the salience of a normative dimension to the conduct of international politics. At the forefront of the first wave of this research programme were major studies into the emergence and spread of prohibitions, such as on nuclear weapons (Tannenwald

---

[4] However, while I develop this approach to explain my three cases, it should be applicable beyond them.

1999), chemical weapons (Price 1995), and slavery (Keck and Sikkink 1998). By the end of the 1990s, scholars had developed complex models of norm 'life cycles' (Finnemore and Sikkink 1998) and of the reasons why some norms endure while others disappear or fail to become prominent in the first place (see, among others, Klotz 1995; Keck and Sikkink 1998; Bernstein 2000; 2001).

The second wave, beginning in the early 2000s, partially de-reified norms and attended to their dynamic nature more fully than the scholarship of the first wave. Actors themselves played a more prominent causal role, contesting and interpreting norms rather than passively internalising them through processes of socialisation (Acharya 2004; Cortell and Davis 2005; Sandholtz 2008; Wiener 2004; 2008; Krook and True 2012; Wiener 2004; 2007; 2008; 2009; 2014; Hofferberth and Weber 2015). Scholars of this wave analysed norm change at a finer resolution, temporal or institutional, whereby a single norm may be interpreted or manifested differently across social time and space. In this literature, norm change arises out of a temporary settling of ongoing contestation and interpretation, which can arise out of anything from a 'ground-up' shift in institutional culture to 'top-down' executive imposition. Wiener offers the most articulate direct theorisation of norms here, advising scholars to focus on 'meaning-in-use', contingency, and the 'micro-level ... settings of interaction' (2009, 178). Her broader project is to capture the 'dual quality' of norms (2007), whereby they serve both as routinised social agreements, constituting areas of cultural and political life, and as essentially contested discursive objects undergoing continual interpretation (2008; 2014). Warning scholars not to 'ontologise' norms as objects (2008, 46), she advises instead to focus on how arguments about norms perform simultaneous constructive and deontic functions for actors, as it obliges them to determine the meaning of a norm by using it to justify their actions (see also 2009 on 'meaning-in-use'). Hofferberth and Weber (2015) propose something similar, arguing that norms be approached through an 'interpretive' methodology (75) whereby they serve as sense-making and linguistic devices. These scholars have thus confronted the problems of treating norms as social objects and sought to resolve them by taking seriously their hermeneutic and deontic dimensions, along with the changeability of content those dimensions imply.

These attempts to contextualise 'norms' already start to dissolve them as an ontologically meaningful category, to focus instead on the broader constituents of normativity. When norms are entirely products of interpretation, they become the epiphenomena of the 'cultural practices' (Wiener 2009, 181) that determine their form and content or otherwise are simply focal points of discourse rather than something more or different. However, by still treating norms as causes or as features of social structures with their own qualities, this work retains the 'norms-as-units' ontology. Asserting that norms are both discourses and objects at once can certainly help scholars better appreciate how contestation and normativity work in multiple ways, but it does not resolve the basic contradictions that can arise in associating normativity with a specific social object. Nor does this completely surmount the analytical problems that some questions or some cases of normative transformation raise. In other words, the turn towards contestation and interpretation may de-reify norms but only by relinquishing the robust causal role that normativity can play outside of discourse, and it can regain that role only by reverting to reification.

The recent work of Wiener, Hofferberth and Weber, and others studying norms in similar ways reflects increasing, though still limited, engagement or convergence with critical constructivist research. Critical constructivists, taking after Kratochwil (1989) and Onuf (1989) rather than 'soft constructivism' (Wendt 1999), have long examined discursive processes of normative interpretation (Epstein 2008; Towns 2012), but their work has largely remained on the margins of more conventional norms research – in a sense, as part of 'the constructivism that wasn't' (Jackson 2012). They have studied the ways interpretation and practice establish the ends and ethics of world politics but not how norms transform, which is the preoccupation of the first wave, however problematic the 'life cycle' model may be.

The different strands of norms scholarship thus embrace ontological dualism. Early work, employing a definition still in use today, approaches norms as reified social objects: 'standard[s] of appropriate behavior for actors' (Keck and Sikkink 1998, 891) possessing both subjective and inter-subjective dimensions (Hoffmann 2010), respectively shaping actors' moral opinions and featuring in processes of socialisation and social regulation. Norms are parts of the social world that guide people in how to live – and make up the context for much of their life in the first place. On this view, norms are discrete, causally efficacious 'things' (Krook and True 2012) that can feature in claims of cause and effect. To be sure, scholars have recognised that norms are enmeshed in a given context. Finnemore, for example, avers 'the importance of viewing norms not as individual "things" floating atomistically in some international social space but rather as part of a highly structured social context ... a fabric of interlocking and interwoven norms rather than individual norms of this or that' (1996a, 161). Nevertheless, by orienting analysis around specific norms, both in theory and in practice, the ultimate result is atomistic. Norms still end up existing as travelling units of moral information, embodied in social and psychological form, influencing the course of events.

Conversely, critical constructivists and some second-wave norms scholars approach norms as points of discursive contestation or orientation, which avoids reifying them but also significantly constrains their potential role in explanations of change. In this approach, 'norms' change, but there are no consequences to this because they are the outcomes of underlying processes of interpretation, and thus they are outcomes rather than causes of events. Rather, a change in a norm indicates that something else has changed, discursively or hermeneutically – a form of ontological reductionism.

To be sure, many cases of institutional transformation involve breaks from the past or revolve around distinct rules, principles, or values so pronounced and obvious in substance that they can be (and have been) productively explained through norms-talk. However, some other cases of transformation, because they are uneven or internally inconsistent, span a heterogenous set of practices or are the outcome of a range of agendas and instruments. These cases do not admit of neat division into old norms, new norms, norm entrepreneurs, and discourses of contestation revolving around the interpretation of a discrete standard or value.

Yet these kinds of cases are still of interest to relational and practice-theoretic IR scholars, focusing on institutionally situated processes of evolution or transformation rooted in greater micro- and meso-level sensitivity to agency (see McCourt 2016; see also Jackson and Nexon 1999; Adler and Pouliot 2011). Moreover, when relational IR scholars do take a macro-sociological perspective, they often pay attention to the dispersed and plastic nature of values and conventions (see, for example, Nexon 2009; Linklater 2011), further limiting the usefulness of a 'norms-as-things' ontology, compared to one in which norms are de-reified into configurations of processes and relations of interaction. Indeed, relational and practice-theoretic IR research has thus largely left behind norms research for this reason (McCourt 2016), despite the evident potential for contributing to it.

Some scholarship on norms recognises this same problem and offers possible solutions that do not completely discard 'norms' as entities, by way of semi-de-reifications of 'big norms' into arrangements of 'smaller norms'. This is in many ways a logical and reasonable approach. It retains a concept that has a large and productive literature behind it and that often also aligns with actors' own ontological and discursive worlds – for actors themselves often conceive of norms as existing in some meaningful way and orient their actions in relation to them. One example of this is in Winston's (2018) concept of 'norm cluster', which she develops to better appreciate the indeterminate range of possible forms a seemingly singular 'international' norm can take when it is concretised in practice by some specific set of actors. Winston defines a norm cluster as

a bounded collection of interrelated specific problems, values, and behaviors that are understood to be similar enough that their adopters form a family group [within which] problems, values, and behaviors may be combined, depending on state context or other factors, into a number of distinct but acceptable combinations of problem, value, and behavior. (Winston 2018, 647)

As a concept, norm clusters are a helpful way to study the relationship between arrangements of norms and institutions that flexibly shift, admit of multiple interpretations, and inform actions may look normatively inconsistent but nevertheless sit within the same broader constitutive and justificatory complex. This offers a finer-grained ontology of the dual character of norms that Wiener establishes in her work on contestation and shows the direction available to the norms research programme as it better appreciates contestation and multiplicity as parametric conditions.

There are nevertheless two problems with this. First, it does not actually resolve the methodological dilemma of an inability to distinguish new norms from 'old' ones that have changed; it merely kicks the dilemma down to a different ontological level or resolution, in the hope that at some point there exists enough consistency in action or discourse for sustained concretisation. Once consistency is found, the analysis then scales back up to show how actors resolve the normative inconsistency. Second, it leaves out the processes and mechanisms by which various practices or relations of ethical analysis, professionalisation, organisational steerage, or institutional management generate normativity but are not easily summarised – or are not even experienced or approached by actors themselves – as principled positions on the good, right, or true. In other words, 'more norms, higher resolution' may work for some specific cases, but it does not fundamentally address the ways some other cases might just not look like examples of norm change even though they exhibit an evident normative transformation.

One possible place to find this new perspective may be in the 'critical constructivist' literature on norms, taking after Kratochwil (1989) and Onuf (1989) rather than the 'soft constructivism' (cf. Wendt 1999) of the norms scholars of the 1990s. Their pioneering books treated norms as means and contents of communication and human reason, performing functions beyond just regulation (Kratochwil 1989, 9–11), admitting of an interpretive understanding of the causes of human actions (27), and serving as the ontologically primitive building blocks of all social life (Onuf 1989, 66). However, while critical constructivist research attends closely to diffuse discursive processes of normative interpretation (Epstein 2008; Towns 2012), it has disengaged from more conventional research on the causal impact of normative forces as such – in a sense, it is part of 'the constructivism that wasn't' (Jackson 2012). By this I mean that, while critical constructivists have studied the ways interpretation and practice establish the ends and ethics of the conduct of world politics, this has not taken the form of theorising the causal mechanisms through which one norm may come to replace another, spread throughout the international system, and influence state conduct. As a result, it also offers limited potential to explain how prohibitions transform and how those transformations relate to changes in practice.

Another good approach might lie in rationalist theorising, which tends to focus on strategic action within an environment of constraints and opportunities, typically where the goal of action is to favourably transform that environment. Yet the weakness of rationalist explanations lies in their inability to account for the apparent moral element of norm dynamics. In the cases I study, actors make reference to, and base actions in part on, principled notions of right and wrong, or legitimate and illegitimate, in defending or criticising a proposed course of action.[5] While some scholars in the field have suggested that this problem can be resolved simply by identifying moral concerns with preference formation prior to strategic interaction (Legro 1996), this approach seems to elide the inherent normative aspects of discourse (Finnemore 1996b; Risse 2000), where standards of appropriateness play an important institutional role. This is certainly true in my three cases and has more generally been established as an essential feature in norm dynamics by international relations scholars (Hoffmann 2010). There is undeniably an instrumental aspect to the process by which actors contend and propagate new norms, and this aspect extends into discourse itself (Krebs and Jackson 2007; cf. Risse 2000), but the deontic and cognitive features of normativity – the way it establishes both ethical imperatives and shapes the way actors think – render the rationalist ontology simply inadequate to make sense of the cases I investigate here.

Furthermore, rationalism provides no satisfying answer to the question of 'where do we go from here?'. Even if the rationalist approach were correct in an overall sense, and the United States simply began to engage in previously prohibited practices because the institutions that would make these practices costly deteriorated or transformed, it is unhelpful for anyone interested in maintaining prohibitions in the future. Insights into the tactics and tools that security practitioners employ in order to overcome prohibitions will help rights campaigners design better such regimes and enable better accountability processes by providing information on who and what is responsible for causing key changes for the worse and for the better. Or, to put it much more simply, it is both conceptually inadequate and ethically unsatisfying to theorise norms from a rationalist perspective.

Given these limits on existing ways of conceptualising norms in IR scholarship, I develop an alternative by drawing upon a range of literatures in philosophy and sociology. I try to retain the analytical value of 'norms' as a central theoretical concept, but nevertheless replace fundamental ontological features of it as a way of capturing

---

[5] For empirically driven criticisms of the rationalist approach on these grounds, see, for example, Price (1995).

normativity as a causal force and variable of interest. In the next section, I present this alternative.

2.3 From Norms to the Normative Configuration

Normativity, in very general terms, is the arrangement of experiences and social dispositions generated by values, virtues, and imperatives – or, more accurately, by the processes by which these things are established, contested, and managed. I draw on pragmatist and relational social theory to make sense of normativity, which builds on a small but potent set of existing criticisms of the norms research programme from other IR scholars. By placing situated creativity and a processual view of social relationships at the centre of this approach, I join with Hofferberth and Weber (2015) and with Wiener (2008; 2014) in tracing the multi-dimensionality and interactivity of normative dynamics. Indeed, Hofferberth and Weber (2015) themselves advance some of the theoretical positions that I propose here, drawing on pragmatist theories of action (Joas 1996) and relational sociology (Emirbayer 1997; Jackson and Nexon 1999) to try to access the dynamic processes of innovation and social interaction that constitute norms. However, I do something these scholars have not done, and which is likely to be contentious: I abandon the concept of 'norm', at least for some analyses, in favour of 'normative configuration' as an alternative that better captures the relational and processual qualities of normativity. In doing so, I join Adler-Nissen (2014), who prefers to talk about 'normative order' rather than norms, but I have focused less on theorising order itself and instead on the question of what normativity is and where it comes from.

This should not be treated as a categorical attack on the conceptual value of 'norm', which productively organises a wide range of thought across many of the social sciences and humanities.[6] The reason why

---

[6] In psychology, norms refer both to conventions of ethical conduct that shape individual behaviour (cf. Dubois 2003) and to cognitive categories into which information may be sorted (Kahneman and Miller 1986). In moral philosophy, a norm is generally understood to be a rule of conduct that carries moral force, and there is a robust debate over the epistemic and metaphysical or ontological status of norms as such (Von Wright 1963; Searle 1995). Economists and rationalist social scientists (such as in political science or sociology) treat norms as determinants of preferences (Axelrod 1986; Fearon and Wendt 2002) and view them in functionalist terms, as means of coordinating social action, either

I still propose dropping 'norms' from my analysis, in favour of 'normative configurations', owes to the ontological implications carried by most uses of the term. IR scholars still mainly conceptualise norms in line with the deontic or 'logic of appropriateness' view (March and Olsen 1998), whereby norms serve as the cultural origins and cognitive underpinnings of rule-following or morally driven action. This view, which is not unique to IR and is rooted in a functionalist social ontology (Hofferberth and Weber 2015; see also Parsons 1937), unidirectionally links the constitutive role of normativity, as a source of values or goals, to its role in orienting action; norms are not implicated in causal processes but serve merely as initiators of them. Moreover, it also leaves little room for agency as a force for the emergence of new normative horizons; agents may spread norms but not innovatively remake them.

Yet there is not a clear alternative. Rationalist views of norms as emergent patterns or instrumentally established coordination principles offer no traction on the obvious ethical character of many empirical cases. Caught between the 'upward conflation' of a voluntaristic overemphasis on agency and a 'downward conflation' of an overemphasis on the determining properties of structure (Archer 1995; see also Loyal 2003), IR scholars have few good options for conducting norms research in cases of institutional politics and innovation. In such cases of creativity and social plasticity, fixating on 'norms' presumes answers to interesting questions and leaves opaque many processes that matter.

A 'normative configuration', as defined at the beginning of this chapter, is an arrangement of ongoing, interacting practices establishing action-specific regulation, value-orientation, and avenues of contestation. Normative configurations are processual, are heterogenous, and provide both ends and means to actors, by directing action towards

intentional or as the unintended and emergent result of collective social interactions over time (Opp 1982; Elster 1989). In much sociology, anthropology, and cultural studies, norms may refer to values, mores, conventions, identities, classificatory schema, shared expectations of behaviour, and associated practices (Cancian 1975; Moore 1993; Bicchieri 2005; Elster 2009b). As noted in the introduction to the book, the norms research programme in IR has converged on a view best (and popularly) summarised by the definition of norms as 'standard[s] of appropriate behavior for actors with a given identity' (Keck and Sikkink 1998, 891), with both subjective and inter-subjective dimensions (Hoffmann 2010), shaping actors' moral opinions and featuring in processes of socialisation and social regulation, respectively.

the attainment of particular outcomes and by treating certain kinds of symbols and performances as authoritative. They gain concrete form when they are institutionalised, but they are never static. Not every arbitrary assortment of practices constitutes a normative configuration by this definition, but every practice is necessarily part of one, as normative configurations provide direction and cultural depth to social life. Hence the task for the investigator is to find which practices come together to generate a particular set of regulative or evaluative outcomes and to study in particular their normativity-producing dimensions.

Investigating what normative configurations do and how they transform clarifies the causal processes underlying social regulation, shows how normativity is involved in the constitution of social arrangements and orders, and can reveal the complex and reciprocal interplay of morality and instrumentality in action and agency. To explain how it offers all this, I first discuss what it means to position normativity *within* an understanding of action and why pragmatist philosophy helps us understand the implications of doing so. I then how discuss how relational sociology relates the outcomes of action to the formation of institutions, practices, and political organisation – and therefore why it is such a strong basis for theorising normative transformation.

2.3.1 Pragmatism and the Normativity of Action

I propose that normativity exists within action. Acts carry an implication of their own goodness or rightfulness. Almost nobody consciously does something without also thinking that there is a compelling or justifying reason for it, and actions taken without conscious thought are conditioned by learned and habituated standards of propriety. Meanwhile, action provides the generative and disciplinary force for normativity in social orders in general. In this sense, so-called norms are not substantive objects in the world but momentary situational summaries of the 'rules of the game', anchoring social understandings and values for both scholars and their subjects alike but open to transformation as 'players' continually renegotiate and reinvent them. Beneath seemingly settled regimes of human rights, sovereignty, and cooperation lies a fractal of nested deliberate and accidental revision of practices and institutions, for status, for efficiency, or principle.

Normativity is established, enforced, and interpreted by ongoing processes of social interaction.

This view grants normativity a pervasive and persistent role in the ongoing creation of social worlds and subjects alike, as the aspect of action that extends beyond the purposes of the individual actor, and establishes seemingly independent or impersonal sources of meaning, value, and justification. Normativity is a dimension of action, but so too is instrumentality – the linking of means to ends – and moreover, normativity is both an 'objective' and forceful feature of the social world actors must account for in their strategies and habits, as well as a 'subjective' orientation towards particular values and ends. This raises a question: how do we describe potential for self-reformation and world-transformation definitive of agency, without neglecting the dispositional role that values and meanings play, both by orienting action around particular ends and by supplying a repertoire of known means? Or, put most simply, how are creativity, as the capacity to invent new worlds, and sociality, as the orientation towards meaningful collective life, knit together in practice?

Pragmatist philosophy offers a compelling answer to this question. A pragmatist theory of action begins not with wilful actors, nor with the dispositional properties of social structures, but with a certain kind of relation: the transaction. Acts are transactions between the body, or organism, and its physical environment – they are arrangements of unfolding processes which cannot be specified apart from one another, extending in time as well as space, and which, in the case of the organism and its environment, deny the independent pre-existence of either one (Dewey and Bentley 1949, 137). Acts often take place with little conscious reflection, as 'an acquired predisposition to ways or modes of response' (Dewey 1983, 32). But these 'habits', as Dewey called them, are more than simply *individual* expressions of acquired dispositions. They are part of the environment in which the organism lives and acts: they are 'situational structures rather than individual reflexes, psychic associations, or repeated actions' (Alexander 1987, 142). They are part of a relational process of adjustment to the contingencies of experience, and they generate both self and world.

For pragmatists, habits are not always sub-intentional or unconscious, and they can be subject to modification. When habit is interrupted or inhibited, an organism must select from a wide range of mutually exclusive responses. The way by which it does so is through reflective self-awareness, from the consideration and selection of alternatives (Hildebrand 2008, 28–30). Thus, unlike in theories of practice or habit where action lacks conscious intentionality, for pragmatists action moves in and out of self-awareness, and cognition occurs at both levels. This approach rests on a counter-intuitive theory of mind: that it exists in the doing rather than as a distinct faculty applied to action and decision as needed. In Dewey's own words:

> [Mind] never denotes anything *self-contained*, isolated from the world of persons and things, but is always used with respect to situations, events, objects, persons and groups … *Mind is primarily a verb.* (Dewey 1987, 268; my emphasis)

Put more simply, action is what produces minds because minds are actions: they are ongoing processes of reflection and habit-modification, directed at coping with the inhibitive or indeterminate features of the world. For humans, mind is therefore social, because we live in a world of other people.

The pragmatist view of agency is thus that it arises from an inherent human capacity for continual innovation, rather than the outcome structured relations of enablement and constraint. Agency does not refer to a capacity of individual persons to act with freedom or flexibility but rather to the capacity of action itself to change the world. This understanding of agency moves away from the established 'structure/agency' binary and towards something closer to the agency *of* structure – or at least of the social arrangements that theorists have named 'structures'. In other words, agency is the power *of* action, rather than the power *for* action. That capacity receives its expression in the relationship between action and its ends:

> [New] goals will arise on the basis of newly available means. … This reciprocal process between means and ends structures action. It anchors the notion of goals firmly in the action process itself and argues against the external setting of goals as advocated in teleological theories of action. This allows one to perceive perception and cognition not as acts preceding action but as part of the action process that is inherently connected to the situational context. (Joas and Beckert 2001: 273)

This focus on evolving transactions covers both the creativity of action and the way it is shaped, oriented, and directed by historically determined, institutionalised social settings, imposing pressures and offering opportunities. The process of inhibition and reorientation of habit explains both how normativity persists in familiar forms and also how it may change rapidly in form or content. It grants actors the possibility of significantly reinterpreting their goals and obligations without denying the value-laden nature of both.

A pragmatist view of agency also starts with a phenomenological and cognitive account of an activity or practice. This is epistemologically significant, because it calls into question any explanation that describes action as the outcome of some overarching or disposing social structure. Boltanski refers to this analytical mode as 'the sociology of translation':

> Instead of defining agents by means of stable attributes, endowing them with interests and tendencies that are inscribed in the body and capable of generating objective unconscious intentions, and then assigning itself the task of explaining the actions of these agents when they encounter external obstacles, the sociology of translation shows how actors develop discourses about these actions, how they shape their action into a plot. (Boltanski 2012 [1990], 29–30)

This view of action makes especially clear why a pragmatist analysis of normative transformation may be preferable to a conventional constructivist explanation of 'norm change': precisely because it does not take a norm to necessarily exist, or be causally significant, to account for normativity, the pragmatist view does not take for granted that a 'norm' has changed. This matters when actors, such as those in the cases I examine, all deny that this has happened even as they engage in activities that imply an evident normative shift.

Yet the pragmatist account of action lacks a well-specified theory of social environment. It focuses on the capacities of the 'human organism' to adapt but does not offer any clear way of describing the institutional settings in relation to which adaption occurs, nor of grasping political struggle between persons and groups. While Boltanski, both on his own (2012) and with Thévenot (Boltansky and Thévenot 2006), attempted to provide this, that approach is less helpful because of its focus on justifications and justificatory discourses. In the cases I examine, justification is one component of a broader set of processes of institutional change, and thus, while pragmatism offers a strong basis for approaching them, it is not analytically helpful without connecting it up to a sociological account of institutional arrangements. In the next sub-section, I suggest a way of doing so.

2.3.2 *From Action to the Normative Configuration*

A pragmatist theory of action is not a full-fledged sociological account of how normativity forms and transforms – but it does suggest how such an account might be built. By analysing social arrangements through the lens of pragmatist action theory, a certain conception of their normative dimensions emerges, and this is what yields the concept of 'normative configuration'. It refers to many of the same kinds of things that scholars have called 'norms' and their effects, but it replaces that vocabulary with an alternative one – for new language often carries with it new sensitivities and opportunities for novel theories.

I advance four propositions about how its role in generating and shaping social order and practice, built on the foregoing discussion role of normativity in action through a pragmatist lens. First, as normativity inheres in the action process, the mechanisms of normativity are the ways it features in evolving transactions linking actors to one another and to their worlds. This grants normativity a causal role and implies that an analysis of normativity is, whether hermeneutic or otherwise, an analysis of what creates or transforms a social arrangement.

Second, as normativity provides subjects with ends, with means, and with the symbols, performances, and social skills through which to link the latter to the former, it inscribes or institutionalises culture into the action environment such that it becomes a resource for action as well as an outcome of it. This means that normative transformations become components of subsequent action. It introduces an iterative element to how we conceptualise change by accounting for how it shifts from an outcome to a cause.

Third, normativity enables the recursive transformation of ends and means. It orients action around certain ends but also makes possible ethical change, as ends are rarely consistent, featuring competing imperatives and values-in-tension which must be resolved through creative problem-solving. This is how normativity generates agency and should not be viewed in opposition to it, as is common in functionalist or structural views of norms as determinants of ends alone or as constraints to action.

Fourth, normativity takes the form of institutions. They become ongoing components of formal and informal social arrangements, gaining legitimacy from their position within broader authority structures and becoming part of the expected and reproduced array of activities associated with a particular role or profession. This process of institutionalisation is the concrete manifestation, or 'crystallisation',[7] of values, standards, principles, and commitments into ongoing components of formal and informal social arrangements, gaining legitimacy from their position within broader authority structures. Once institutionalised, normativity enters into processes of reproduction and disciplining, and the actions through which it is expressed are less prone to radical transformation because they have been routinised, formalised, and to some degree sacralised. Institutionalised normativity is what observers are concretising when they speak of seemingly enduring 'norms'.

Collectively, these propositions provide a meta-theoretical approach to the understanding what normativity is and how it works, as well as a basic analytical architecture for examining historically specific processes of social change. They rest on an examination of the strengths and weaknesses of influential relational and practice theorists who wed their theory of action with one of social order. Pragmatism implies that social arrangements are not only an outcome of organism–environment transactions but feed back into the environment itself and thus are part of a recursive process that generates actors as fully fledged subjects. Moreover, because action is a process, it has a history and a boundary (Rescher 1996): it has physical, temporal, and conceptual edges that give it presence in space and time. A range of broadly relational social theories already speak to this in various ways, from the capillary operations of power/knowledge discussed by Foucault (1980) to the practice-oriented synthetic social theory of Giddens (1979; 1984; in IR, see Steele 2008) to the Marxian-inspired agent-structure co-determinism of critical realism (Bhaskar 1998; Archer 1995; in IR see Wendt 1987; Wight 2006) to the Wittgensteinian constructivism, building off the notion of 'language games' (Wittgenstein 1958), advanced in philosophy by Winch (1958), in sociology by Schatzki (1996), and in IR by Onuf (1989).[8] Crucially, in ways that I will presently discuss, these

---

[7] To borrow Mann's (1993) term for describing how power gains concrete forms.
[8] Language games are bundles of practices and habits, and their form generates both the player and the 'rules of the game' alike. Yet because rules must be interpreted, there is always room for creative revision, and thus language games

sociological wagers also accord with many of the critiques and projects advanced by scholars in IR's 'practice' turn, who draw especially from Bourdieu but also, increasingly, from a more diverse set of theorists, many of whom (such as Goffman 1959; 1969; 1983) already sit within the broad tent of pragmatism. Beyond that affinity, the relationality of the conception of normativity I propose is sympathetic with certain strands of English School scholarship, such as Linklater's (2011) application of Elias's figurational sociology (1978; 1994).[9]

This diverse array of sociological affinities reveals one of the main benefits to adopting the concept of the normative configuration: it links the investigation of norms to a number of other projects in IR. In the next section, I consider these links, showing how the view of normativity I propose implies a broader and more progressive social theory than is often attributed to scholarship on norms.

2.4 Normative Configurations in the Study of Practices, Relations, and Fields

In a provocative essay, McCourt (2016) argued that practice theory and relationalism are the 'new constructivism', doing the work that was once but now is no longer done by scholarship on norms. Rather than treat these new trends as ruptures or radical reorientations, the view of normativity I advance instead offers a critical continuation of many of the same themes.

First, it is consistent and sympathetic with the particular ways IR scholars have approached and employed Bourdieu's theories of practice and field. Bourdieu has enjoyed a recent renaissance amongst IR

feature continual, dynamic transformations of the conventions that define them and the actors that play them. This suggests a view of social settings as plastic, horizontally distributed interchanges of rule-following performances, in which action is normatively oriented but retains creative and interpretive features.

[9] While relatively few IR scholars have applied Elias's insights, I see considerable sympathy in his work for the study of normativity. At the core of his approach is the concept of a 'figuration': an interwoven complex of individuals living within a form of life, 'characterized by socially and historically specific forms of habitus, or personality-structure' (van Krieken 1998, 52–3). Stable figurations not only condition actor identities but also sustain the action environment, making politics possible in the first place: 'At the core of changing figurations – indeed the very hub of the figuration process – is a fluctuating, tensile equilibrium, a balance of power moving to and fro, inclining first to one side and then to the other' (Elias 1978, 131).

scholars, for whom he has offered a potent means of theorising the habitual, embodied, and localised communities of practice that constitute key international institutions (Pouliot 2010; Bigo 2011), the dispositional metaphysics of power (Guzzini 2013), and much of the foundation for the 'practice-turn' that has more generally taken shape in the field (Adler and Pouliot 2011; Bueger and Gadinger 2015). Notably, IR scholars whose earlier work sat more firmly within an 'orthodox' interpretation of Bourdieu's theory of practice have begun to hybridise their approach with pragmatist sociology, such as in Pouliot's (2016) incorporation of Goffman's work on image management to study diplomatic 'pecking orders' and Adler-Nissen's (2014) application of Goffman's pioneering work on stigma management to international orders. Bourdieu's concept of the 'field' is also growing in popularity amongst IR scholars (Nexon and Neumann 2018). Bourdieu defined fields as social spaces made up of asymmetrical relations of power and exchange, envisioning an objective domain in which the artefacts of culture are produced and actor-positions of advantage are captured, defended, secured, contended, and expanded (Bourdieu 1984). In these terms, fields are considerably more structural and concrete than the shifting and unfolding arrangements that comprise normative configurations. However, as a concept, 'fields' have developed a sociological scope beyond orthodox Bourdieu, in ways not yet well explored by field theorists within IR.

This is related to the second way normative configurations link the norms research programme to another progressive trend in IR theory. Field theory owes its growing popularity in part to its expansion beyond Bourdieu and into a broad, relational theory of organisational, bureaucratic, and social movement politics. In *A Theory of Fields*, Fligstein and McAdam redefine definition field as a 'mesolevel social order in which actors … interact with one another on the basis of shared (which is not to say consensual) understandings about the purposes of the field, relationships to others in the field (including who has power and why), and the rules governing legitimate action in the field' (Fligstein and McAdam 2012, 1). On their understanding, fields display a higher degree of plasticity as contestation occurs within them, through a range of mechanisms and processes that Fligstein and McAdam draw from earlier work in relational social movement theory (McAdam, Tarrow, and Tilly 2001). Perhaps unsurprisingly, given the various affinities between Tilly's work and pragmatism (see Gross

2010), the view of normativity I propose offers a contribution to this approach to fields.

Similar to normative configurations, 'fields' describe an institution-alised but changeable normative context for action as an ordered terrain of social life, wherein manoeuvres and stratagems establish new cultural materials and new pathways for future actions. However, as 'fields' are constitutively arranged around struggles for domination and supremacy, they feature a thin notion of normativity seemingly based on a quasi-instrumental view of action. Actions appear cynical and lack the aspirational creativity that drives norma-tive transformation on the pragmatist view. Moreover, transform-ations in fields are temporally detached from transformations of actors themselves; while a changing field should feature changing sub-jects, the two processes do not need to occur with any immediate reciprocity – and, indeed, actors may possess a form of subjectivity ill-suited to life in their field (Bourdieu 1984; Steinmetz 2013). By fixing attention on transformations in normative configurations *within* fields or as sources of influence *upon* fields, the growing community of field theorists can overcome some of the functionalism and instrumentalism that still persists in their approach – or at least be better attuned to these tendencies in their logic.

Third and finally, the approach to normativity I propose aligns with a growing body of pragmatist-inflected network theory in IR, in ways that carry reciprocal value added. Goddard (2009) examines how network structure and the position of *brokers* – entrepreneurs in positions of particular significance in linking together fragmented relations – makes possible the emergence of new norms and empowers their spread/imposition. Defining agency as something that 'inheres' within networks, Goddard (2009, 258) explains creativity and innov-ation as the result of brokers' structural position, as being at inter-change points allows them to 'combine together divergent symbols and norms, and introduce novel ideas in international politics ... [to] have more capacity for cultural invention than other actors in inter-national politics' (Goddard 2009, 259). It is this process that drives normative transformation. Nexon (2009) introduces what he terms the 'relational-institutionalist' approach, per which international structure and state boundaries may be understood as networks and transform over time due to the mechanisms and positions of social movements therein. While broader in scope than norms literature,

Nexon is still studying normative change in conceptions of sovereignty, authority, and legitimacy and doing so by incorporating insights from both pragmatist relational sociology and network theory. Avant (2016) also merges these two bodies of thought, albeit without the same focus on network structure as an explanatory variable; rather, Avant builds on pragmatist problem-solving theory to show how networks, loosely theorised as dense and ongoing relational ties, are conditions of possibility and facilitation for effective governance and regulation.

While networks have long been part of the norms research programme, this scholarship by Goddard, Nexon, and Avant comprises a much smaller body of work building on the relational turn to approach the issue of normativity without falling into the binary of structure and agency; rather, agency sits *within* arrangements of relations.[10] However, missing from the more network-theoretical side of this project is a robust account of creativity. As Goddard (2009, 259) notes, 'The ideas brokers introduce are never entirely new [and w]hether or not ideas resonate, in turn, is not so much a matter of content as context – it depends on whether or not entrepreneurs incorporate material found in existing networks'. Meanwhile, while Avant's (2016) approach does foreground creativity, it does so at the expense of theorising the structure of networks. The pragmatist theory of action does allow for the content of ideas to matter and locates the creation of something novel in every act of problem-solving. In the next chapter, I discuss at greater length the role of brokerage and position in facilitating normative transformation, which will better establish why network-theorising provides such a sympathetic body of thought to thinking about normative transformation in relational terms. But it is worth emphasising here that the approach I propose in this chapter offers a way to consider both structural position and creativity without treating them as opposing forces or depicting their relationship as a binary. This arises from the particular 'co-evolutionary' ontology advanced in pragmatist relational sociology, and, while I do not explicitly portray the social settings I examine as networks, I can both draw from and contribute to this branch of network theorising in the field.

---

[10] The observation that some IR scholars are hybridising pragmatism and network theory was made to me some time ago by Lucas Dolan.

One of the most important implications of this approach lies in the collapse of the ontological distinction between the material and the 'ideational'. Pragmatism is a form of materialism, as it defines cognition and representation as concrete processes rather than abstractions or idealisations. Culture, for pragmatists, is not something non-material layered atop the material world but itself a material arrangement – an insight recognised by new materialists in Science and Technology Studies for decades (Latour 2005).[11] In IR, this ontological dualism has a deep legacy in mainstream constructivism, featuring even in sophisticated and path-breaking scholarship (see, for example, Ruggie 1998). While practice theorists have broadly eschewed it, they have done so mostly in implicit ways; by developing an explicitly materialist conception of normativity in action, my approach provides the 'practice turn' in the field with a clear alternative: practice is always material, always social, and always concrete.

This discussion of related IR literatures should show the intersections at which my own proposed approach to normativity sits. While I develop it mainly with reference to the trajectory and objectives of the norms research programme, it contributes to a range of other conversations and is likely to have applicability outside of the specific questions that norms scholars tend to ask about regulation and restraint. The conclusion I have tried to draw out of these intersections, broadly, is that a number of research communities in the field are converging, or at least can choose to converge, on pragmatism and relational sociology as a way of going beyond some of the binaries and boundaries that limit us.

2.5 Summary

The foregoing pages presented the theoretical foundations for a conceptual and ontological alternative to 'norms': the normative configuration. I argue that normativity is not the property of social objects (norms) but a property and dimension of action itself – all action carries its own normative force. By adopting a pragmatist understanding of action, it also becomes possible to view normativity as a force not just for the maintenance of social relations but also for

---

[11] New materialist scholarship still comprises a relatively small body of work in the field, but I engage with it at greater length in the next chapter.

their transformation, as part of an ongoing process of creative revision of habit.

The value of this new approach lies in the way it permits practice and action to be studied without reifying their normative dimensions. This offers something that other theoretical approaches lack – or at least do not offer without notable trade-offs or limits. The same is true of a number of prominent sociological and philosophical approaches more broadly, especially those associated with relational sociology. Some existing IR theory already proceeds from similar such foundations, but, as I have sought to show, it has not approached the dimensions of normativity with the scope or specificity that I have here.

In the next chapter, I expand on that foundation to discuss the causal mechanisms of normative transformation. I also outline a general methodological approach to defining and analysing the key elements of cases of normative transformation. Finally, I overview the key sources and methods I use to gather data on my cases and develop explanations of them.

3 | *Tracing Normative Transformations*

3.1 Introduction

This chapter explains how I trace the causal processes responsible for cases of normative transformation – meaning how normative configurations change – and how I identify what, exactly, has changed in the first place. As noted, existing critical constructivist approaches to normative transformation typically lack the methodological instruments for identifying causal relationships, instead offering thick description of the cultural formations and implications surrounding particular discourses or normative configurations. Even in the case of other pragmatist scholarship on the subject (Schmidt 2014), a general pragmatist theory of action is offered in place of a more specific pragmatist theory of how that action works within institutions to generate lasting change in practice. While a number of scholars have recently sought to develop systematic approaches to the analysis of the effects and evolutions of practices (Pouliot 2007; 2011; Adler 2019), these approaches are not specifically aimed at studying normative transformation, nor for the specific task of de-reifying a 'norm' or 'prohibition' in order to clarify a situation of possible transformation. I formulate both a set of causal mechanisms and an analytical approach for locating their operation in particular episodes. This facilitates an examination of my three cases and contributes to ongoing methodological conversations amongst theorists of practices and norms.

This chapter has two main sections. In Section 3.2, I propose three mechanisms of normative transformation: convention reorientation, technological revision, and network synthesis. I describe what they are and how they work in practice, and I connect them to existing bodies of literature in IR scholarship – on norms and practices and on institutions. I take an abductive, analytical, and process-oriented view of mechanisms. They are not deduced logically from the theoretical

38

premises set forth in the preceding chapter, nor inductively from a close consideration of patterns in the data of the three cases I examine. Instead, I consider the implications of my proposed approach to normativity *alongside* the cases themselves, and I look for a way of accounting for them that is both ontologically consistent with how normativity works and epistemically consistent with what interests IR scholars studying norms and international security.

While social scientists have proposed a range of abductive research design strategies (Reichertz 2007; Thomas 2010; Timmermans and Tavory 2012), I hew fairly closely to pragmatist understandings of the logic of enquiry: that explanation is a concept-driven attempt to 'enable orientation in a relevant field [consisting] of mapping a class of phenomena to increase cognitive understanding and/or practical manipulability' (Friedrichs and Kratochwil 2009). First, I identify what about a case (or set of cases) warrants explanation, based on a general account that highlights what is confusing and what is clear. Second, I develop a conceptual vocabulary around the processes or dynamics in these accounts that are currently hard to understand. Third, I use this vocabulary, and the new sensitivities it cultivates, to re-describe what occurred in the case(s) in ways that adequately resolve my initial confusion, by using theory to reveal or make tractable symbolic and causal operations that previously defied description. Moreover, they are methodological tools – hence their inclusion in this chapter rather than in the preceding or following ones – because they permit data to be coherently ordered to make causal processes analytically tractable. This is why I do not follow a more conventional process of first presenting my theory, then presenting 'empirics', and finally applying the theory to those empirics. I instead present each of my three cases in a more active dialogue between description and theorising, blending chronology and theorisation rather than treating the former as *explanandum* and the latter as *explanans*.

Methodologically, this is a form of process tracing, built around key premises of practice theory and pragmatist sociology. It provides a single case analysis of the over-time operation and, crucially, the interaction of the three posited mechanisms, to account for how normative obstacles to targeted killing, torture, and private military and security contracting were overcome by proponents of these things, through a mixture of technological, discursive, and bureaucratic-political manoeuvres. I define a causal mechanism as a specifiable arrangement of unfolding actions – what Guzzini has called an 'action-complex' (2011, 336) – that when triggered will produce an observed outcome. Focusing on the role of practitioners as drivers of institutional change, I foreground creative problem-solving, where actors search for ways to resolve proximate impediments in applying means to ends, as the trigger for these mechanisms. I treat them as transactional – a term from pragmatist philosophy (Dewey and Bentley 1949) referring to ongoing processes that simultaneously constitute both actors and their worlds alike.[1] Using this approach, I show that while technology, rhetorical contestation, and bureaucratic politics may already be the object of investigation by IR scholars of norm change, they drove norm transformation in this case in simultaneous and mutually reinforcing ways – a causal interaction not currently well studied or theorised in the field. That is, the three mechanisms worked in concert. The outcome is that a prohibition on assassination still persists, but it is not the same prohibition as it was at the outset of the case. It has changed in form rather than having been eliminated.

In Section 3.3, I propose an analytical approach consisting of three stages: de-reification, attribution of agency, and tracing transactions. I explain how this approach is an outgrowth of pragmatist and relational sociology, and (as in the previous chapter) I connect it to existing approaches in the field. The purpose of the approach is to make it easier to locate and trace the three mechanisms in action. It is a way of determining what information is important and how it should be treated. In this section I also identify the specific kinds of data and tools of data collection most likely to enable this kind of analysis. Following others, I differentiate between methodology and method. The former is a conceptual apparatus of analytical assumptions about how the world should be studied. The latter is the set of research instruments it informs. I conclude with some observations on the specific ways the mechanisms and analytical approach shape how I examine my cases.

---

[1] This view of causal mechanism rests upon premises elaborated at greater length in Gross (2009) and shares a relational view of agency drawn from Emirbayer and Mische (1998). It turns on an understanding of creativity and action developed by Joas (1996; see also 2000). For the sake of brevity I will not re-examine these sources here, as they are covered in the preceding chapter, but reference them as a way of situating the particular way I discuss causality and agency here.

3.2 Mechanisms of Normative Transformation

To analyse transformations in normative configurations, investigators need a way of describing what has changed and how those changes have occurred. Because the specific mechanisms through which normative configurations transform will vary across historical contexts, other scholars attempting to theorise normative change through pragmatism (Schmidt 2014; Hofferberth and Weber 2015) have provided only a general account of action and ethical reinterpretation.[2] They may be correct in only going this far; if norms scholars take the creativity of action seriously, a truly general theory of normative transformation is impossible, and we should instead look only for a helpful analytical approach that allows us to identify and describe the contextually specific mechanisms that interest us. It is, however, a limited alternative to the defined theories of change already offered by norms scholars in IR. Yet, I argue, it is possible to offer a more defined theory of change from pragmatist premises.

I propose that three causal mechanisms drove the normative (and institutional) transformations underlying the emergence and institutionalisation of targeted killing, torture during interrogation, and extensive employment of armed contractors. This proposal rests on two bases. The first is a *prima facie* plausibility test, in line with an abductive research mindset: the data I have collected, and the historical accounts of the cases I can provide, suggest some interaction of technology, normative framing, and bureaucratic politics are behind the rise of these practices, and it is hard to imagine an adequate explanation of them without reference to all three dynamics. Actors revised their normative stances alongside their strategies in recursive ways, meaning counterterrorism or military efficacy influenced discourses on what is right or proper, just as normative influences shape discourses on strategic choice. Meanwhile, normativity not only provided moral guidance to actors but also supplied rhetorical and institutional resources for contesting various practices. The second basis lies in a reading of existing literature on changes in norms and institutions. To varying degrees, technology, framing and discourse, and bureaucratic politics have all been part of existing theories of norms in IR. These bodies of

---

[2] For example, Schmidt (2014, 821) simply reframes norms as habits and places them within the process of inhibition, deliberation, and revision of habit definitive of a pragmatist view of action.

scholarship provide guidance on how best to specify and trace causal mechanisms in my three cases.

These mechanisms may show up in any given situation but are likely to be especially salient or potent in cases involving states that generally orient policy around the formal and informal conventions of international humanitarian law and adhere to a broadly liberal view of warfare – one guided by principles of proportionality and discrimination, with protections for non-combatants and fought by a professionalised armed force.[3] These mechanisms also have relatives in other theories that will be familiar already to IR scholars of norms; it is not that they denote a radically novel process of normative transformation but rather that they describe normative transformation in ways especially well-suited to offering an account of practice-driven changes 'from below' within institutions. For this reason, they should be taken together with the three-stage analytical procedure discussed later in this chapter, to see how they facilitate better explanations of particular cases.

The first is *convention reorientation*: the re-description of a situation to reposition it within a different set of definitional and regulatory terms (subject to institutional availability),[4] changing critical features of the normative configuration to entail different obligations, actor identities, and local ends. By 'convention' I mean an institutionalised standard of right conduct that effectively serves as a professional or practical device for adjudicating disputes over what should be done. Invoking and referencing conventions are a routine part of both contestation (Wiener 2008; 2014) and the evolving process of social construction (Adler 2019) and obliges actors to articulate (and contend) a narrative about what situation they are in, what dilemmas they confront, and what criteria must be satisfied by any solution to them.[5] Similar mechanisms are discussed in the literature on framing

---

[3] This category more or less encapsulates most industrially advanced and non-pariah states within the 'Western-dominated' international community. It is a modest scope condition but refers more to an ideal-typical case than an absolute and real boundary past to which the theory is applicable.

[4] This mechanism relies on the existence of more than one existing conventional framework, and the options for repositioning or 'swapping' the situation–convention match are limited by the number of available frameworks and avenues for situating actions within them.

[5] In this sense, invoking and referencing conventions is an exercise in framing, as it involves applying a communicative device to 'fix meanings, organize experience,

(Barnett 1999; Payne 2001; Kornprobst 2019) and 'rhetorical coercion' (Krebs and Jackson 2007), while ontological security explanations (Rumelili 2015) and securitisation theory (Buzan et al., 1998; Shannon (2000) in particular explore debates over whether an action falls within the regulatory scope of a norm, termed 'justification', through a psychological framework. While diverse, these scholars share an interest in showing how the classification of a situation positions it within particular normative configurations, and reclassifying that situation often moves it to a completely new such configuration. As classifications are the outcomes of creative and competitive transactions, they fit well within a relational theoretical framework such as the one I use here. Moreover, a pragmatist perspective takes this beyond a purely instrumental account of framing or of strategic speech-acts to include how actors are themselves changed along with their situations. The common thread unifying different possible instances of this mechanism is that the way a situation is classified situates it in particular normative configurations, and to reclassify that situation is often to normatively relocate it.

This mechanism is likely most potent as a force for transformation when the situations in which state actions may be used, such as the employment of political violence, are comprehensively defined by formal conventions; by switching the gestalt of the social configuration, a new horizon of possible actions emerges. It is activated when existing social configurations are unsettled by the emergence of a new dilemmas or crises where – in line with a pragmatist view of action – familiar routines of convention invocation and reference no longer offer satisfying ethical and strategic answers. For example, by presenting its counterterrorism practices as a war, the United States places them within the broader normative framework of Just War Theory, which in turn implies certain obligations of proportionality and discrimination, codified in international law and liberal political thought (Crawford 2003). This was facilitated by widespread anguish and anger in the aftermath of the 11 September 2001 attacks. When critics of US practices discuss them according to the language of crime and

and alert others that their interests and possibly their identities are at stake, and propose solutions to ongoing problems' (Barnett 1999, 25). Unlike IR scholars researching framing, however, I do not explore the 'resonance' or cultural 'congruence' (Kornprobst 2019) to explain their relative persuasiveness or how they trigger popular mobilisation (see, for example, Zellman 2015).

punishment, such as by referring to killings as 'extra-judicial executions' (cf. Kretzmer 2005), they are seeking to reorient the situation such that a different set of conventions apply – ones that permit far less extensive violence and entail far greater institutional oversight. Over time, these discursive manoeuvres produce broader transformations, with changed classifications and their associated conventions crystallising into new normative configurations.

The second mechanism is *technological revision*: the redirection of action through new media of intervention into the world – both new physical tools but also new skills or bodies of technical knowledge – which carry different normative connotations and enable new transactions subject to different regulations, standards, or evaluations. While scholars of international politics usually understand technology to mean equipment or devices produced by feats of engineering, such as aircraft or computers, I use the term more broadly. Technology also encompasses 'skills, routines, and methods as well as the knowledge needed to operate devices . . . technique, a way of doing something [or] organizations of practices' (Massey 2011, 112).[6] As noted, technological innovation is directed by value-driven and cultural processes and is only one part of a broader set of enabling conditions making normative transformation possible at a systematic scale. Technological determinism alone is wholly inadequate to understand this, but an analysis that omits technology ignores key instrumental factors – on this view, technology *does not determine* actors' choice of actions but rather offers *new possibilities* to them, for them to evaluate, select, or synthesise as they see fit.

Again, IR scholars have articulated some aspects of this mechanism in existing work. The clearest example is recent scholarship drawing upon new materialism to bring assemblage theories to the study of international politics (Coole 2013; Acuto and Curtis 2014; Dittmer 2017). However, while the broader approach to normative transformation

---

[6] Few IR scholars have understood technological change to involve a transformation of these things (rather than the development of new devices or artefacts), and to my knowledge only one study on the interaction of technology and normativity in military or national security practices uses this definition: Liivoja's (2015) discussion of the ways technological change prompts changes in the laws of war. While broader in scope, and focused neither on technology nor war, Toope and Brunée (2011) offer an interactional account of the production of laws by, and within, communities of practice that similarly supports the view that the law evolves alongside other forms of social transformation.

I take bears some similarities to new materialist assemblage theorising, the specific mechanism I isolate here is not one that new materialist scholars typically explore. Assemblage theorists treat objects and people as entangled in a subjectivity-producing mesh that gains agency in totality, often to make critical interventions aimed at showing how some objects carry and sustain complexes of action and meaning (see, for example, Mac Ginty 2017). I am more interested in a specific recursive dynamic: the way the search for new problem-solving instruments – technologies – establishes new environments that in turn impel the evolution of action (and actors) within them. Deliberate attempts to resolve dilemmas through feats of engineering or skill development may not be major parts of all cases of normative transformation, but they are manifestly important in the cases I examine in this book, and especially in the first two, where 'drones' and interrogation techniques such as waterboarding are publicly notorious as factors.

There are, however, other points of contact with the way IR scholars have approached technology and order, where technologies and sciences are embedded within evolving institutional arrangements. Most of this is macro-level, from Ruggie's early examinations of 'asymmetric interdependences' (1975) in the governance of new technologies to more recent longue durée historical studies into the material foundations of international systems (Deudney 2000) and into the complexification of war (Bousquet 2008). Something closer to what I try to do here can be seen in work by Carvin and Williams (2014), who take an explicitly practice-theoretical approach to look at the emergence of a liberal way of war, in which specific devices such as aerial bombers introduce new ethical possibilities for engaging in 'just' warfare but presented new challenges to doing so as well. A last point of intersection lies with the IR-adjacent literature in political geography on materialism and war, which has specifically engaged with how drones alter the landscape of combat (Holmqvist 2013; Shaw 2013; Grayson 2016). What distinguishes the pragmatist take on technological revision is an emphasis on the relationship between technological development and *creative possibility*, with new means of action disclosing new horizons of ends and values. What matters most here is how the pursuit of new instruments and techniques leads to unforeseen and often significant reformations of actors, environments, and problems.

The third mechanism is *network synthesis*: the formation of new organisational structures able to authorise new actions and reform interpersonal arrangements, producing new normative configurations. It is so named because creation of new institutional relationships in this way is synthetic, involving the joining of existing networks at key 'interchange' nodes connecting institutions, extending existing power arrangements through new spaces. Network synthesis is thus the outcome of *brokerage*: 'the linking of two or more previously unconnected social sites by a unit that mediates their relations with one another and/or with yet other sites' (McAdam et al. 2001, 27). Goddard (2009) explains the power held by brokers capable of linking bundles of ties in non-dense networks, which suggests that network densification may be either a form of or a relative of network synthesis, while Castells (2009) shows how those brokers who sit at points of interchange between networks are influential switches determining when and how relations proceed. I propose this mechanism not to talk about the power of brokers but to look at what happens as they establish new institutions out of different pre-existing ones – a process Jackson and Nexon (1999, 314), building on Andrew Abbott's term, call 'yoking' (see also Abbott 1995). In this sense, while the relationship between brokers and network structures matters in explaining why network synthesis has transformative power, the impetus for the process is the outcome of bureaucratic politics.[7]

This mechanism is most potent in situations where new and insurgent actors emerge or where existing social networks are, as with convention reorientation, unsettled by the emergence of pressing new challenges. In many respects, network synthesis has already been the subject of sustained attention by norms scholars. For example, in their account of the demise of the transatlantic slave trade, Finnemore and Sikkink (1998) study the successes of Christian activists in influencing

---

[7] It is worth noting that while 'bureaucratic politics' is a well-explored concept in IR (Allison and Halperin 1972; Halperin and Clapp 2006), I do not know of any major work bringing it together with network theories. For the sake of brevity I will not go into detail about how specific forms of bureaucratic politics influence the operation of network synthesis, both because I think that for the purposes of my case studies I do not need a highly articulated account of this to achieve an adequate explanation and also because unifying these two theories likely requires a lengthy discussion of ontological commensurability. It should suffice to say that network synthesis happens because actors look to appropriate and build authority by exploiting their connections to yoke together institutions, in ways that alter bureaucratic scope.

the British government to employ naval power against ships involved in transporting slaves. Acharya (2004) also examines a form of network synthesis in how individual states 'localize' international conventions, gaining influential foreign support but reshaping those conventions in the process. More recently, studies of private security companies show how closer ties between government elites and corporate executives challenge and transform perceptions of mercenaries and of legitimate combatants (Avant 2005; 2016; Percy 2007a; 2007b). Network synthesis has thus been well studied as a mechanism of alliance building. Yet it also builds worlds, resulting in often sweeping transformations of normative confirmations as actors engage the novel situations. It produces new kinds of actors and with them new moral authorities – along with often unforeseen new problems.

Table 3.1 summarises the three mechanisms. However, it is also important to note that all three mechanisms may occur at once, and they may reinforce each other (Figure 3.1 illustrates this process).

Table 3.1 *The mechanisms of normative transformation and their effects*

Mechanism	Normative Effect
Convention Reorientation	Redefines the situation to involve a new set of laws, authorities, agents, and agencies, changing its normative dimensions.
Technological Revision	Shifts action onto new media, establishing new means with different normative connotations to their use.
Network Synthesis	Brings actors together in new ways, creating new alliances able to authorise new kinds of action.

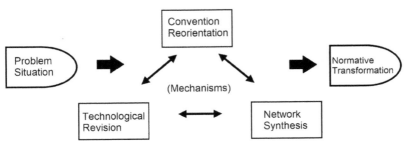

Figure 3.1 The process of normative transformation.

In describing the three mechanisms, I have repeatedly discussed how they are activated or intensified by situations of dilemma, crisis, unprecedented challenge, or some other impediment. In line with the pragmatist view of action, I propose that all three mechanisms only begin to operate once a 'problem situation' emerges. By 'problem situation' I mean a situation in which existing habits or routines of action are inhibited and in which whatever people were doing before no longer offers an adequate way to 'go on' with a particular way of being. This can take the form of major crises, such as spectacular terrorist attacks and the initiation of wars, serving as 'exogenous shocks' that significantly unsettle existing institutional arrangements.[8] However, as others have already observed, fixing on major crises as the primary activating conditions for change ignores the possibility for ongoing agency and for endogenous dynamics to produce change over time (Widmaier and Park 2012; see also Adler 2019, 257). Through a pragmatist lens, the inhibition of action – and the emergence of a problem situation – can also come from more immediate, institutionally specific dilemmas, such as inadequate means to ends for a given practice, or gradually emerging ethical challenges to employing means to ends in a legitimate way. It is thus a kind of conceptual fractal, representing triggers for the transformation of action at any analytical resolution.

Whether it arises from crisis or gradual disruption, a problem situation only becomes a stimulus for transformation when it is intelligible as such. As a premise of pragmatist metatheory, the inhibition of action obliges actors to actively reflect on, and represent to themselves, both their environment and their existing habits.[9] A more substantive specification of this, however, may be found in the concept of 'attribution of threat and opportunity' – a process of interpretation that resolves into a coherent range of avenues for new action often only after collective discussion, collaborative or contentious (McAdam et al. 2001;

---

[8] The concept of an 'exogenous shock' is commonly used in economics to refer to violent perturbations of existing markets, such as due to natural disasters. It enters into political science in Hall's (1989) study of how the Great Depression of the 1930s created the space for political elites across a range of countries to promote Keynesian economics as an alternative to laissez-faire. In IR, Wendt (1999, 188) has stressed the role of exogenous shocks as a condition of possibility for change in international order, as have later scholars (Widmaier, Blyth, and Seabrooke 2007).

[9] See, for example, its role as a trigger for the operation of social mechanisms of any type, as Gross (2009) discusses.

Fligstein and McAdam 2012). This process in turn may feature its own smaller problem situations, its own mechanisms, and its own fractalised dynamics of inhibited and revised action. Without getting lost in layers of taxonomy, it should be enough to direct attention to the hermeneutic and sociological aspects of the problem situation as an institutional moment rather than merely one of individual cognition.

As actors respond to a problem situation and begin revising their practices, the three mechanisms are the outcome, operating when action changes both actors and their environments. Moreover, the mechanisms are not merely additive in their effects but interact in mutually reinforcing or multiplicative ways. Finally, though this is not implied by the figure, they can also manifest in 'fractal' ways – that is, a given instance of one or more mechanisms at work, spanning a time period of months or years, may, if examined closely, feature numerous, concatenated iterations of those mechanisms occurring over relatively short time-scales, and those mechanisms may in turn feature the same mechanisms working at the level of brief interpersonal exchanges such as conversations, meetings, or short correspondences, for example, across formal levels of bureaucracy.[10] In other words, the transactional forms identified are not specific to one ontological 'level' or timescale and instead describe more general kinds of processes that yield more specific explanations when placed within appropriate historical context.

In the next section, I set forth a method by which scholars may do just that, by identifying and analysing empirical evidence of normative transformations in particular cases.

3.3 The Three-Stage Approach

In order to identify when these mechanisms are at work, describe when and how they interact, and explain how they produced a particular

---

[10] A board of top executives may contend a policy, reach an agreement, then advise the divisions of their organization of the new policy. Top management in each division may then engage in their own contention over the policy before reaching agreement and advising middle management, who may then contend the new policy with lower management or rank-and-file workers. In each case, the outcomes of previous normative transformation will alter the context for subsequent periods of contention, yet the same mechanisms may nevertheless operate to transform the same form of normative configuration. Note, however, that this is not the same as a mechanism working across *levels of analysis* – the context to this process is still ontologically flat.

normative transformation of interest, I use a three-stage analytical process: *de-reification, attribution of agency*, and *tracing transactions*. In simple terms, it is a process of historicising a normative configuration, locating sites or instances of agency, and then crafting an account of how those instances lead to social change. This is the second way this account adds value to IR scholarship on norms. Pragmatism and relational sociology offer a basis for developing more detailed and case-specific mechanisms of normative change than the field has leveraged to date. My goal here is to draw from them a well-specified methodological framework for doing so.

In the first stage, *de-reification*, the researcher disaggregates a given standard, convention, or prescription – something that IR scholars might want to call a 'norm' – into its constituents. This means specifying a configuration of institutions, actors, and practices featuring both mechanisms of reproduction, defined by historical place as well as regulatory function, and describing how it generates stability, where it contains places or relations of tension, and where problems of implementation or disagreement may spark innovation and transformation. This provides the information needed for the researcher to identify causal sources of transformation, along with the media through which sources influence and interact with the broader relational field in which they are situated.

This already has some precedent in sociology. De-reification has much in common with the Bourdieuian approach of mapping fields of structural and semiotic relations (Bourdieu 1993; Pouliot 2007; Epstein 2013), expanded by later field theorists to also involve identification of actors and specialised structures of institutional governance (Fligstein and McAdam 2012). Examples of skilful normative de-reification by IR scholars include enquiries into cosmopolitan views on harm (Linklater 2011), into the foundations of human rights in Israel (Krebs and Jackson 2007), and into the challenges to Turkish and Japanese identity presented by war crimes allegations (Zarakol 2010) – all marked by an attention to process and to relational analyses. Simply put, this stage means identifying the *who, what, when*, and *where* of a given case of normative transformation.

The second stage, *attribution of agency*, draws heavily on the pragmatist and relational view that agency is not something *possessed* by actors but an outcome of transactions between organisms and their environments (Emirbayer and Mische 1998). This is likely counterintuitive for many scholars because conventional views of agency associate it with *agents* rather than situations. The approach I take may seem overly meta-theoretical. However, it has analytical value in three ways. First, it makes it easier to examine the interaction effects of causal mechanisms working in concert. Even if each individual mechanism refers to intentional attempts to create change, the outcomes of their interaction may be unintended, and describing them as situational avoids the problems that attributing intentionality raises. Second, it links explanations to relationships rather than decisions, which is helpful when empirical data more clearly depicts the former than the letter. In this book I deal with testimonies and statements, in many cases self-exculpatory, by officials who are used to dissembling and who are interested in protecting their reputations. They may misrepresent their reasons, subtly or significantly, but their relationships are harder to conceal, and a relational understanding of agency makes those the centre of gravity for analysis. Finally, this approach makes it easier to see the role of technology as a powerful component of normative transformation (Latour 2005). This inclusion makes intuitive sense, given how important it often is to the narratives of change actors in these cases offer. However, technology diminishes in relevance in most accounts of normative change unless given agency of its own – and hence why I find value in new materialist social theory, as discussed earlier in this chapter.

However, attributing agency is not the same as treating an assemblage as an agent. Rather, it involves locating and specifying the particular transactions within a normative configuration most likely to encounter disruption and where the resolution of disruption is most likely to have a powerful effect in driving a broader transformation of interest. For example, in her discussion of brokers, Goddard (2009) observes that the actions of brokers are more influential in less dense networks because they mediate a greater share of connections. Before even studying exactly what choices or actions a broker takes, it is therefore possible to look at the structure of a network and assess, tentatively and preliminarily, where and for whom a change in circumstances is most likely to cause a broader transformation. However, rather than identify a broker as an *agent*, attribution of agency identifies significant sites or regions within a social arrangement, on the premise that agency emerges from a situation rather than from the individualised decisions and behaviours of a person.

Applied to cases of normative transformation, attribution of agency requires an investigator to look at a normative configuration and mark out the situations where mechanisms are likely to work with efficacy and potency. In the cases I examine here, this means deciding where to look to account for how the three proposed mechanisms operate: the discursive and disciplinary centres of gravity for conventional frameworks, rapid or threshold-level processes of technological innovation, or points of inter-network connection where brokerage can occur.

As such, attribution of agency is also a hypothesis: it is an initial proposal about who and what was instrumental in producing changes, and if it is incorrect then it will not be possible to complete the third stage of the analysis, as I will presently explain. It is part of the abductive research design I employ, where to offer an adequate explanation of the right parts of a case I first must first determine where to begin those accounts and what kind of theory is likely to enable an adequate explanation in the first place. Hence, attribution of agency does not involve denoting something ontologically distinct from a process of change itself, as it proceeds, works, and evolves, but is a temporal and cognitive step in making sense of a question. It also provides methodological room for researchers to consider a range of competing explanations and to test them by examining whether they specify processes that can, based on the data at hand, plausibly account for the observed normative transformation.

Several existing traditions of institutional analysis all feature some form of attribution of agency already, albeit in ways that deviate from the pragmatist approach I use. Beyond the already-provided example of network theory, historical institutionalism does so through the examination of exogenous shocks as destabilising influences, as this requires investigators to identify situations of crisis and actors with ambitions for change, the combination of which establishes the conditions for transformation (Thelen and Steinmo 1992; Steinmo 2008). Though not explicitly conducted using this approach, IR scholarship into the rise of new prohibitionary regimes in the wake of the Cold War (Nadelmann 1990) offers a good example of analysis that relates major upheavals to new space for normative change. Complexity theory directs attention towards non-linear forms of interaction and towards thresholds at which small changes in particular interactions can lead to large changes across an entire system (Mitchell 2009), granting particular situations and factors the causal power to generate significant transformations (Byrne 1998; Jervis 1997), such as in warfare (Bousquet 2008) or global climate governance (Hoffmann 2011). Finally, practice theorists do not just map fields but also identify kinds of practices or types of practitioners with unusual transformative potential (Schatzki et al. 2001; Adler and Pouliot 2011), through indicators of rising pressure, friction, or institutional weakness. Though a pragmatist approach to attributing agency focuses specifically on sources of situated creativity, the foregoing discussion shows that doing so is an established methodological technique, able to fit within a range of analytical frameworks.[11]

The third stage, *tracing transactions*, is a form of 'process tracing': 'the analysis of evidence on processes, sequences, and conjunctures of events within a case for the purposes of either developing or testing hypotheses about causal mechanisms that might causally explain the case' (Bennett and Checkel 2015, 7). What distinguishes tracing transactions from other forms of process tracing is the attention paid to reciprocal re-constitution. By looking at a string of transactions, the investigator searches for the ways actors transform, with each transformation leaving the situation and everyone involved different from before. In other words, it emphasises the embeddedness of actors within their own problems, such that both are transformed through situated action. For the study of normative transformation, this offers an especially important benefit: it makes it possible to see how existing prohibitions can be 'side-stepped' not by changing what is prohibited but by transitioning out of a given category of regulated actor, with the ultimate effect of a new relationship between a normative standard like a prohibition and the conduct of those supposedly bound by it.

I use a Bayesian approach to process tracing. I identify key observable implications of my explanation, which, if they obtain, should increase confidence in operation of that mechanism over explanations which would not feature it, such as norm alienation, norm death, or the predominance of any one mechanism over the others (Humphreys and Jacobs 2015; see also Nexon and Musgrave 2018). While process tracing may take a range of methodological forms (Bennett and Checkel 2015), I have chosen this approach to make transparent my

---

[11] Other approaches with an existing presence in IR include network analysis (Hafner-Burton et al. 2009) and Actor–Network Theory (Nexon and Pouliot 2013). Constraints of space limit deeper engagement with them here, however.

selection of single-case-study evidence: I focus on documenting the kinds of institutional processes that are most likely to yield evidence attesting to the operation of these three mechanisms in particular – the presence of which is enough to warrant some confidence in the explanation I offer.

In other words, the more the case evinces the most likely observable implications of the three mechanisms, the more confidence is warranted to accept that they account for the underlying causal story. Convention reorientation, as it refers to discursive attempts to reframe situations to place them within different normative frameworks, implies key discussions around definitions. Specifically, there should be clear evidence of a definitional dispute, the outcome of which determines the essential normative valance of a contested practice; whether the practice is forbidden or permissible will depend on its place within an already articulated set of conventions, and thus discourse revolves not around whether an action is right or wrong but which conventional framework should apply. Technological revision does not imply that technology alone is the 'master variable', but it does imply that the development of new tools plays an observable role in making normatively contentious action more palatable – that it reduces moral or strategic costs in ways that empower proponents of the action over opponents. Finally, network synthesis should imply observable patterns of bureaucratic alliance-making as a key component to the triumph of a 'winning coalition' of proponents of a normative transformation, as well as of the new practices or actions associated with it. These mechanisms are summarised in Table 3.2.

It should be possible to sketch, in general terms, what an analysis of normative transformation would look like according to this process. After identifying an interesting case, the investigator looks at the relevant institutional 'playing field' just prior to the period of transformation and maps it out. Doing so both defines the social relations which come together to produce the normative configuration in question and defines positions of influence and points of pressure or instability – the people who can make changes and the places where change happens. Then the investigator, based on some existing familiarity with the history of the case, identifies which people and situations were causally instrumental in causing the normative transformation in question. The investigator may also identify several mutually incompatible possible

Table 3.2 *The mechanisms of normative transformation and their observable implications*

Mechanism	Normative Effect	Observable Implication
Convention Reorientation	Redefines the *frame* of a situation to involve a new set of laws, authorities, agents, and agencies, changing its normative dimensions.	Definitional disputes over action classification, rather than over overarching legal/moral principles.
Technological Revision	Shifts action onto new media of intervention into the world, establishing new means with different normative connotations to their use.	Use of new tools to reduce moral/strategic costs of a contentious action.
Network Synthesis	Brings actors together in new ways, creating new alliances able to authorise new kinds of action.	Partnerships of actors from different institutional networks to push a common agenda.

sites or sources of agency, as hypotheses. Finally, the investigator traces the activity of designated agents, showing how it did (or did not) produce transformation through a process of causal interaction. The outcome is an analysis clarifying how and why practices emerge or change, in situations where the relatively macroscopic category of 'norm' encompasses too much of interest and where disaggregation is the only means of investigating the outcome of interest.

3.3.1 Data, Evidence, and Explanation

Investigative procedures for gathering data on normative transformations encompass an array of qualitative methods and tools. Official records – such as internal memos, executive reports, press releases, legal arguments and court records, and legislative or judicial testimonies – constitute one rich body of information on the institutional cultures, key personalities, and major events of a given case. Official records may feature a combination of retrospective narratives (such as in the case of congressional hearings) and contemporaneous manoeuvres themselves designed to effect normative change (such as white papers or legal warrants). Elite interviewing provides an ideal avenue of supplementing and moving beyond existing primary- and secondary-source evidence when key actors are accessible. In cases where academic researchers have also been able to achieve a high degree of trust and have access to sites during ongoing episodes of normative transformation, ethnographic methods provide another approach. Secondary data sources may include not only other academic accounts but also autobiographies – to be taken, of course, with a grain of scepticism. Journalistic investigations may be another invaluable source of data, particularly in cases such as those studied in this book, where key persons and events are often only accessible to those who have devoted years to cultivating a network of trustworthy sources – and to becoming trusted figures themselves. The common thread tying all these data sources together is that they provide historical insight into background conditions, important moments or periods of tension and transition, and relevant actors and their relationships.

Techniques for analysing data collected from these sources may be found in several approaches to process tracing and to historical sociology more generally. As I have already discussed the most immediately applicable such techniques, it should only be necessary to mention only one more. Tarrow's (2010) method of 'paired comparison' offers a way of setting two cases of normative transformation against one another, in order to accentuate relevant points of divergence and to call attention to causal processes unique to each one.[12] This is not covered in the three-step analytical process for studying normative transformation but is a technique capable of illuminating causal dynamics that a single-case analysis would leave opaque. In this book, three paired comparisons are possible, and in the concluding Chapter 7 I will use this method of analysis to discuss some of the broader patterns and

---

[12] In the Conclusion to this book, I employ this approach to comparison by examining the cases of targeted killing and 'enhanced interrogation' as examples of enduring and non-enduring normative transformation, then the cases of targeted killing and private contracting as working through centralised and diffused causal processes.

variations across all three cases, along with some discussion of additional 'partial' cases. Ultimately, however, I will analyse data through the approaches already described in this chapter.

3.4 Summary

In this chapter I proposed three substantive mechanisms – convention reorientation, technological revision, and network synthesis – and outlined a three-stage analytical process for enquiring into when and how those mechanisms generate normative changes of interest. I finished with some discussion of kinds of data I use in my three case studies. I move on to the bulk of my empirical analyses in the coming three chapters. I now turn to the case of the USA's targeted killing programme and to the prohibition on assassination.

4 | Case 1
Targeted Killing and Assassination

Armed drones are weapons of assassination, not of war as we know it.

Eugene Robinson[1]

[A] US passport shouldn't be a shield [...] If a guy is an international terrorist, determined, has murdered innocent Americans, then personally and legally I don't think there's any bar to undertaking that action. But I think it is a big step, just psychically [...] Had there been a proposal when I was there to go out and target for assassination an American citizen, boy, I mean, I definitely think there would be a very, very high standard there. Just, simply, the image of, the thought of it, killing one of your own.

John Rizzo[2]

4.1 Introduction

The emergence of the US targeted killing programme, which has come to play a major role in US military and counterterrorism actions in numerous conflict zones, is a clear case of normative transformation. The story of its development and institutionalisation shows significant bureaucratic, legal, and operational revisions in how the US security apparatus employs force and also in interpretations of national and international prohibitions on assassination. In other words, it is a prime example of transformation across a normative configuration, spanning civil–military relations to technologies of war to diplomacy.

Beginning in late 2002, under the Bush administration, the CIA began air strikes, launched from remotely piloted, propeller-driven aircraft – the MQ-1 Predator – on a small number of 'high-value

---

[1] 'The End of the "War on Terror"'. *Washington Post*, 2 May 2013; available at www.washingtonpost.com/opinions/eugene-robinson-the-end-of-the-war-on-terror/2013/05/27/5ef7a4a2-c4b4-11e2-8c3b-0b5e9247e8ca_story.html; accessed 2 July 2016.

[2] Interview with author.

targets' comprising al-Qaʿida and Taliban leaders (Plaw 2006). Under the Obama administration, these strikes increased considerably in frequency, reaching a peak in 2010 of at least 128 in Pakistan alone. Since then they have declined as a result of the end of US military expedition in Afghanistan, and with the focus of the War on Terror shifting to Yemen and the Horn of Africa, but they continue to be a routine activity.[3] Besides becoming more frequent over the first decade of the War on Terror, these killings also became more expansive, both in terms of who was targeted and in terms of who carried them out. As will be discussed presently, the US military began a parallel targeting programme, while at one point the CIA briefly considered using private contractors to carry out some killings (Mazzetti 2013).[4] There is no indication that these kinds of actions will cease in the future, even if they may diminish in scale proportional to larger US military commitments abroad.

The evolution of targeted killing in the United States is already the subject of a large body of research. This literature falls into four categories. Two concern 'objective' evaluations of targeted killing. The first examines assesses the effectiveness of the programme as a military or counterterrorism instrument, with some finding it to be a poor such instrument (see, for example, Jordan 2009) and others concluding the opposite (Price 2012). A few investigators find it is simply not possible to evaluate absent better data (Carvin 2012). For my purposes, this discussion is not salient, insofar as it is concerned with the 'objective truth' of whether targeted killing works rather than the perceptions of those engaged in it as a practice. The second evaluates the legal and ethical legitimacy of the programme under prevailing conventions of armed conflict and killing in war. This concerns the particular definition of assassination under international law (Beres 1991; Pickard 2001; Thomas 2001), questions of imminence and pre-emption (Kasher and Yadlin 2005; Gordon 2006), the space in which a formal armed conflict is occurring, and the status of combatants (Blum and Heymann 2010). It is also largely irrelevant to this case,

---

[3] For these statistics and others pertaining to the USA's use of armed UAVs, see the Bureau of Investigative Journalism: www.thebureauinvestigates.com/projects/drone-war.

[4] Though, significantly for my argument, this prospect proved beyond the pale and was scrapped. This limit is also explored in the third case, which tackles contracting practices more generally.

because, as with the previous category of literature, it is concerned with the 'objective' ethical or legal status of targeted killing, rather than the status key actors assigned to it or constructed for it.

The final two categories of literature are more salient. The third provides an institutional and strategic history of targeted killing, explaining how the programme emerged and developed (see, among others, Zenko 2013; Carvin 2015; Fuller 2017). Such work covers some of the same processes and interactions that I do here but is much less engaged, theoretically and analytically, with the question of normativity. Nor is it particularly interested in the material or technological basis for targeted killing, although it provides valuable context for those who are interested in this.[5] The fourth examines targeted killing as a new norm or conversely as the erosion of an existing one. Some of this appears in a special issue of the journal *Contemporary Security Policy*, edited by Hurd (2017), who largely avoids comment on the origins or implications of targeted killing practices but who calls attention to the significance of an interaction effect of international law and technological change underlying the 'reciprocal' relationship between norms and practices. Jose (2017b) approaches targeted killing as a new norm and shows how the US government engaged in a process of contestation over its legitimacy with Human Rights Watch, an NGO opposed to the practice. Großklaus (2017) argues that targeted killing is a new norm enabled by friction between 'meta-norms' of sovereignty and liberalism. All three are significant because they present targeted killing as a new norm rather than the erosion of an old one – Jose (2017a) makes this especially clear elsewhere by examining targeted killing by the United States according to the familiar life-cycle model. Banka and Quin (2018), conversely, argue for the 'erosion' thesis through an institutional analysis to look at the role of secrecy in enabling targeted killing to escape early censure until it was well established.

All of this work, however, remains wedded to an approach that separates norms from practices. It is thus committed to explanations focused on norm emergence or erosion, which, as I have argued, carves cases up into shapes or periods that smuggle in normative judgements and impose boundaries not reflected in practice. Only Grayson (2016)

---

[5] Though Carvin, in a later book (Carvin and Williams 2015), considers the intertwining of technology and normativity quite carefully.

examines the normativity of targeted killing without reference to unit norms, by focusing on cultural 'assemblages' that make it possible, although, in this account, bureaucratic politics and strategic innovation are largely absent. Collectively this presents an enormous body of discussion of what targeted killing is and how it might be practised.

It is the intersection between the institutional and normative histories – the third and fourth categories of the literature – where I contribute most to these existing perspectives. I try to show that the strategic history of targeted killing must be bound up in a normative one, and vice versa. The institutionalisation of targeted killing by the United States suggests a significant transformation in its interpretation of, and adherence to, conventions of war-fighting and counterterrorism. This transformation is distinct from – though certainly entangled with – formal or legal rules and extends throughout the practices and institutions composing the US counterterrorism apparatus.[6] Significant actors involved in that apparatus articulated concerns over what was right or proper, making reference not just to laws but to embedded institutional norms, organisational history, and experience with scandal, professionalism, and other dynamics warranting focused sociological investigation. In particular, their concerns pertain to the salience and nature of international and domestic prohibitions on assassination *as interpreted* by ranking figures in the CIA and in the Bush and Obama administrations.

This shows that a normative transformation took place, as part of the process by which targeted killing came to be institutionalised. Had there been no normativity 'in practice', none of the involved actors would have referred to the prohibition or oriented their actions around it; had it 'died' in the process of the construction of the targeted killing programme, actors would have initially felt it mattered but then stopped caring much about it as it underwent normative erosion. The evidence shows, however, that the prohibition on assassination – when properly understood as a normative configuration – continued to play a role over the development and employment of targeted killing practices, even though it underwent a process of reformation.

In this chapter, I explain how the US targeted killing programme emerged and evolved, what kind of normative transformation took place, and what the practices associated with it tell us about the normative

---

[6] With the exception of Jose (2017), who examines the status of the normative shift but not the institutional process leading to it.

character of assassination. I do not question the strategic need for new and effective instruments in the struggle against terrorism, nor the actual efficacy of targeting and killing specific terrorists or insurgents. From a methodological standpoint, what matters here is that actors within a community felt a need for improvement and had legible reasons for doing so. Necessity breeds innovation, but it is not the mechanism by which innovation takes place; that is, strategic pressures trigger the engagement of creative attempts at revising existing practices to incorporate new techniques, solutions, and materials. Through tracing the causal activity of the three posited mechanisms – convention reorientation, technological revision, and network synthesis – I show how attempts to respond to these pressures lead to change. Tracing the causal influence of all three mechanisms shows how the specific features of drone technology, the kind of strategic challenges posted by al-Qaʿida and its allies, and the bureaucratic-legal features of the US security apparatus connect to one another. In doing so, I identify the nature and origins of the normative transformation accompanying the USA's use of targeted killing.

4.2 De-reification: Targeted Killing and the Prohibition on Assassination

To de-reify the prohibition against assassination and show how it relates to the USA's use of targeted killing, I organise its history along two dimensions. First, I describe the emergence and development of the prohibition as an international convention, with both formal and informal normative status. Second, I describe the emergence of a prohibition at the domestic level, as part of the culture guiding, and the laws regulating, the conduct of the US security apparatus and in particular the CIA. Though domestic US law and security culture is deeply intertwined with international conventions, it is analytically necessary for the purposes of my discussion to separate the two. Specifically, it makes it easier to account for particular scandals and watershed moments in past CIA activities that heavily influenced how targeted killing was initially perceived by key actors in the initial conditions or outset of this case. This section is thus about outlining a normative configuration before its transformation took place; its purpose is to draw a picture of a state of affairs prior to causal intervention, to situate later analysis within an adequately fleshed-out environment.

4.2.1 Targeted Killing and the International Prohibition on Assassination

The international prohibition on assassination dates back several centuries[7] and has been a factor in discouraging the killing of political leaders (Thomas 2001) and military officers (Solis 2010), with the hunting and killing of 'named' individuals lying outside of the conventional morality of permissible killing in war. This was bound up in operational assumptions about how assassination would work: while ambushes were permitted in times of war, the infiltration of undercover operatives appeared 'perfidious' and therefore was forbidden. Moreover, assassination was associated primarily with political disputes between conflicting elites, wherein the method and the target sat outside normative military affairs (Thomas 2001). Without technology or tactics that allowed uniformed forces to target specific persons, Western military norms cemented assassination as illegitimate by nature, nearly impossible to perform honourably. For example, the Lieber code of 1863, a manual of military conduct issued by Abraham Lincoln to the Union Forces of the United States during the American Civil War, states in Section IX ('Assassination'), Art 148:

> The law of war does not allow proclaiming either an individual belonging to the hostile army, or a citizen, or a subject of the hostile Government, an outlaw, who may be slain without trial by any captor, any more than the modern law of peace allows such intentional outlawry; on the contrary, it abhors such outrage. The sternest retaliation should follow the murder committed in consequence of such proclamation, made by whatever authority. (quoted in Melzer 2008, 48)

Earlier treatises, such as those by Gentili, Vattel, and Grotius, do not present such a categorical condemnation of killings of specifically targeted persons. They appear to distinguish between legitimate wartime killings, which may be performed stealthily (such as by sneaking into an enemy camp), and treacherous killings, in which the killers abuse some good-faith trust put in them by their victim (such as by posing as, or bribing, a servant in the household of the target); nevertheless, they discourage the

---

[7] Renaissance-era politics and warfare, conversely, were frequently characterised by assassination, and the practice was widespread throughout Europe during the era (Thomas 2001). For example, as Morgenthau wrote, 'Venice, from 1415 to 1525, planned or attempted about two hundred assassinations for purpose of its foreign policy' (1967, 225).

killing of enemy leaders except in cases of dire necessity and exception (Zengel 1991). As Thomas (2001) observes, these ethical understandings of treacherous killing correlate with the rise of the sovereign state and should be placed in a broader normative context of the growing fixation on decisive battles between massed forces as the only legitimate means of settling military conflict – and of the view that political leaders act not in private capacities but as the agents of impersonal sovereigns.

In a modern context, at least prior to 9/11, there is further evidence for a customary prohibition on assassination that might also cover targeted killing in a wartime context. Assassination, even during war, is specifically prohibited under the Hague Convention IV of 1907[8] and, whether it targets officials or enemy personnel, would contravene *jus in bello* laws concerning combatant, civilian, and *hors d'combat* status (Beres 1991). As a number of legal (Schmitt 1992; Pickard 2001) and IR scholars (Thomas 2000; 2001) have observed, the targeting of combatants during times of war is less obviously prohibited under international law and custom than the killing of non-combatant political leadership outside of a wartime context.[9] Nevertheless, even this was contentious, as shown by the extraordinary Nazi response to the assassination of General Reinhard Heydrich.[10]

The international prohibition on assassination had three key features salient to this case. First, it prohibited selective or 'named' killings of political leaders and high-ranking officers. Second, it associates such killings with punitive execution, which violates the moral innocence of combatants, whereby being a soldier in an enemy army is not enough to

---

[8] Article 23(b) of the Hague Convention IV of 1907 states that 'it is especially forbidden . . . to kill or wound treacherously, individuals belonging to the hostile nation or army' (quoted in Beres 1991, 236).

[9] For example, when asked about Executive Order 12333, in which President Clinton authorised the killing of Bin Laden should capturing him not be possible, Roger Cressey replied, 'It's very easy for the legal community in government to separate Bin Laden and the efforts to hunt him down from what would traditionally be viewed as assassination, because he wasn't a candidate to be assassinated because he didn't fall into that category.'

[10] Heydrich was killed in 1942 by eight members of the Czech resistance, whom the British trained and parachuted into Bohemia. On 27 May, two of the agents, dressed in plainclothes, intercepted Heydrich's vehicle and injured him with a grenade; he died on 4 June of blood poisoning. In response, Nazi forces razed the nearby village of Lidice, executing 198 men on site, sending 184 women to a death camp, and abducting 98 children whom they forcibly had adopted by German families (Solis 2010).

make someone an outlaw. Third, it establishes as illegitimate most non-conventional means of such killings, where most means of infiltration are dishonourable or treacherous.

However, when it comes to the emergence and development of the US targeted killing programme, there is also a strong domestic prohibition on assassination. This prohibition is in part shaped by the international context[11] but is largely rooted in a specific history of scandalous intelligence operations and an institutional commitment to liberal values. Moreover, as confirmed in interviews with key Bush administration officials John Rizzo[12] and Roger Cressey,[13] the specifics of international law mattered less to policymakers and practitioners close to the programme than did US law and bureaucratic division of authorities. This implies the international normative context was generally stable, despite plasticity in the way the United States positioned itself with reference to the international prohibition – this being demonstrative of how normative configurations may span multiple policy spaces or domains. Put differently, the normative instability here lies in the institutionalisation of the international prohibition within a domestic legal and organisational context. It is to this process I now turn.

4.2.2 Targeted Killing and the Domestic Prohibition on Assassination

The presence of an international prohibition has not stopped the US government from getting directly involved in 'assassination-like' activities in the past. The most salient example of this was the Phoenix

---

[11] As Thomas (2001) notes, US reputation would suffer, with diplomatic costs, if it were known to engage in treacherous or perfidious killings.

[12] As Rizzo states, 'The notion of international law is not a consideration. I mean it's simply what every spy organization does in the world, is violate some form of international law, you're [acting innocent] in front of democratic and non-democratic countries. Espionage is basically another activity to violate other countries' sovereignty, that's just what it is, so it's US law that you keep. So that was, that would be the first consideration, does this program, does any program the CIA would undertake for that matter, is there a US law that governs here and is the CIA's actions within the scope of that law?'

[13] As Cressey states, 'it was making sure that at the end of the day, if they were successfully able to capture or eliminate Bin Laden, they could explain to congressmen and Senators that this was done within existing Presidential authority and within legal parameters and within existing authorities that the intelligence community operated under'.

Program, in which CIA agents partnered with South Vietnamese police and military personnel to 'capture or kill' Viet Cong agents and which thus resembled targeted killing in some ways. However, it does not appear to have left an institutional legacy or precedent. An exchange during my interview with John Rizzo illustrates this:

RIZZO: Well I think, again, these are unprecedented, certainly in my career. We ... hadn't done really a program that involved killing, involved killing people, a killing program. I mean we'd done paramilitary programs but not targeted killing.

AUTHOR: Not the Phoenix Program?

RIZZO: I said in my career. I'm not that old. [During] the Phoenix Program I was in high school, so–

AUTHOR: But these things have an institutional legacy to some degree?

RIZZO: Well, not really. Believe me, no one was around at CIA in 2001 who'd been around for the Phoenix program. I mean, that was William Colby's generation, that wasn't, so that was all ... I had been there twenty-five years, and I came in after the Phoenix Program. And I certainly didn't have any, any, first-hand experience or knowledge about it. So we knew these were unprecedented activities we were being asked now to take, and we knew, I certainly knew, of the risks.

By the late 1980s, there were strong legal and informal conventions against the practice. A history of scandal – mainly associated with the CIA's involvement in Latin American coups – and a lack of institutional memory surrounding the use of assassination in counterinsurgency meant that Agency officials 'grew up' in an environment where targeted killing was seen as prohibited in the minds of many within the CIA and in other arms of government, at least before 11 September 2001.[14]

First, it was explicitly forbidden by Executive Order 11905, signed in 1976 by President Gerald Ford: 'No employee of the United States Government shall engage in, or conspire to engage in, political assassination.'[15] Ford's order was later reinforced by Executive Order 12036, signed in 1978 by President Jimmy Carter. Both orders were

---

[14] Note however – as will be expanded upon later in this chapter – that initiatives to develop targeted killing were already in motion prior to 11 September 2001, even if less widely supported than they would be in the aftermath of the attack.

[15] A copy of the order may be found at https://fas.org/irp/offdocs/eo11905.htm; accessed 10 May 2017.

reinforced again by Executive Order 12333,[16] signed by President Ronald Reagan in 1981,[17] which reiterated that employees of the intelligence services were forbidden from engaging in assassination. The 1976 ban on assassination came after public investigation and exposure of a number of unsuccessful CIA operations to assassinate foreign leaders, and it established firm boundaries constraining the scope available to the US intelligence community for covert action. As Grayson (2016) notes, this ban was 'generously narrow' (54) and geared more towards mechanisms of transparency and executive control rather than permanent prohibition – indeed, employing the legal instrument of an executive order may have been to specifically preempt a legislative ban, which would have denied future presidents the power to approve of assassinations should they see fit. Nevertheless, until overridden the Order carried legal and institutional weight, redirecting the CIA away from any routine paramilitary operations.

Second, beyond its apparent illegality, assassination also fell within the range of activities associated with 'policy' rather than intelligence collection, which ran afoul of the principles internalised by the CIA in the wake of the Iran-Contra scandal; as James Pavitt, deputy director for operations for the CIA from 1999 to 2004, would later tell the 9/11 Commission, 'We don't do policy from Langley . . . and you don't want us to' (National Commission on Terrorist Attacks upon the United States 2004a).[18] As testimony in the 9/11 Commission report, discussing Clinton-era attempts to neutralise the threat Bin Laden posed, states:

CIA senior managers, operators, and lawyers uniformly said that they read the relevant authorities signed by President Clinton as instructing them to try to capture Bin Ladin [sic], except in the defined contingency . . . [T]wo senior CIA officers told us they would have been morally and practically opposed to getting CIA into what might look like an assassination. One of them,

---

[16] A copy of the order may be found at www.archives.gov/federal-register/codifi cation/executive-order/12333.html; accessed 10 May 2017.

[17] A copy of the order may be found at https://fas.org/irp/offdocs/eo/eo-12036.htm; accessed 10 May 2017.

[18] Pavitt's reluctance is not unique; during the mid-1980s, President Reagan's security executive made some attempts to establish CIA-run teams of local commandos to target and kill terrorists in Lebanon but was forced to scrap the plan in the face of strong resistance from both the CIA and the State Department, both of which cited the illegality of assassination and the likelihood of strong public relations blowback should the operation be exposed (Mazetti 2013).

a former CTC chief, said he would have refused an order to directly kill Bin Ladin [sic]. (National Commission on Terrorist Attacks upon the United States 2004a)

Or, as Richard Clarke, a top adviser to the White House on counterterrorism to both Clinton and later Bush, explained: 'The corporate view inside CIA was "We don't want to do covert action. And if we do covert action, we want it to be neat and clean. We don't want to be involved in killing people. Because we're not like that. We're not Mossad"' (quoted in Mazetti 2013).

This is consistent with expectations stemming from the explanation I advance for this case. First, it shows how key actors both defined targeted killing as assassination and were opposed to it on that basis as well as on the basis of deeper institutional conventions concerning the appropriate powers of the CIA versus other arms of the US defence and security apparatus. Second, it shows that, despite the obvious role that advanced technology has since then played in US use of targeted killing, major objections revolved also around propriety rather than solely the absence of adequately precise means. The form opposition to targeted killing took thus makes norm alienation unlikely, while suggesting that whatever changes later took place cannot solely be a product of the technological revision mechanism alone.

Yet while the above may have reflected the 'corporate view' inside the CIA, the prohibition was at its weakest in CIA's Counterterrorism Center (CTC), where attitudes towards the appropriate role the organisation should play in combating terrorism tended towards the bellicose. In other words, in the CTC, practitioners were more weakly socialised into the prohibition on assassination and more likely to consider practices that could conflict with it. The CTC was established during the Reagan administration, on 1 February 1986, in the aftermath of the deaths in Beirut of a number of ranking CIA officers, along with numerous American military personnel, at the hands of the Lebanese Hizbullah. Its first director, Duane 'Dewey' Clarridge, was chosen precisely for his aggressive and action-oriented reputation, and he pushed heavily for a pre-emptive, global counterterrorist doctrine making use of elite military forces (Fuller 2015). Clarridge even appears to have proposed the use of armed drones, though this project did not come to fruition before he was sacked in the wake of the Iran-Contra scandal (Fuller 2015, 783).

This evidence that the CTC chafed under the prohibition on targeted killing is unsurprising. The global orientation of the CTC, and its mandate to target violent non-state groups rather than to conduct more traditional intelligence duties, placed it at the seam between espionage and military action, in a unique, novel institutional space where the conventions of neither were clear. This speaks to the institutional plasticity of a relatively stable international prohibition and a relatively unambiguous – at least for most practitioners – domestic one. As a normative configuration the prohibition lies in the grounded practices of personnel working not just in the context of US law and of executive, top-down directives but also in an environment of localised habits, understandings of strategic challenges, and learned ethical sensitivities. In the CTC, practitioners had developed an orientation in line with its mandate but less consistent with the broader and more consistent prohibition on assassination as institutionalised throughout other branches and agencies of the US security apparatus.

Conversely, the prohibition was more strongly established in the other executive branches of the government, where it fit more broadly within an increased sensitivity to accidental civilian casualties of military action. This was a consistent feature in relations between the White House and the CTC over the years (Fuller 2015) and had significant operational consequences even as the prohibition on targeted killing began to relax. This is well illustrated by the way President Clinton approached an opportunity to kill Bin Laden when the first Predator UAVs began flying over Afghanistan, in mid-September 2000. In a trial run for expanding their use as a surveillance platform, one of their pilots had observed, at Bin Laden's Tarnak Farms compound outside Kandahar, a figure apparently matching Bin Laden's description (National Commission on Terrorist Attacks upon the United States 2004a, 190). The option of launching a cruise missile at that location existed, but Clinton was unwilling to approve a large strike upon a settlement in which children were very likely present (Coll 2014). Even once targeted killings had begun, under Bush, the reticence to employ the measure widely over concerns about civilians dying in the process persisted, as seen in the aborted 2007 attempt to kill Hizbullah commander Imad Mugniyeh.[19]

---

[19] On this, see Adam Entous and Evan Osnos, 'Qassem Suleimani and How Nations Decide to Kill', *New Yorker*, 10 February 2020, available at www.newyorker.com/magazine/2020/02/10/qassem-suleimani-and-how-nations-decide-to-kill.

In other words, this was not merely a particularity of Clinton but a well-established concern for the executive branch.

However, targeted killing was, by this point, under consideration. Attempts to arm the Predator were under way, and indeed, on 4 September 2001 approval was eventually given to employ an armed drone to target Bin Laden (Fuller 2017). However, government officials were all extremely hesitant, at least up until that point, to engage in targeted killing; the executive arm of the US government lent the prohibition strength, largely by hitching it to other conventions regarding the distribution of powers across the arms of the state – according to which the CIA had no legitimate powers to engage in killing – and to a particular, liberal vision of how states should apply lethal violence or wage war in a post–Cold War era. For the executive branch, therefore, it was not just the specific international prohibition on assassination that mattered in shaping the prohibition on targeted killing but broader cosmopolitan norms concerning interventions abroad.

As this all shows, the prohibition against assassination emerges from a plastic normative configuration stretching across multiple institutions and linking up to a range of other conventions and practices. It was not uniform. The CTC's position in this institutional field was initially subordinate, and thus, even though it housed proponents of targeted killing, those proponents were deprived of opportunities to mount a real challenge to the status quo. However, developing technologies, the nature of the threats posted by Islamist militancy, and the expansive reaction to the attacks of 11 September were to change this.

4.3 Attributing Agency: Technological and Ethical Potential for Change

In this section, I identify where, within the relevant normative configuration(s), practical tensions, technological pressures, or ethical discontentment established moments or spaces especially conducive to generating change. To clarify the pragmatic and multidimensional nature of the normative configuration in this case – and others like it in which standards or principles change significantly across time and social place – I show the interaction of all three of these things. This is part of what sets the approach I take apart from other approaches to 'norm change' in the field: a focus on the *interaction* of strategic/instrumental, technological/material, and ethical/moral sources of social change. I find that the potential for significant transformations in the US stance towards targeted killing lay in an individually necessary and jointly sufficient combination of new technology and a new executive orientation towards the use of military force abroad – in other words, in the symbiotic interaction of contentious or insurgent bureaucratic 'entrepreneurs' and the emergence of new material capacities.

As noted, one of the major executive inhibitions surrounding targeted killing related to accidental deaths of civilians. However, a remotely piloted aircraft armed with a smaller and more accurate missile offered a far more discriminating use of force than did a cruise missile, such as that which had previously been considered and rejected as a means of targeting Bin Laden. In my interview with him, Roger Cressey confirmed this in stark terms:

AUTHOR: How did people feel about accidentally killing civilians, kids? How bad of an outcome would that have been if you also got Bin Laden?

CRESSEY: So that's a big argument why you want to use the Predator instead of cruise missiles. It's the difference between a hundred-pound warhead and a thousand-pound warhead. It's the difference between line-of-sight shooting with laser precision and shooting a cruise missile from several hundred miles away and hoping to hell the gyroscopes work the right way to go on target.

His response shows importance of attempts to arm the MQ-1 Predator, a remotely piloted spy plane initially designed for surveillance only. Though not specifically related to any desire to engage in targeted killing, these attempts proceeded throughout the late 1990s, with successful tests taking place throughout 2001 (Whittle 2014), and appeared to provide the ideal platform for killing with adequate precision. A Predator armed with a Hellfire anti-tank missile was preferable to a cruise missile, which, as noted, had previously been considered and rejected as a means of targeting Bin Laden (Fuller 2017). As Cressey later explained, it offered a 'little boom' rather than the 'big boom' produced by larger ordnance (Roger Cressey, interview with author), while offering means of killing that, crucially, did not require commandoes to place 'boots on the ground' of another sovereign country and did not entail the risk of dead American personnel (and especially not the desecration of their bodies, as infamously occurred to American peacekeepers slain in the 1993 Battle of Mogadishu).

Unmanned aerial vehicles also provided an important solution to problems of intelligence collection. Cressey emphasised this:

[T]he Predator program, which really started a lot of this, was created out of the frustration we all shared over the lack of actionable intelligence on Bin Laden senior leadership and what they were doing. And the idea was to use an aerial platform that could loiter for hours upon hours over a part of Afghanistan to identify activities on the ground and then hopefully develop an understanding of predictive movement of individuals . . . . You can start to predict that if it's Monday he's in Kandahar, on Thursdays he goes to Jalalabad. And if you can have that type of data, you know, cross-referenced with whatever SIGINT [signals intelligence] you have ... [I]t's a mosaic that is then created from all these individual disparate pieces of data that gives you an intelligence picture. And what we were looking to do was to develop the kind of intelligence that would allow us to predict where Bin Laden would go, so that we could then present to the President and his advisors, 'Bin Laden is going to be in Jalalabad on Thursday, at five o'clock, and this is the building he traditionally goes into at this time. This is an opportunity to eliminate him.'

Moreover, further developments would later take place after targeted killings had begun, both in optical technology and in the form of entirely new aircraft such as the MQ-9 Reaper, contributing to the further use of unmanned airpower once the targeted killing programme was already ongoing (Coll 2014). These developments did so by making it possible to gather higher-quality tactical information and spend longer periods of time loitering in the skies over target areas. Also key were improvements in electronic and signals intelligence collection, offering new opportunities to learn the locations of desired targets in time to strike them (Miller et al. 2013). In other words, these technological developments, which allowed would-be targeted killers in the CIA to better remain within the parameters of cosmopolitan warfare while still employing effective force, provided a prior enabling condition and source of institutional leverage for normative transformation.

Yet technological revision, with its attendant ethical concerns, was not the only potential mechanism for driving normative change over this period. Under the Bush administration, another key role was played, both initially and during later expansions of targeted killing practices, by the added impetus of involvement by the White House, intervening on behalf of the CTC against directorial opposition to targeted killing – in other words, by the additional and supportive involvement of new networks containing actors with the power to reorient extant conventions in ways the CTC could not. Then, under the Obama administration, further executive involvement enabled an escalation in the number of strikes and the range of targets. I will go into greater detail on the role of executive involvement in the next section, discussing causal mechanisms; the important point to be made here is that normative transformation was possible not simply because the president willed it to happen but because the administration found allies within the CIA whom it could empower and help out-manoeuvre bureaucratic rivals – and because it did these things effectively in practice.[20]

Finally, the nature of 'the enemy' also established a strategic impetus, constituting the sort of threat that could motivate or legitimate normative transformation. Targeted killing was appealing because the enemy was otherwise hard to reach through more conventional means, making use of organisational structures and geographic spaces that made other kinds of intervention or uses of force difficult, legally and technologically. Hence the emergence of 'norm change' here came, at first, out of a response to a specific problem with a circumscribed context. Moreover, as Cressey explains, the status of the enemy as a non-state actor operating in the sovereign territory of other countries introduced diplomatic problems with higher-profile military means:

There has to be a level of cooperation between governments on these type of programs, otherwise it doesn't work. Otherwise you fly in a B-2 bomber at, you know, 80,000 feet, that no other government could shoot down, and you drop [large munitions]. The precision nature of the Predator became very compelling. Because for the other governments, it allowed them to minimize the collateral damage.

As this shows, the unusual organisational and legal position of al-Qaʿida established the operational need that drones could provide, while foreclosing on other, more conventional avenues of capturing or attacking terrorists – or at least making these other avenues highly problematic, given diplomatic and public conventions on use of force abroad.

---

[20]   One implication of this account is that theories of bureaucratic politics are rooted in relational sociological assumptions – indeed, Fligstein and McAdam (2012) go to lengths to demonstrate this.

But this does not account for normative transformation on its own. Policymakers and practitioners might instead have altered their ends to be more in line with the means available to them or chosen to forgo targeted killing for normative reasons despite its supposed strategic advantage. In other words, the characteristics of terrorist and militant groups introduced new strategic calculations to the pursuit of security-related ends, but this neither determined nor (absent discursive and cultural engagement) legitimated a major transformation in the prohibition on assassination.

4.4 Tracing Transactions: The Three Mechanisms at Work

In this section, I provide a causal account of the targeted killing programme and of the normative transformation it involved. I show how the operation and interaction of the three proposed causal mechanisms – convention reorientation, technological revision, and network synthesis – explain how targeted killing came to be and how it evolved from its origins into its current form. While this account thus focuses on the specific processes generating change, it is situated within contextual and background information provided in the preceding two sections. It rests not just on its own specific sources but also on the existence of established normative prohibition on assassination and on the technological and institutional sources of agency previously identified. For analytical clarity, I divide the account into two sub-sections: I examine first the emergence under Bush of a targeted killing programme; and second the expansion and legal normalisation of that programme under Obama.

4.4.1 *The Emergence of a Targeted Killing Programme*

The potential for significant transformations in the US stance towards targeted killing lay in a combination of new technology and a new executive orientation towards the use of military force abroad. As noted earlier, arming the MQ-1 Predator allowed would-be 'targeted killers' in the CIA to better remain within the parameters of cosmopolitan warfare, provided an enabling condition and source of institutional leverage for normative transformation. Yet technological advances were not the only factors enabling normative change. According to available accounts, the possibility of using drones to carry out targeted killings was first raised by Cofer Black, the director of the CTC, in mid-2000. Black, alongside Richard Clarke, had been searching for a way to damage al-Qaʻida and Osama Bin Laden. However, the proposal that the CIA engage in targeted killing met with strong legal and bureaucratic opposition (Mazetti 2013). Director of Central Intelligence George Tenet was highly resistant to the prospect of his organisation engaging in what appeared to be assassination. To quote the final report of the 9/11 Commission:

Tenet in particular questioned whether he, as Director of Central Intelligence, should operate an armed Predator. 'This was new ground', he told us. Tenet ticked off key questions: What is the chain of command? Who takes the shot? Are America's leaders comfortable with the CIA doing this, going outside of normal military command and control? Charlie Allen told us that when these questions were discussed at the CIA, he and the Agency's executive director, A. B. 'Buzzy' Krongard, had said that either one of them would be happy to pull the trigger, but Tenet was appalled, telling them that they had no authority, nor did he. (National Commission on Terrorist Attacks upon the United States 2004b, 210 and note 241)

Tenet's reticence delayed further serious consideration of the use of CIA resources to engage in any killings for over a year. This appears to have been in line with broader executive policy. In July 2001 the US government made a firm public statement against targeted killings when the US ambassador to Israel at the time, Martin Indyk, condemned Israel's assassinations of Palestinians suspected of terrorism: 'The United States government is very clearly on record as against targeted assassinations . . . . They are extrajudicial killings, and we do not support that' (Meyer 2009). The US government thus publicly and internally took a dim view of targeted killings; significant normative transformation had yet to take place.

Yet even prior to the 11 September attacks and the commencement of a 'War on Terror', White House executives under the new Bush administration sought to circumvent the opposition of leadership of the CIA to targeted killing by soliciting ideas from lower-ranking members of the agency. As early as mid-2000 – and expressed opposition to extensive CIA involvement in 'policy' notwithstanding – Clarke was looking into ways of striking at Osama Bin Laden. He went so far as to call a meeting at the White House for drone warfare's main advocates in the CIA and the DoD but excluding Tenet (Mazetti 2013). While it was not out of the ordinary for Tenet to be absent from routine briefings, convening a meeting to gather together proponents of a course of action Tenet opposed, and including a dissident subordinate from the CIA, clearly demonstrates the operation of *network synthesis*. Clarke's actions indicate a reforming of the normal chain of authoritative relationships through which the executive and the CIA made policy and communicated directives. By investing the White House connection with Cofer Black with greater significance and using it to bypass bureaucratic obstacles, Clarke made the CTC into a new and more important node in the networks that make up the US security apparatus.

The 11 September attacks, unsurprisingly, set the stage for a significant escalation in the slower and smaller normative transformation already under way. Despite organising advocates of targeted killing in the form of that White House meeting, Clarke's enthusiasm for targeted killing was not limitless. As he later would explain, he was invested in maintaining 'assassination' as a distinct and forbidden practice:

We didn't want to create a broad precedent that would allow intelligence officials in the future to have hit lists and routinely engage in something that approximated assassination ... . There was concern in both the Justice Department and in some elements of the White House and some elements of the CIA that we not create an American hit list that would become an ongoing institution that we could just keep adding names to and have hit teams go out and assassinate people. (quoted in Scahill 2013)

Black, however, had a well-established reputation amongst his colleagues for enthusiastically supporting paramilitary counterterrorism activities. Following the 11 September attacks and with the Bush administration's interest in aggressive counterterrorism, he soon became a popular figure at the White House – essentially bypassing Clarke, in a further and perhaps ironic example of continued *network synthesis*. Black and the CTC were very quickly given the authority to begin targeted killings, following a White House briefing to which only Black, senior personnel under his command, and select foreign intelligence officials were invited (Scahill 2013).

While this clearly demonstrates the escalating transformative power of the *network synthesis* set into motion by Clarke, it was not the only mechanism active during this time. *Convention reorientation* also operated through the introduction of novel ways of framing and justifying a militarised response. The legal permissions offered by the new *Authorization for the Use of Military Force*, passed on 14 September 2001 and authorising the use of military forces against those responsible for the attacks, introduced a broad military logic to the CIA's counterterrorism initiatives – a point emphasised to me by a former counterterrorism adviser to the Bush administration (Roger Cressey, interview with author). In other words, executives in the Bush administration out-manoeuvred Tenet to partner with a lower-ranking CIA official who did not share his director's distaste for clandestine killing, and they supplied those in favour with a new set of conventions governing use of force in counterterrorism or counterinsurgency operations.

Here it is helpful to explicitly revisit the observational implications of the proposed causal mechanisms and to consider whether those implications obtain in ways that should increase confidence in an explanation involving all three. The role of new technology as a way to overcome the disadvantages of previous means, both operational and normative, is the easiest to discern. This strongly attests to the role of technological revision. Moreover, the importance of executive enthusiasm for aggressive counterterrorism, post-9/11, is consistent with network synthesis; the intervention of the White House in support of targeted killing proponents neutralised the previously more dominant CIA actors opposed to it. Perhaps hardest to discern in this phase is the role of convention reorientation. At first glance, it may be possible to imagine all this taking place without redefinition of targeted killing; more consistent with norm death, this explanation would simply point to new technologies and executive impetus. Speaking to the operation of convention reorientation is only the importance of the AUMF (Authorization for Use of Military Force) in resituating counterterrorism activities within a logic of armed conflict. However, further evidence more supportive of including that mechanism in an explanation for the emergence and institutionalisation of targeted killing can be found in the actions of the Obama administration, discussed presently.

Crucially, this account does not make sense if each of these mechanisms worked in isolation from the others; each mechanism necessarily helped sustain and intensify the conditions for the others to operate. New technologies could be used because the possibilities for action they generated were given bureaucratic and conventional legitimacy. Conventions could change because the concerns that motivated them had technological work-arounds and because powerful backers of new practices could overrule risk-averse officials who still hesitated. New executive authorities could extend through bureaucratic networks because they could supply insurgent practitioners with the means of technologically and legally bypassing internal obstacles oriented around previous technological and legal constraints. Moreover, it is also difficult to make sense of the origins of targeted killing solely in terms of contention or as simple strategic exigency; discursive and rhetorical factors play an obvious role, but so too do the material possibilities established by technological development, and the interaction between discursive frames and technological means is evidently reciprocal.

4.4.2 *The Expansion and Normalisation of the Targeted Killing Programme*

Despite the rapid re-orientation of the CIA towards targeted killing, engineered by the Bush administration and its supporters within the agency, the practice met with mixed reception from the defence community at large. As former CIA general counsel Jeffrey Smith claimed in an interview with the *Washington Post*, targeted killings may 'suggest that it's acceptable behavior to assassinate people . . . . Assassination as a norm of international conduct exposes American leaders and Americans overseas' (Meyer 2009). The Bush administration and the CTC, however, were certain they were dealing a significant blow to al-Qaʿida and its allies. They even for a time considered using private contractors on the ground to carry out killings in areas where drone strikes were not feasible, such as in urban spaces. In 2004 the CIA contracted with Blackwater to provide deniable, arms-length paramilitary teams able to target al-Qaʿida leaders, but the plan was scrapped due to internal and executive concerns over its legitimacy.[21] In the end, however, both the CIA and the Defense Department, through the expansion of JSOC (Joint Special Operations Command) and its own

---

[21] Specifically, Director Panetta is on the record as opposing the use of non-governmental, civilian agents to carry out state-directed killings, as expressed in the aftermath of the breaking of this story (see Mark Mazzetti, 'C.I.A. Sought Blackwater's Help to Kill Jihadists', *New York Times*, 19 August 2009, available at www.nytimes.com/2009/08/20/us/20intel.html; accessed 10 April 2017).

intelligence infrastructure, had by and large accepted if not embraced their roles as counterterrorists fighting on a global battlefield.

Once President Obama took office, network synthesis changed in form, mostly working through his increased personal involvement in the targeted killing process, while technological revision diminished in salience. Nevertheless, surveillance and drone technology continued to increase in precision and scale, providing further material evidence for proponents of targeted killing to adduce in establishing the legal character of targeting as militarily normal and ethically more humane than putatively less precise uses of force. The decreased salience of technology does not mean its irrelevance, and the interweaving of the three mechanisms still are essential to an adequate causal account of what took place.

With the end of the Bush administration, Obama would have had an opportunity to limit the scope of drone warfare or otherwise to put a halt to further targeted killings, but he instead did the opposite: he escalated and expanded the programme. Within the first year, the Obama administration had presided over more drone strikes than the Bush administration had in its entire eight years in office, and Obama took a far more personal role in the programme immediately upon entering office, signing off on lists of targets in weekly meetings between himself and the director of the CIA (Meyer 2009). He relied on a former head of the CTC and long-time veteran of the CIA's clandestine service, John Brennan, as his counterterrorism adviser and later appointed him to the position of director of the CIA – a role for which he had considered Brennan from the very beginning of his presidency.[22] Brennan's prominence began during Obama's presidential campaign, in which he served as a foreign policy adviser and advocate of a multi-arm governmental approach to covert action; this would surely have been a clue that Obama intended from the beginning of his administration to pursue a bellicose and intelligence-driven counterterrorism strategy. That Brennan became Obama's counterterrorism 'priest'[23] speaks to the growing centrality of the CTC within

---

[22] Micah Zenko, 'The Lethal Bureaucrat', *Foreign Policy*, 11 September 2012, available at https://foreignpolicy.com/2012/09/11/the-lethal-bureaucrat/.

[23] Micah Zenko, 'The Seven Deadly Sins of John Brennan', *Foreign Policy*, 19 September 2012, available at https://foreignpolicy.com/2012/09/19/the-seven-deadly-sins-of-john-brennan/.

the CIA during this period. The CTC, increasingly, *was* the CIA – or at least was its most prominent and significant internal unit.

There are two reasons why Obama may have committed so extensively to targeted killing as an instrument. The first is the desire to step up the 'good' fight against al-Qaʻida while stepping down the 'bad' fight the Bush administration had started in Iraq. The second, at least according to some within the government, was that, as the Obama administration abandoned the infamous 'enhanced interrogation' programme, targeted killings became a much more significant defence against terrorism (Scahill 2013).[24] As this deprived the CIA of significant human intelligence sources, the killings had to shift from a pre-emptive to a preventive mode, lest another major attack against the United States take place and result in great political cost to Obama and his government. Though this second reason may imply a rather more cynical motive, it highlights the perceived value of targeted killing and drone warfare as a key instrument for the Obama administration to fight terrorism while showing how different their approach to the War on Terror was from that of their predecessors.[25]

One of the clearest indicators of the Obama administration's attempts to legally normalise targeted killing is a leaked, undated State Department white paper.[26] Entitled 'Lawfulness of a Lethal Operation Directed against a U.S. Citizen who Is a Senior Operational Leader of Al Qa'ida or an Associated Force', it was confidentially provided to members of the Senate Intelligence and Judiciary committees in June 2012. The memo went beyond simply outlining the circumstances under which a US citizen may be targeted and killed, to state, in legal language, much of the Obama administration's case for

---

[24] The new administration's desire to distance itself from the Bush-era interrogation programme is taken up further in the next chapter, focused specifically on that programme and its relation to the prohibition on torture.

[25] Whether this perception was accurate lies outside the remit of my book.

[26] Another memo, dated 2011, outlines a more specific justification for the targeted killing of Anwar al-Awlaki, an al-Qa'ida leader and US citizen. Here the US government claims the authority to target him under the AUMF, positioning the operation as a military action directed at an imminent threat rather than a punishment for terrorist crimes; it acknowledges but dismisses civil liberties concerns surrounding extrajudicial execution. A copy of the memo may be found at www.washingtonpost.com/r/2010-2019/WashingtonPost/2014/06/2 3/National-Security/Graphics/memodrones.pdf?tid=a_mcntx.

targeted killing in general. First, it firmly differentiated such killings from 'assassinations':

In the Department's view, a lethal operation conducted against a U.S. citizen whose conduct poses an imminent threat of violent attack against the United States would be a legitimate act of national self-defense that would not violate the assassination ban. Similarly, the use of lethal force, consistent with the laws of war, against an individual who is a legitimate military target would be lawful and would not violate the assassination ban. (US Department of Justice 2012)

Second, it stated when targeting is permissible, including a broad definition of imminent threat: 'The condition that an operational leader present an "imminent" threat of violent attack against the United States does not require the United States to have clear evidence that a specific attack on U.S. persons and interests will take place in the immediate future' (US Department of Justice 2012). Beyond presenting an imminent threat, two other conditions must be fulfilled: 'law of war principles' must in general be followed; and capturing the target, at least when they are an American citizen, must be practically unfeasible, or at least not without considerable risk to US personnel.

It is here that convention reorientation can best be observed, as efforts to define targeted killing as something distinct from assassination are the clearest indication that this mechanism is at work. This is not simply a move within legal discourse but, given the formal and informal channels through which the law influences the normative sensitivities and orientations of the CIA, a bureaucratic and institutional move as well. If the Obama administration could simply have decided, regardless of legal or conventional status, to escalate and institutionalise targeted killing, there would be no reason for the white paper. By going to the efforts of intervening in the definitional dispute over whether targeted killing was or was not assassination, therefore, the administration's actions attest to the operation of something other than just the network synthesis mechanism.

Also key to the Obama administration's approach was that targeted killing be closely managed and coordinated by executive involvement – in particular, by Obama himself in close partnership with his adviser John Brennan. Brennan was a former CTC analyst, assistant to Director George Tenet, and later the station chief for Saudi Arabia, before leaving the CIA to work in private consulting. He returned to political influence as a significant source of advice for Obama, as the president's chief counterterrorism adviser from 2008 to 2013, and then as director of the CIA from 2013 to January 2017. Brennan staunchly advocated extensive use of targeted killings from the start of his tenure as adviser, and he was responsible for liaising with the CIA, presenting target lists to Obama for approval, and for institutionalising the 'disposition matrix' – a database of intelligence allowing for streamlined selection and pursuit of targets (Miller 2012; Zenko 2012). While Obama has often been presented as a singularly supportive force for targeted killing, Brennan's involvement from the start of his presidency constitutes an essential piece of the puzzle in understanding the executive and structural influences behind the expansion of targeted killing, compared to the scale of the programme during the Bush years (Zenko 2012).

By this point, the second major phase of normative transformation had taken place, with US use of targeted killing looking mostly as it does today: legally normalised at the domestic level, prominent in US security policies in several regions, and a fixture of political discourse on countering terrorism. The Obama administration sought to normalise and institutionalise targeted killing as a major policy instrument, to an extent that went beyond what Bush-era proponents such as Clarke had originally desired. Technological revision diminished in salience, but UAVs and surveillance technology nevertheless had increased in sophistication in ways that permitted a greater scale to the targeted killing programme, even though the major change – the development of a means of precision killing – had already taken place. Convention reorientation and network synthesis synthetically interacted, as shown by the effects of Obama's personal involvement in the targeted killing programme, along with his extensive reliance upon John Brennan to provide both his vision and bureaucratic experience within the intelligence community. By taking a hands-on approach, the administration injected considerable executive authority to help push through extensive measures of legal normalisation, shifting the killings from an executively determined state of exception to a well-defined institutional role.[27] Of the two periods of transformation, in other words, the first

---

[27] By comparison, this process of legal normalisation took place with Israel's targeted killing programme far sooner, in part because the programme was led by the military and prosecuted in places visible to the public eye (Pratt 2013).

was of significant normative reorientation, the second of consolidation and expansion of the change in practice and institutional structure. Moreover, just as in the first phase, this second phase shows the irreducible interaction of all three mechanisms, where it is difficult to imagine such a significant normative transformation if they were not collectively present and mutually reinforcing.

4.5 Summary

It impossible to understand the evolution of US targeted killing practices without examining the mutually supportive interaction of discursive contestation, technological innovation, and bureaucratic politics. The strategic pressures of the War on Terror incentivised new practices and new technological developments, but the emergence of the targeted killing programme also involved evident struggles over right and wrong by practitioners, in ways that influenced the trajectory of technological development itself. Despite the evident appeal of drones as 'flying sniper rifles', officials in both the CIA and the Bush administration were hesitant to heavily invest in targeted killing due to concerns about bureaucratic authority and the legal status of targets. They were both utilitarian *and* normative in their decisions. In other words, rather than normative transformation being propelled by the suasive activities of entrepreneurs (Finnemore and Sikkink 1998), *or* the rational calculations of actors responding to strategic pressures (Morrow 2014), *or* intra-institutional competitions by elites (Allison 1971; see also Fligstein and McAdam 2012), the account I provide shows that all of these processes were interwoven together, such that each mechanism established the operative conditions for the others.

There was not a single prohibition on assassination to be changed or overcome but rather a complex set of normative imperatives and orientations, ranging from concerns over use of military force in general to the specific authorities held by each institution within the US security apparatus. Hence, unlike approaches that fix analysis on uptake (Finnemore and Sikking 1998), interpretation (Acharya 2004), contestation (Wiener 2008), or erosion (McKeown 2009) of specific norms, I find the greatest analytical value comes from orienting analysis around a constellation of commitments, standards, and principles – what I have termed a normative configuration. Taken together, these render sensible the US targeted killing programme in ways that established theories of norm change, whether focused on contention or rational choice, do not.

Moreover, this analysis of the US targeted killing programme suggests several things about the current state of the international prohibition on assassination and on the extent to which it has changed. It suggests that the international prohibition is largely intact, as the primary conventional logic behind the US practices is broadly drawn from international humanitarian law and from the laws of armed conflict, because the targets remain relatively limited to combatants in non-state militant groups, and because the means – aerial bombing – avoids use of poisons, double agents, or other 'treacherous' instruments of delivering a killing blow. However, there is reason to think the prohibition is weakened. Both Osama Bin Laden and Anwar al-Awlaki, another senior al-Qaʿida leader, were targeted, yet Awlaki did not have a combatant role in the organisation,[28] and – while information suggests that Bin Laden still did at the time of his death – this came as somewhat of a surprise.[29] Moreover, though the killing of Bin Laden was initially framed in public as a 'kill or capture' operation – in self-conscious contravention of a range of international laws – later reports showed that the order was in fact simply to kill,[30] and the killing of Awlaki has been widely viewed as an extrajudicial execution by the United States of one of its citizens.[31]

[28] Awlaki played a role as recruiter and ideologue, both of which established him as a threat to US security, but intelligence indicates negligible involvement in specific planning and execution of attacks (see Mark Mazzetti, Charlie Savage, and Scott Shane, 'Anwar al-Awlaki, a U.S. Citizen, in America's Cross Hairs', *New York Times*, 9 March 2013, available at www.nytimes.com/2013/03/10/world/middleeast/anwar-al-awlaki-a-us-citizen-in-americas-cross-hairs.html; accessed 10 April 2017).

[29] Nicolas Schmidle, 'Getting Bin Laden', *New Yorker*, 8 August 2011, available at www.newyorker.com/magazine/2011/08/08/getting-bin-laden; accessed 10 April 2017.

[30] Charlie Savage, 'How 4 Federal Lawyers Paved the Way to Kill Osama bin Laden', *New York Times*, 28 October 2015, available at www.nytimes.com/2015/10/29/us/politics/obama-legal-authorization-osama-bin-laden-raid.html; accessed 10 April 2017.

[31] See, for example, Conor Friedersdorf, 'A Ray of Sunlight on Obama's Extrajudicial Killings', *The Atlantic*, 24 June 2014, available at www.theatlantic.com/politics/archive/2014/06/a-ray-of-sunlight-on-obamas-extrajudicial-killings/373247/; accessed 10 April 2017. Also see Michael Ratner, 'Anwar al-Awlaki's Extrajudicial Murder', *The Guardian*, 30 September 2011, available at www.theguardian.com/commentisfree/cifamerica/2011/sep/30/anwar-awlaki-extrajudicial-murder; accessed 10 April, 2017.

On the one hand, this suggests that targeted killings still can generate broad pushback, affirming the continued existence of a prohibition on assassination and a relationship between that prohibition and the legitimacy of targeted killing. On the other hand, the willingness to engage in these actions and the lack of subsequent diplomatic or legal consequences for the United States implies that they are, at least internationally, within de facto normative boundaries.

The analysis I offer in this chapter has implications going beyond the specific case of targeted killing. Many international relations scholars show an interest in the apparent deterioration or demise of a number of prohibitions in the context of Western counterterrorism and counterinsurgency practices (Percy 2007a; 2007b; McKeown 2009; Panke and Petersohn 2011). I show that what took place in this case was not erosion, although it could be easily mistaken for such from a reified view of norms. Rather, the prohibition on assassination changed, with some practices becoming permissible whereas before they were not, while nevertheless the *idea* remained that assassination was forbidden. Changes in the classification of certain kinds of killing shifted the boundaries of permissible and impermissible. Moreover, I show that there is no way to make sense of that change by focusing exclusively on strategic or technological pressures; while the 'asymmetrical' nature of the US war on terror clearly incentivised new methods of fighting, the institutional evolution that took place is laden with obvious ethical deliberation and contention.

In the next chapter, I examine a case with some institutional and strategic similarities but a strikingly different normative outcome: the USA's 'enhanced interrogation programme' and the prohibition on torture.

| *Case 2*

'Enhanced Interrogation' and the Prohibition on Torture

At least five CIA detainees were subjected to 'rectal rehydration' or rectal feeding without documented medical necessity. The CIA placed detainees in ice water 'baths'. The CIA led several detainees to believe they would never be allowed to leave CIA custody alive, suggesting to one detainee that he would only leave in a coffin-shaped box. One interrogator told another detainee that he would never go to court, because 'we can never let the world know what I have done to you'. CIA officers also threatened at least three detainees with harm to their families – to include threats to harm the children of a detainee, threats to sexually abuse the mother of a detainee, and a threat to 'cut [a detainee's] mother's throat'.

United States Senate Select Committee on Intelligence, 'Committee Study of the Central Intelligence Agency's Detention and Interrogation Program' (2014, 4).

5.1 Introduction

President Obama's blunt statement that the US government 'tortured some folks' is an astonishing admission of guilt.[1] It placed the CIA's detention and interrogation programme, which lasted from 2002 to 2009, along with the use of the 'enhanced interrogation techniques' (EITs) developed as part of that programme, beyond the supposed moral pale. A prohibition on torture is well established in both international and US domestic law and may even be seen as a fundamental tenet of a liberal approach to law enforcement and war –namely, that prisoners have a right not to be assaulted by captors seeking confessions or information. The strict avoidance of torture is embedded in long-standing US military and law-enforcement interrogation practice. Given the bureaucratic and executive scale of the US use of coercive or

---

[1] See https://obamawhitehouse.archives.gov/the-press-office/2014/08/01/press-conference-president.

violent interrogation methods, a major normative transformation appears to have taken place during the Bush administration, involving a departure from convention at many levels.

Perhaps surprisingly, there is still debate over whether the EITs in fact constituted torture, years after they ceased to be used (as far as public knowledge goes) by any employee of the US government. Though numerous academics (McKeown 2009; Panke and Petersohn 2011; Steele 2017), prominent defence journalists (Mayer 2008; Ackerman 2014), and politicians (Dianne Feinstein in SSCI 2014)[2] endorse the view that the EITs were acts of torture, the legal experts (John Rizzo, quoted in Moughty 2015; Yoo 2014[3]) and practitioners (Tenet et al. 2014; Rodriguez 2015) associated with the CIA's detention and interrogation programme disagree. They argue that their methods – which included waterboarding (a form of simulated drowning previously used to elicit confessions by the Spanish Inquisition and later by the Khmer Rouge [Solis 2010]) – as well as extended sleep deprivation and forced rectal penetration[4] – do not violate any legal prohibition on torture and are not outside the established boundaries of permissibility. However sceptical one might be of this position, the defenders of EITs articulate it without blushing, implying that it carries at least some normative weight amongst target audiences.

This suggests two things: contestation over whether a prohibition on torture exists and has been transgressed; and a transformation in the prohibition's contents or social 'shape' in the relevant normative environment. This is made apparent by the fact that EIT defenders base their defence so much on claims of efficacy.[5] If there is an ongoing debate over whether potentially torturous actions are effective ways to educe reliable

2 See also the previously cited Obama statement at https://obamawhitehouse .archives.gov/the-press-office/2014/08/01/press-conference-president. See also John McCain, quoted in 'Sen. McCain's Full Statement on the CIA Torture Report,' *USA Today*, 9 December 2014, www.usatoday.com/story/news/polit ics/2014/12/09/john-mccain-statement-cia-terror-report/20144015/.
3 See also www.nydailynews.com/opinion/john-yoo-torture-report-dustbin-article -1.2039758.
4 On several occasions, Khalid Sheikh Mohammad's interrogators roughly inserted a tube into his anus as means of delivering food. While this was not on the list of approved EIT, the lack of medical justification for rectal feeding implies that it was a method of coercive interrogation (SSCI 2014).
5 While prominent accounts, such as those provided by former FBI interrogator Ali Soufan (2011) and by the SSCI Report (2014), suggest that EITs were comprehensively ineffective if not counterproductive, several former top-level

information, the implication is that if the answer is 'yes', then torture may be permissible under certain circumstances. The language of contestation over EITs shows not only that the boundary between torture and non-torture may have shifted but also the status and content of prohibition itself.[6] While at no point did proponents of EITs within the US government argue torture should be permitted as such, the intensity with which they continue to assert the efficacy of their methods implies a complex and murky relationship between whether a wrong act has taken place and whether a contested act is useful – that is, between a logic of appropriateness and a logic of consequentialism.

In this chapter, I explain the development of EITs and show how they were linked in practice to the normative status of torture. While there is evidence to suggest widespread public support, in the United States, for violent interrogations as a method of counterterrorism intelligence gathering,[7] my analysis focuses on the emergence, evolution, and application of the EITs – and of coercive interrogation methods more broadly within the US security apparatus. In this context, a prohibition on torture was firmly established by law and institutional convention. EIT proponents developed new technology, in the form of techniques designed to induce 'learned helplessness'. They formulated and applied new conventions for categorising both detainees (as enjoying fewer protections from harsh treatment) and those techniques (as not torture, because not designed to elicit answers during their immediate use). They operated through and from new structures of authority and secrecy, generated by increased involvement of the executive and of the CIA in handling interrogation. As with targeted killing, the development and institutionalisation of EITs thus rested on a synthesis of convention reorientation, technological revision, and network synthesis.

CIA and Bush administration executives involved with their use claim otherwise (Tenet 2007; John Rizzo, quoted in Moughty 2015; Harlow 2015).

[6] It should be noted that enquiring into the 'objective' effectiveness of EITs, or the 'objective' fact of whether they were or were not torture, is not the focus of this chapter. In the interest of transparency on these questions, I will state that I concur with the conclusions of the Senate Select Committee on Intelligence – namely, that EITs crossed the line into torture and were not any more effective than non-torturous alternatives. However, what matters here is not whether this position is defensible but rather how proponents and opponents of EITs have contended the matter in practice and in the process generated normative transformations.

[7] See www.pewresearch.org/fact-tank/2016/02/09/global-opinion-use-of-torture/.

As with the previous case, I begin by de-reifying the prohibition on torture through historical overview of the relevant institutional and legal conventions, both establishing that this prohibition *prima facie* pertains in some ways to the legitimacy of EITs and mapping out how that prohibition worked in practice during the time period of the case. I then identify sources of technological, bureaucratic, and strategic pressure and innovation, attributing agency to the actors and means that played a key transformative role. Finally, I provide a process-based account of the emergence and evolution of EITs, first as they became part of the CIA's detention and interrogation programme, then as they became, in part, a component of the military's own interrogation practices, and finally as they were phased out due to intense opposition from several influential quarters. In so doing, I show that the prohibition itself remains intact but that this case nevertheless indicates the persistent insurgent potential of small numbers of highly placed officials to transform even well-entrenched normative configurations through creative technological and bureaucratic manoeuvring.

5.2 De-reification: The Prohibition on Torture in Convention and Practice

To de-reify the prohibition on torture and show its connection to the US government's interrogation practices, I divide between legal or formal conventions establishing torture as impermissible and the informal conventions of interrogators in military, intelligence, and law enforcement agencies favouring other methods of interrogation. These informal conventions deserve attention because they prohibit torture not (only) on categorical moral or legal grounds but on the grounds that it is ineffective, unprofessional, and, in an aesthetic sense, inelegant. In both sub-sections, I identify not only where the prohibition was strongest but also where, in the normative configuration, the opportunities lay for the transformative attempts that made EITs possible.

5.2.1 Formal and Legal Prohibitions on Torture

Torture is the subject of numerous international legal and diplomatic prohibitions. Internationally, torture is banned under several treaties, most notably in the 1949 Geneva Conventions (Article 12 of the First and Second, Articles 17 and 87 of the Third, and Article 32 of the Fourth), the Universal Declaration of Human Rights (Article 5), the 1984 Convention Against Torture and Other Cruel, Inhuman or Degrading Treatment or Punishment, and the 1998 Rome Statute of the International Criminal Court (Articles 7 and 8).[8] These prohibitions do not seem to have routinely been violated by any major liberal state (Foot 2006),[9] at least not recently.[10] US law prohibits the use of torture by law enforcement personnel,[11] disqualifying any confessions or statements made under torture from consideration as evidence in court and putting those who torture at the level of slave-traders, labelling them 'enemies of mankind'.[12] The prohibition on torture is a peremptory norm (Foot 2006) to which the United States is committed in numerous treaties and in central documents of domestic law. It would have been nearly inconceivable to imagine, prior to 2001, that unambiguous torture by US government personnel could receive executive and legal endorsement, and, as I will discuss, proponents and defenders of EITs traded heavily on the supposed ambiguity of EITs in this respect.

5.2.2 Informal Practitioner Aversions to Torture

Interrogator accounts and manuals show a widespread aversion to torture and indicate an informal prohibition in communities of practitioners in the United States. These sources show the pervasive view that inflicting intense physical pain or discomfort to coerce a person into revealing information is an ineffective and unnecessary means of intelligence-gathering. There are noteworthy exceptions by counterterrorists of other states with similar principles of justice and military professionalism: France and Israel both institutionalised torture at times, yet did not do so overtly or explicitly,[13] while security forces in Northern

---

[8] For more, see www.icrc.org/eng/resources/documents/faq/torture-law-2011-06 -24.htm.

[9] Acknowledging the fuzziness of this category, I use it generally to denote those states which have robust protections for human rights and a relatively high degree of democratic accountability and transparency.

[10] Though as I will discuss presently, the United States during its counterinsurgency in the Philippines, and during the 1980s, did engage in coercive interrogation practices that arguably qualify.

[11] 18 U.S. Code § 2340.

[12] For details, see www.cfr.org/terrorism-and-the-law/torture-united-states-laws- war/p9209.

[13] The French in Algeria, during the Battle of Algiers (http://warontherocks.com /2014/12/torture-in-a-savage-war-of-peace-revisiting-the-battle-of-algiers/) and

Ireland engaged in torture on several occasions but not on a pervasive and institutionalised basis ('Case of Ireland v. the United Kingdom' 1978). Nevertheless, something like EITs appears firmly outside the normative and historical precedent for the US security apparatus.

Military interrogation accounts from the Second World War up until 2001[14] (and beyond)[15] claim professional interrogators opposed anything resembling torture. Instead, interrogators used rapport-building approaches and forms of low-level deception designed to gain prisoners' trust and to relax them. At a 2007 reunion, Second World War era US military interrogators described their approach in pointed contrast to the post-9/11 use of EITs. According to one: 'During the many interrogations, I never laid hands on anyone ... I never compromised my humanity.' According to another: 'We got more information out of a German general with a game of chess or Ping-Pong than they do today, with their torture'.[16] A similar approach characterised interrogation practices in the Pacific Theatre.[17] Later, during the Vietnam War, US military

Israel during the 1980s and 1990s, until a Supreme Court ruling moderated the practice somewhat, albeit without ceasing it entirely (http://scholarship .law.berkeley.edu/cgi/viewcontent.cgi?article=1202&context=bjil).

[14] At the beginning of the century, in the Philippines, US military personnel achieved some notoriety for routine use of the 'water cure', a form of waterboarding. This practice does not appear to have persisted following the end of counterinsurgency operations there, and it was the subject of public scandal in the US (www.newyorker.com/magazine/2008/02/25/the-water-cure; see also Miller [1982]).

[15] For example, in an address to troops in Iraq in 2007, General David Petraeus made the following remark: 'Some may argue that we would be more effective if we sanctioned torture or other expedient methods to obtain information from the enemy. They would be wrong. Beyond the basic fact that such actions are illegal, history shows that they also are frequently neither useful nor necessary'. See www .washingtonpost.com/wp-srv/nation/documents/petraeus_values_051007.pdf.

[16] See www.washingtonpost.com/wp-dyn/content/article/2007/10/05/A R2007100502492.html; note, however, that this is perceived efficacy and is not presented here as evidence for a claim as to what works best in an objective sense – again, that question is beyond the scope of my enquiry in this case.

[17] See Stephen Budiansky, 'Truth Extraction', *The Atlantic*, June 2005, available at www.theatlantic.com/magazine/archive/2005/06/truth-extraction/303973/; accessed 14 April 2017. This attitude is likewise prominent in accounts by British wartime interrogators as well. For example, with reference to the interrogation of suspected Nazi spies – who did not benefit from Geneva Convention protections – one interrogator explained his unwillingness to use physical violence to elicit information: 'For one thing it is the act of a coward. For another, it is unintelligent, for the spy will give an answer to please, an answer to escape punishment' (Shoemaker 2008, 96).

interrogators continued to prefer the same approach – though their close relationship with South Vietnamese military interrogators, who routinely tortured, introduced some ambiguity into the broader normative picture (Spracher 2008).[18] In other words, for most of the century prior to the emergence of EITs, prisoners of the US military were not typically subject to torture, and military interrogators did not view torture as a productive or appropriate method of gathering intelligence.

Military interrogation manuals further confirm this aversion to the use of physical violence by interrogators. FM 30–15, titled *Intelligence Interrogations* (first published in 1967, revised again in 1969 and 1973), initially stated that force was an unnecessary interrogation technique, then, in its final revision, was expanded to contain a specific section on a 'prohibition on the use of force'. This section reiterated both Geneva Convention and US military laws prohibiting torture and more forcefully dismisses 'threats of force, violence, and deprivation' as useless (Gebhardt 2005, 49). All three versions of the manual contained the following paragraph in the chapter titled 'Tactical Interrogations':

[F]orce is neither an acceptable nor [an] effective method of obtaining accurate information. Observation of the Geneva Conventions by the interrogator is not only mandatory but advantageous because there is a chance that our own personnel, when captured, will receive better treatment, and enemy personnel will be more likely to surrender if the word goes out that our treatment of PW [prisoners of war] is humane and just. (Gebhardt 2005, 49)

In 1987, FM 30–15 was replaced by FM 34–52 (revised again in 1992), titled *Intelligence Interrogation*, which included all of its predecessor's strong language on the impropriety and inefficacy of force or violence. Moreover, other manuals not specifically devoted to intelligence and interrogation but relevant to the military conduct also forbade torture. FM 31–73 and FM 31–16, for example, both state the need for humane treatment of prisoners even when those prisoners are not accorded POW status, such as if they are guerrilla forces (Gebhardt 2005, 48). On their own, these manuals would not necessarily indicate that any prohibition on torture existed in actual interrogation practice, but, together with the foregoing accounts by interrogators themselves,

---

[18] Some incidents of torture of North Vietnamese or Viet Cong prisoners by enlisted troops are also clearly documented, though these acts were neither systematic nor part of the routines of professional interrogation.

they lend weight to the claim that such a prohibition did exist in notable ways.

Law enforcement interrogations in the United States are intended to secure confessions and the information needed to secure additional warrants for search and detention; while torture historically played a role in this – with police giving suspects the 'third degree' – it rapidly ceased as a routine practice when judges began dismissing confessions or statements acquired through its use (Rejali 2007). While this context would ordinarily be less salient to national security intelligence-gathering, it matters a great deal in this case: prior to the development of the CIA's detention and interrogation programme, the FBI was primarily responsible for interrogating al-Qaʿida-affiliated prisoners (Soufan 2011). In other words, in war zones interrogators had a strong aversion to torture, and so too did those interrogators tasked with domestic counterterrorism intelligence gathering.

The CIA, by contrast, has historically had a more ambivalent relationship with torture. Close cooperation between CIA personnel and South Vietnamese security forces, particularly within the context of the Phoenix Program – a Vietnam War–era collaboration with US military units and South Vietnamese security forces to target Viet Cong cells – placed the CIA in a position of cooperation with, and authority over, extensive use of torture as a method of interrogation (Weiner 2007). However, contemporary accounts claim CIA interrogators themselves did not engage in torture, even if they were not above threatening to transfer prisoners from American to South Vietnamese custody, nor making use of information gleaned by South Vietnamese interrogations.[19] Close relationships between CIA personnel and the security forces of a number of Latin American countries – known for their use of torture notably Chile and Guatemala – also imply ambivalence. The clearest demonstration that the CIA, as an institution, approached physical violence as a potentially effective and morally unproblematic interrogation method comes in the forms of the Agency's two training manuals on the subject. *KUBARK Counterintelligence Interrogation* (1963) and *Human Resource Exploitation Training Manual* (1983) both include entire chapters on 'coercive' interrogation, advising interrogators on how best to use 'threats

---

[19] See also the account hosted on the CIA's own publicly accessible website, available at www.cia.gov/library/center-for-the-study-of-intelligence/csi-publications/csi-studies/studies/vol48no1/article06.html.

and fear', 'pain', and 'debility' (KUBARK 1963, 83). These manuals were meant for the training not of CIA officers, however, but of intelligence personnel in the Latin American countries with which the CIA was partnered, in their joint struggle against communist insurgencies throughout the continent. Hence, as with CIA involvement in the Phoenix Program, Agency personnel were not themselves detaining and torturing anyone – at least not as a matter of routine or official practice.

Also crucial to understanding how the EITs emerged, moreover, is that the CIA also simply had *no* real first-hand culture of interrogation by the time 9/11 occurred. While the CIA knew of and facilitated South Vietnamese and Latin American use of torture, during the 1960s and 1980s, respectively (Weiner 2007), no institutional precedent existed for running an in-house detention programme and carrying out interrogations entirely alone. The Agency's policy was to defer to military interrogation practices and standards.[20] The CIA did not, in 2001, employ its own interrogators capable of handling the questioning of terrorism suspects (SSCI 2014). A *New York Times* investigation quotes A. B. 'Buzzy' Krongard, executive director of the CIA in 2002, admitting this: 'I asked, "What are we going to do with these guys when we get them?" I said, "We've never run a prison. We don't have the languages. We don't have the interrogators."'[21] John Rizzo expanded on this:

[Detention and interrogation] are unprecedented, certainly in my career. We never held people incommunicado, we never built prisons to hold people. I mean, notwithstanding all the myths about CIA being this rogue elephant, we hadn't done anything close to that.[22]

Because there was no extensive existing culture of interrogation, and because the FBI had until that point handled counterterrorism

[20] To quote from the SSCI report: 'Testimony of the CIA deputy director of operations in 1988 denounced coercive interrogation techniques, stating, "[physical] abuse or other degrading treatment was rejected not only because it is wrong, but because it has historically proven to be ineffective". By October 2001, CIA policy was to comply with the Department of the Army Field Manual "Intelligence Interrogation".' (17). A notable exception here is the CIA's interrogation of Soviet defector Yuri Nosenko, who from 1964 to 1967 was subjected to sleep deprivation and forced standing during his detention by the CIA (17).
[21] See Scott Shane, 'Inside a 9/11 Mastermind's Interrogation', *New York Times*, 22 June 2008, available online at www.nytimes.com/2008/06/22/washington/22ksm.html; accessed 14 April 2017.
[22] Interview with author, 2015.

interrogation, informal prohibitions of torture – born, as they were, from practitioner experience and professionalism – were at their weakest in the CIA.

5.3 Attributing Agency: Technological and Ethical Potential for Change

A key source of agency in this case stems from the aforementioned absence within the CIA of existing institutional culture and precedent for maintaining a detention and interrogation programme. When directed to step up human intelligence-gathering efforts, the CIA was not limited by an extensive existing structure of normatively constrained or settled practices. It was free to consider new actions without encountering as much internal opposition – compared to the targeted killing programme, which did indeed encounter internal dissent from powerful official voices within the Agency. Rizzo's recounting of friction between the FBI and the CIA is illustrative here:

FBI did say at the time, that I heard, was that, okay, if you're going to undertake these kinds of techniques we cannot participate, because this is violative of FBI policy. You know, they have certain rules and regulations about conducting investigations, and this program was going to go obviously way beyond that.

This is further confirmed in the SSCI report's 'Findings and Conclusions': 'The use of coercive interrogation techniques and covert detention facilities that did not meet traditional U.S. standards resulted in the FBI and the Department of Defense limiting their involvement in CIA interrogation and detention activities' (SSCI 2014, 7). This suggests that the departure of the FBI removed a major bureaucratic obstacle to the CIA's plan to depart from normative interrogation practices. The FBI had supplied practitioners with a robust interpretation of the applicable conventions and authorities definitive of the interrogator's role. Once they left, the CIA was free of the existing normative constraints of law enforcement and military intelligence interrogation, as well as empowered by legal and executive support. At this point, the process of innovation surrounding 'enhanced interrogation' could accelerate and be institutionalised.

Technology also constituted a major source of transformative agency in this case and was a key component of the already-described origins of the transformation in interrogation practice. While not 'high-tech' in the sense of new feats of aeronautical engineering or electronic intelligence collection, behavioural science presented by psychologists nevertheless should be treated as a crucial technological development.[23] Based on remarks he made in a December 2001 meeting of a number of psychologists and intelligence officers, held to brainstorm methods of interrogation, the CIA approached James Mitchell, a Survival, Evasion, Resistance, and Escape (SERE)[24] instructor, for guidance on how best to 'break' al-Qaʿida prisoners during questioning.[25] This led Mitchell to recruit his friend and colleague Bruce Jessen, and together they designed a new approach to interrogation built around the concept of 'learned helplessness', which they understood to render subjects mentally incapable of non-compliance with, or resistance to, commands. On their own initiative, the two psychologists drew on past methods used by enemies of the United States to secure false confessions, reconstructing them to produce compliant interrogation subjects (SSCI 2014). Mitchell and Jessen thus appropriated techniques typically understood to be torture, and not otherwise in use by US interrogators, and connected them to a broader psychological theory Mitchell had developed and then marketed to CIA officials desperate for new options. They promised that with the right infrastructure in place – the right conditions of detention and physical coercion – subjects would reveal any information they had. They also experimented with new methods: waterboarding was not something the CIA had previously carried out,[26] but they were able to develop it and other techniques into standardised procedures once they engaged in hands-on interrogations, starting in April 2002 in Thailand, with the questioning of Abu Zubaydah (Soufan 2011; SSCI 2014). In other words, through

[23] While scholars of international politics and security tend to mostly associate technology with digital and mechanical artefacts, the development of new instrumental practices on the basis of new scientific theories is no less an example.
[24] SERE training is designed to prepare military personnel at high risk of capture, such as special forces troops or air crews, to withstand the ordeals of capture and abusive treatment.
[25] See Scott Shane, '2 U.S. Architects of Harsh Tactics in 9/11's Wake', New York Times, 11 August 2009, available at www.nytimes.com/2009/08/12/us/12psychs.html, accessed 14 April 2017.
[26] See Joseph Tanfani and W. J. Hennigan, 'Two Psychologists' Role in CIA Torture Program Comes into Focus', Los Angeles Times, 14 December 2014, available at www.latimes.com/world/afghanistan-pakistan/la-fg-torture-psychologists-20141214-story.html; accessed 14 April 2017.

technical innovation and progressive evolution, the CIA gained new material capacities able to fill the otherwise-empty institutional routines needed to build from scratch an interrogation programme.[27]

A final source of agency lies in the extent to which the prohibition on torture depended on a diverse set of legal categories. As I will discuss in the next section, legal space for EITs rested on the ability of lawyers from the CIA and the Departments of Defense, Justice, and State to permissively interpret what counted as torture and what protections prisoners enjoyed. For example, a 1 August 2002 Department of Justice memo states:

[T]orture as defined in and proscribed by Sections 2340–2340A [of the Convention Against Torture] covers only extreme acts. Severe pain is generally of the kind difficult for the victim to endure. Where pain is physical, it must be of an intensity akin to that which accompanies serious physical injury such as death or organ failure. Severe mental pain requires suffering not just at the moment of infliction but it also requires lasting psychological harm, such as seen in mental disorders like posttraumatic stress disorder.[28]

This passage excludes EITs from the category of torture, because they are designed primarily to evoke acute and powerful distress, as with waterboarding, or great exhaustion and frustration, as with sleep deprivation or noise bombardment.[29] As the SSCI Report (2014) succinctly put it, the memo established that 'the criminal prohibition on torture would not prohibit the methods proposed by the interrogation team because of the absence of any specific intent to inflict severe physical or mental pain or suffering' (34). Nor was this passage, excerpted from a larger document infamously known as 'the torture memos', the only key form of legal empowerment salient to the case.

---

[27]   To be clear, 'learned helplessness' is not the same as 'enhanced interrogation'; the former was the technological or scientific basis for the latter. There is no evidence to suggest the CIA solicited coercive interrogation techniques from the beginning. Rather, the progression appears to be that the CIA approached psychologists for ideas, became interested in learned helplessness, and then contracted Mitchell (and later Jessen) to build a new set of practices around this 'scientific' theory. In a sense, then, 'learned helplessness' was a technology much as drones were; just as drones became part of the broader set of practices comprising the CIA's targeted killing programme, so 'learned helplessness' became part of the broader set of practices comprising 'enhanced interrogation'.

[28]   Quoted in Miles (2016), 12.

[29]   Indeed, it would also appear to exclude the removal of fingernails with pliers, as this likely would not match the intensity of pain produced by 'death or organ failure'.

Before employing any EIT, at least during the early stages of the interrogation programme,[30] interrogators sought specific and explicit approval from legal counsel (SSCI 2014). Through this ongoing supervision, legal legitimacy was regularly extended into all ongoing contentious practices and replenished through regular endorsement. The transformative agency offered by legal interpretation and argument thus appears greater than in the case of targeted killing; EITs required more precise and elaborate definition to establish their permissibility.[31]

5.4 Tracing Transactions: The Three Mechanisms at Work

In this section, I provide an account of the causal process behind the emergence of the CIA's use of EITs and of the normative transformation it involved. Specifically, I show how the operation and entangled interaction of the three causal mechanisms – convention reorientation, technological revision, and network synthesis – explains how these interrogation methods came to be and how they became increasingly institutionalised before being rapidly phased out. For analytical convenience and clarity, I divide the account into three sub-sections. First, I examine the initial development and application of EITs for use in interrogating a small number of high-value al-Qaʻida prisoners. Second, I examine the expansion and institutionalisation of the CIA's detention and interrogation programme to encompass a number of secret facilities and a much larger population of prisoners. Third, I examine the end of EITs and the re-institutionalisation of a prohibition on torture.

5.4.1 The Emergence of EITs

The origins of the EIT began in the aftermath of 9/11, with the US security apparatus experiencing crisis, upheaval, and a desperate search for improved counterterrorism capabilities. John Rizzo is worth quoting at length here on the depth of this urgency and fear:

[T]here was a sense that we'd let the American people down as an institution. There was also a sense that [the] CIA's very existence was in the balance, that

---

[30] Evidence suggests that as the number of detention and interrogation sites expanded, the level of legal oversight over each use of EITs diminished (SSCI 2014).

[31] For further discussion of this comparison, see the concluding Chapter 7.

it was made clear to the CIA and the FBI, because they had a responsibility too, that there was not to be another terrorist attack. That was a universal cry, do basically whatever you have to do, but do not let this happen again. So there was that sense of urgency. I mean, I'm personally convinced that had there been a second major attack on the homeland in those early months, as everyone predicted was going to happen, I think that would've been the end of the CIA as an institution. So there was that, that sense of urgency, [and] because of this unprecedented catastrophe and the universal fear and dread, inside this country at least, that another attack could be around the corner, that [the] CIA would be directed to do things that it had never done before, that it never dreamed of doing before. So I knew that was inevitable too, and that sense was palpable around the building.[32]

By the end of 2001, the CIA was holding meetings with experts to develop better human intelligence-collecting capabilities. As noted earlier, this began with informal meetings bringing together psychologists and intelligence officers,[33] but, as CIA officials began looking for new practical options, they soon decided on the need for 'non-standard means of interrogation'—ones which Mitchell and Jessen, as psychologists and as SERE instructors, seemed equipped to provide. Quoting a 2013 CIA response to its findings, the SSCI Report states:

Drs. [Jessen and Mitchell] had the closest proximate expertise CIA sought at the beginning of the program, specifically in the area *of non-standard means of interrogation*. Experts on traditional interrogation methods did not meet this requirement. Non-standard interrogation methodologies were not an area of expertise of CIA officers or of the US Government generally. We believe their expertise was so unique that we would have been derelict had we not sought them out when it became clear that CIA would be heading into the uncharted territory of the program. (SSCI 2014, 32/499; italics in the original)

Defence journalist Jane Mayer sheds further light on this. In a passage from her book *The Dark Side*, she recounts:

In early January 2002 … CIA officers at a high-level legal meeting in the Situation Room voiced a problem they were facing. 'The CIA guys said, "We're going to have some real difficulties getting actionable intelligence

---

[32] Interview with author, 2015.
[33] See Scott Shane, '2 U.S. Architects of Harsh Tactics in 9/11's Wake', *New York Times*, 11 August 2009, available at www.nytimes.com/2009/08/12/us/12psyc hs.html, accessed 14 April 2017.

from detainees" if the Agency's interrogators were required to respect the limits for treatment demanded by the Geneva Conventions,' John Yoo told the *Washington Post*. In Yoo's version of events, the impetus to break out of Geneva's strictures thus came from the CIA. Many at the Agency, however, saw this differently, suggesting it was Cheney and his lawyer, Addington, who pushed the Agency to take the path toward torture. (Mayer 2008, n.p.)

There thus existed the normative and institutional space to develop increasingly violent interrogation practices, but not the epistemic or practical content. For this, the CIA needed to build their expertise, and hence, from April of 2002, Mitchell was actively consulting at the CIA's Combatting Terrorism Center (CTC) and proposing new interrogation techniques that appealed to Cofer Black's desire for a tough new approach to counterterrorism. As one witness to some of these consultations recalls, Mitchell suggested a method that would induce in al-Qaʿida prisoners 'a comparable level of fear and brutality to flying planes into buildings' (Mayer 2008). Though coercive interrogation methods were first used in April 2002 and the full list of EITs not codified until later that year, they were thus in development mere months after 9/11 took place.

Already, the above account shows the interactive operation of revision and network synthesis. The executive demand for, and support of, more aggressive counterterrorism actions introduced authoritative impetus for the CIA to develop new possible practices – initially undefined. The expansion of the CTC into an agency-within-an-agency appears to be especially signification, developing the capacity not just for military action (as discussed in the previous chapter) but also detention and interrogation. This was unprecedented bureaucratic territory, requiring the CIA to do 'in-house' what it previously relied on partner actors, domestic and foreign, to do on its behalf. In the case of interrogation, the lack of foundational knowledge and practice increased the CIA's receptivity to outside expert networks, and those networks in turn provided a technical skillset for developing new capacities.[34] It likely mattered that significant figures within the CTC were new to it: both Jose Rodriguez, a veteran clandestine services officer whose main experience was in Latin America and who would eventually become the CTC's director, and Gina Haspel, who oversaw

---

[34] Further details of this may be found as well in Jose Rodriguez's testimony to the USDC for the Eastern District of Washington, filed 22 May 2017, available at www.aclu.org/sites/default/files/field_document/175._declarationj_of_jose_rodriguez.pdf.

an interrogation 'black site' in Thailand[35] and, on 21 May 2018, was sworn in as the director of the Central Intelligence Agency, both began at the CTC on 11 September 2001. However, without the authority provided by urgent directives for tough new means of fighting terrorists, the CIA would have lacked good cause or reason to build a detention and interrogation programme, and without the structure and legitimacy provided by expert input, it would had lacked the technological material to actually institutionalise a new set of interrogation practices, being left only with existing legitimate means or means proscribed more explicitly by anti-torture conventions.

Abu Zubaydah, a Saudi citizen with close ties to al-Qaʿida, was the first detainee subjected to the CIA's still-developing set of new interrogation techniques. Following his capture in Faisalabad on 28 March 2002, the wounded Zubaydah was transferred to a hospital in Thailand,[36] where he was first interrogated by FBI agents using standard law enforcement methods. During initial questioning by FBI agents, Abu Zubaydah appeared fully cooperative, providing valuable intelligence; however, the opinion of the CIA was that he was still concealing important information. Hence the CIA team that arrived mid-April, led by James Mitchell, had prior approval for the use of coercive methods and to temporarily exclude the FBI from further interrogation sessions. Under the supervision of Mitchell, who, in FBI documents quoted in the SSCI Report, had gained 'tremendous influence' (2014, 27), Abu Zubaydah was taken to a secret site where the CIA team interrogated him using a range of new methods including noise bombardment, sleep deprivation, forced nudity, slamming against walls, and confinement in a coffin-like box (Mayer 2008; Soufan 2011; SSCI 2014).[37] This continued for the next several months,

---

[35] These biographical details on Haspel may be found in the National Security Archive maintained by George Washington University and made available at https://nsarchive.gwu.edu/briefing-book/intelligence-torture-archive/2018-05-09/cia-black-sites-program-gina-haspel-nomination.

[36] The choice of Thailand was specifically because it would keep the site outside of US jurisdiction, ensuring against having declare custody over Abu Zubaydah to the International Committee of the Red Cross and against 'possible loss of control to US military and/or FBI' (CIA documents cited in SSCI 2014, 22). The decision was made purely at the executive level, without prior input from the National Security Council Principals Committee, the Department of State, the US ambassador, or the CIA station chief in Thailand (SSCI 2014, 22).

[37] See also Scott Shane, 'Divisions Arose on Rough Tactics for Qaeda Figure', *New York Times*, 17 April 2009, available at www.nytimes.com/2009/04/18/world/middleeast/18zubaydah.html; accessed 18 April 2017.

with the FBI interrogator given occasional access. Abu Zubaydah did not provide the intelligence the CIA suspected him of having – on impending attacks against the United States – and his health deteriorated (SSCI 2014). At this point, the FBI team,[38] already forced to watch as, in Soufan's perception, 'nothing was gained through techniques that no reputable interrogator would even think of using' (Soufan 2011), departed on the grounds that it could not legally continue to participate in coercive interrogations (Soufan 2011; SSCI 2014). The CIA, on the recommendation of Mitchell, decided to make use of its more extreme SERE-imported means (SSCI 2014, 31).

After a July 2002 meeting at CIA headquarters discussing 'novel interrogation methods' for use on Abu Zubaydah, Mitchell proposed a list of twelve SERE-derived techniques and recommended contracting Bruce Jessen, his colleague and friend, to assist (SSCI 2014, 32). The twelve techniques were: the attention grasp; walling; facial hold; facial slap; cramped confinement; wall standing; stress positions; sleep deprivation; waterboarding; use of diapers; use of insects; and mock burial (SSCI 2014, 32). These methods were notable developments for two key reasons. First, they were a significant technical innovation. As the CIA's own internal investigations noted in 2003, they were based on 'physical torture' used by North Vietnamese interrogators on US POWs and were designed not to educe actionable intelligence but to extract false confessions for use in propaganda (interview with senior CIA interrogator in SSCI 2014, 33). Moreover, as the SSCI Report notes, 'Like [Mitchell], [Jessen] had never participated in a real-world interrogation. His interrogation experience was limited to the paper he authored with [Michell] and his work with U.S. Air Force personnel at the SERE school' (2014, 32). Hence they entailed a re-engineering of a largely distinct skill set by two technical advisers with no previous expertise in intelligence interrogation but equipped with theoretical and practical knowledge in how to reduce people to vulnerable psychological states through fear, pain, and violence.

---

[38] Not just the FBI agents left in protest, either. 'One CIA agent', as Soufan recounts, 'had assumed that the madness of [Mitchell's] experiments was over. He protested vigorously to his superiors in Langley but got no satisfactory response. Finally, he announced that he was leaving. He packed up his things. As he waited for a car to pick him up, [he said,] "We are almost crossing the line. There are the Geneva Conventions on torture. It's not worth losing myself for this"' (Soufan 2011).

Second, after these techniques were specified in memo, innovative legal framing (and pre-emptive legal protection) became crucial in offering specific legitimation and authority for the expanded set of coercive interrogation techniques. In mid-to-late 2002, legal counsel for the CTC drafted a letter, intended for Attorney General John Ashcroft but only circulated within the CIA, recognising that the methods were likely to run afoul of legal prohibitions on torture 'apart from potential reliance upon the doctrines of necessity or of self-defense'. The letter requested

a formal declination of prosecution, in advance, for any employees of the United States, as well as any other personnel acting on behalf of the United States, who may employ methods in the interrogation of Abu Zubaydah that otherwise might subject those individuals to prosecution. (quoted in SSCI 2014, 33)

As acting chief counsel for the CIA at the time, John Rizzo formally requested a Department of Justice finding on the twelve techniques, describing them as having been developed by 'expert personnel retained on contract who possess extensive experience, gained within the Department of Defense, on the psychological and physical methods of interrogation and the resistance techniques employed as counter-measures to such interrogation' (quoted in SSCI 2014, 33–4). This legal process was not merely to establish cover should news of Abu Zubaydah's treatment become public[39] but also, it appears, to satisfy professional standards. In telling language, for example, the chief of base at the detention site in Thailand wrote in a cable to headquarters:

We are a nation of laws and we do not wish to parse words ... [W]hile the techniques described in Headquarters meetings and below are administered to student volunteers in the U.S. in a harmless way, with no measurable impact on the psyche of the volunteer, we do not believe we can assure the same here for a man forced through these processes and who will be made to believe this is the future course of the remainder of his life. (quoted in SSCI 2014, 36; emphasis mine)

On 24 July, Attorney General Ashcroft verbally approved all twelve techniques except for waterboarding and mock burial; on 26 July, he

---

[39]   Indeed, his interrogation team sought and received from CIA headquarters reassurances that Abu Zubaydah would be held incommunicado for the rest of his life (SSCI 2014, 35).

gave further approval for waterboarding (SSCI 2014, 36). These, in addition to those already in use by the CIA, comprised the final list of EITs.

Abu Zubaydah was subject to the full range of EITs from 4 to 23 August 2002, around the clock. As his medical officer noted at the beginning of this period in an email to headquarters titled 'So it begins', 'sessions accelerated rapidly progressing quickly to the water board after large box, walling, and small box periods . . . Longest time with the cloth over his face so far has been 17 seconds. This is sure to increase shortly. NO useful information so far' (SSCI 2014, 41–2; capitalisation original). For the duration of the period, Abu Zubaydah spent a total of 295 hours confined to a small box (either coffin-sized or smaller) and was water-boarded '2–4 times a day . . . with multiple iterations of the watering cycle during each application' (daily cables cited in SSCI 2014, 42). Cables note that his responses were to cry, beg, whimper, issue 'hysterical pleas', involuntarily spasm and swallow fluids, and to continue to deny knowledge of any specific plots against the United States, while site personnel voiced written concerns to headquarters that the use of EITs was 'approach[ing] the legal limit' (SSCI 2014, 42–3). Emails from site personnel quoted in the SSCI Report recorded their discomfort: 'It is visually and psychologically very uncomfortable'; 'Today's first session . . . had a profound effect on all staff members present . . . [I]t seems the collective opinion that we should not go much further . . . [I]f the group has to continue . . . we cannot guarantee how much longer'; 'Several on the team profoundly affected . . . some to the point of tears and choking up'; 'two, perhaps three [personnel] likely to elect transfer [from the detention site, should use of EITs continue]' (SSCI 2014, 44–5). In later testimony, Mitchell claimed that, after a few weeks of personally overseeing the use of EITs along with Jessen, he asked senior CIA officials for permission to stop, on the grounds that Abu Zubaydah was fully cooperating. That permission was denied, and, despite having been the progenitor and initial advocate of the waterboard, Mitchell felt it was being employed unnecessarily. Already, then, the EITs were becoming institutionalised beyond the specific experimental team of interrogators tasked with first attempting them.[40]

---

[40] Mitchell actually describes the need to 'put on a show' for officials from the CIA, whom he invited to observe a waterboarding session specifically to persuade them to agree to stop ordering additional use of the method on Abu Zubaydah (Rosenberg 2020).

Eventually, CIA officials and all members of the interrogation team concluded that Abu Zubaydah was truthful in claiming no knowledge of specific plots or attacks. Mitchell and Jessen declared to headquarters that the interrogation had been a success, writing in a cable:

[T]he aggressive phase [of interrogation] should be used as a template for future interrogation of high value captives ... [We brought the] subject to the point that we confidently assess that he does not possess undisclosed threat information, or intelligence that could prevent a terrorist event. (SSCI 2014, 46)[41]

Their cable further recommended that psychologists 'familiar with interrogation, exploitation and resistance to interrogation should shape compliance of high value captives prior to debriefing by substantive experts' (SSCI 2014, 46).

Intersecting the development and first application of EITs are the series of legal memoranda and letters, mainly issued from the Department of Justice at the request of the White House, colloquially known as 'the torture memos'. Not all of these specifically pertain to EITs and Abu Zubaydah – the first several, written in early/mid-2002, sought to provide a legal basis for denying or exempting al-Qa'ida prisoners from Geneva Convention protections. Two others, written in August 2002, directly addressed the issue of torture. The former of these, crucially, argued that a violent or coercive interrogation act would be torture only if it caused pain 'equivalent in intensity to the pain accompanying serious physical injury, such as organ failure, impairment of bodily function, or even death [or] mental pain or suffering [resulting] in significant psychological harm of significant duration e.g. lasting for months or even years'.[42] The latter, as noted earlier, offered a technique-by-technique legal justification for the EITs to be used on Abu Zubaydah. Together these memos provided a novel interpretation of international and domestic law that satisfied institutional and practitioner need for legal cover, empowering the CIA to operate prisons and distinguishing EITs from torture on the basis of their supposed psychological mechanisms – a clear invocation of

---

[41] Note the logic behind this: suspicion that Abu Zubaydah was withholding information was used to justify subjecting him to EITs, then when it proved false, its falseness was again used to justify the use of EITs.

[42] See www.therenditionproject.org.uk/pdf/PDF%2019%20[Bybee%20Memo% 20to%20Gonzales%20Standards%20Interrogation%201%20Aug.pdf.

scientific language as a basis for drawing new moral and legal distinctions.[43] These memos show the increasing salience of convention reorientation as the third mechanism in play, building off the bureaucratic and technological basis for EITs that already had been broadly established.

By this point, the CIA's use of EITs had emerged and solidified, and a normative transformation was under way. All three mechanisms interacted to produce this change. Through extensive legal argumentation, lawyers in several government agencies and branches authorised coercive interrogation methods not by defending torture, though some recognised that the EITs may violate the prohibition on it, but by arguing that EITs were permitted within the existing scope of the prohibition. They argued that the violence during interrogation, despite clearly lying beyond the normative pale for law enforcement interrogators and even for some CIA personnel, was not physically harmful enough to truly be torture. This *convention reorientation* was made possible through high-level support for 'tough' approaches to counterterrorism and by the institutional space for EITs in the CIA, where an absence of interrogators and an historically ambivalent attitude towards coercive methods permitted new practices to emerge. Here *network synthesis* was reinforced by its own successes, because, by driving the FBI away through early use of coercive methods, CIA officials removed what would surely have been a major obstacle for the fuller and more 'aggressive' set of actions that it would eventually engage in.[44] Both of these mechanisms gained potency due to the escalating involvement of James Mitchell and, later, Bruce Jessen, whose presence was itself a product of an executive desire from the Bush administration for tough and innovative means, as well as of the legal benefits of credentialed expert endorsement for otherwise untested techniques. Mitchell and Jessen, through psychological theories and techniques dating back to their SERE days, supplied the epistemic basis for *technological revision* to established interrogation practices, through new psychological theories promising previously unachieved

---

[43] Copies of these memos and a guide to their contents may be found at https://archive.nytimes.com/www.nytimes.com/ref/international/24MEMO-GUIDE.html and www.therenditionproject.org.uk/documents/torture-docs.html.

[44] Given reports that Agent Soufan once, in frustration, threatened to arrest CIA interrogators if he were forced to remain involved in pre-waterboarding phases of Abu Zubaydah's interrogation (hinted at in Soufan 2011 and referenced in SSCI 2014), he might very well have made good on this threat had he been present in what was to come.

leverage on the minds of those interrogated, as well as through the only practical knowledge the United States had of systematic violent interrogation, gained through their involvement in SERE training.

5.4.2 The Institutionalisation and Spread of EITs

By the end of Abu Zubyadah's 'aggressive' interrogation at the hands of the CIA, the EIT had fully emerged as a defined, defended, and established interrogation practice. The CIA had developed an internal training course for new interrogators by late 2002. However, they had not yet spread to the detention facilities at Guantanamo Bay, nor had the CIA yet set up additional secret sites. From the end of 2002 throughout 2003 and until early 2004, this next stage took place.

Though originally intended only to be used on a small number of 'high-value' detainees in CIA custody, EITs began to be used by interrogators, both CIA and military, at Guantanamo Bay Detention Camp (henceforth GTMO), the main US detention site for persons suspected of terrorism or militant activity directed at the United States and its allies. Established in January 2002, the camp was selected for its unusual legal status: as Guantanamo Bay was Cuban territory leased in perpetuity to the United States in 1903, White House lawyers were able to argue that it was not subject to US law, even if it was under US control, allowing the US government to carry out detentions and interrogations outside domestic legal boundaries (Mayer 2008). On 11 October 2002, military officials from GTMO requested permission from Secretary of Defense Rumsfeld for permission to use the same coercive kinds of interrogation techniques the CIA had developed and used on Abu Zubayda – including waterboarding and mock executions (Mayer 2008; Soufan 2011). Though Rumsfeld did not grant his approval until 2 December, interrogators at GTMO had not waited to use EITs and had, later in October, begun the use of stress positions and dogs as a source of intimidation (Soufan 2011). While bureaucratic and legal pressure from opponents of EITs forced Rumsfeld to rescind approval in January 2003, in March 2003 he reissued it in full (Soufan 2011), on the basis of a 14 March 2003 legal memo written by John Yoo.[45]

---

[45] Available courtesy of the American Civil Liberties Union at www.aclu.org/files/pdfs/safefree/yoo_army_torture_memo.pdf; accessed 18 April 2017.

Given that the EITs were supposed to be top secret and designed for the CIA for clandestine use in special circumstances, it may appear strange that military interrogators at GTMO were quickly able to learn about and reproduce them. The EITs were adopted by the military because of close ties between interrogation practitioners. Michael Gelles, chief clinical forensic psychologist for the Navy's Criminal Investigative Service, described the closeness of these professional connections: 'It's a community where people communicate with each other, and there's a lot of sharing of information', and thus the EITs spread 'like a germ' (quoted in Mayer 2008). While this account seems to imply relatively undirected diffusion, there is reason to think that the number of 'vectors' for spreading awareness of the EITs were small in number and not necessarily part of the community of interrogators per se. As Soufan recounts:

[O]n September 16, 2002 . . ., following up on the earlier assistance, a group of military interrogators and behavioral scientists from Gitmo went to JPRA, in Ft. Belvoir, Virginia, for SERE training. On September 25, 2002, a delegation of senior Bush administration lawyers, including Jim Haynes and David Addington, along with John Rizzo and Michael Chertoff, then with the criminal division of the Justice Department (later director of Homeland Security), traveled to Gitmo for discussions on how interrogations should be run. On October 2, 2002, the chief counsel to the CIA's Counterterrorism Center met with Gitmo staff. The Senate Armed Services Committee report notes: 'Minutes of that meeting indicate that it was dominated by a discussion of aggressive interrogation techniques including sleep deprivation, death threats, and waterboarding, which was discussed in relation to its use in SERE training'. (Soufan 2011; see also Committee on Armed Services, United States Senate 2008)

This implies that while some diffusion of SERE techniques took place across groups of practitioners, the substantial driving force behind the use of EITs at GTMO came from legal experts, including – as evidenced by the presence of Rizzo – from the CIA, with extensive existing involvement in the development of the EITs for use on Abu Zubaydah. It suggests the expansion of network synthesis and technological revision beyond their initial institutional context, facilitated by convention reorientation by military officials eager to enhance their human intelligence capabilities along the same lines as the CIA.

Beyond GTMO and Abu Zubaydah, EITs also saw noteworthy use in Afghanistan and Iraq. Some of this may be traceable to the promotion of General Miller, formerly the chief official of GTMO, to command of all detention facilities in Iraq and may owe to Miller's influence and direction (Mayer 2008). Mainly, though, this spread of new practices proceeded through the proliferation of CIA 'black sites'. The second such facility, after Thailand, was in Afghanistan. Referred to as 'Detention Site Cobalt' in the SSCI Report and placed under the command of an early-career CIA officer on his first foreign assignment, it was established in September 2002. Numerous detainees were held there – complete records on how many do not exist (SSCI 2014, 50) – and subjected to coercive techniques, such as sensory and sleep deprivation, noise bombardment, and in some cases waterboarding. These EITs were in some cases used without prior approval from, or later reporting to, CIA headquarters and were found by local US military officials to be too legally problematic for military interrogators to participate in their use (SSCI 2014, 52–4). As of August 2002, the CIA had also established its own internal training programme for new interrogators, taught in part by a former SERE instructor and providing instruction not only on the approved EITs but on an additional two methods not approved in the Department of Justice memo (the 'abdominal slap' and the 'finger press') (SSCI 2014, 58).[46] The CIA was eventually to establish another three sites in Afghanistan, titled 'Gray', 'Orange', and 'Brown' (SSCI 2014, 61).

As the number of CIA detention sites expanded, and with the eventual invasion of Iraq, the CIA further institutionalised its interrogation practices. In late January 2003, in response to the death of one detainee (Gul Rahman) and reports that an interrogator used a gun and a drill to threaten another during an interrogation (both in CIA custody in Afghanistan), DCI Tenet established formal guidelines for CIA detentions and interrogations. These set forth requirements for a basic level of medical care, hygiene, and nutrition (SSCI 2014, 62) – and specified twelve EITs, including two not approved by the OLC (prolonged use of diapers and the 'abdominal slap'), that could be used without prior approval from headquarters (SSCI 2014, 63). By this point, the CIA had multiple interrogation groups working in parallel with different

---

[46] Further details of this may be found in George Washington University's national security archive, in the entry related to Gina Haspel's nomination as director of the CIA, available at https://nsarchive.gwu.edu/briefing-book/intelligence-torture-archive/2018-05-09/cia-black-sites-program-gina-haspel-nomination; accessed 16 May 2020.

standard sets of practices, even if all made use of some combination of EITs.[47]

In both the spread of EITs to GTMO and the military's interrogation program, and in the expansion of the CIA's own detention program, the continued interaction of all three mechanisms is visible. The novel technological promises of SERE-derived techniques, along with their psychologist proponents, worked in tandem with network synthesis through the new alliances and 'study exchanges' that took place in 2002 between GTMO officials, SERE trainers, and administration lawyers. Meanwhile, the role of legal authorisation and indemnification continued to be a crucial form of convention reorientation, with EIT proponents overcoming bureaucratic opposition through arguments that may have appeared problematic in the eyes of many experts on the law – as Mayer (2008) is at pains to document – but became authoritative thanks to the influence of network synthesis in the form of endorsement from top legal counsels in the departments of Justice and State and the support of highly placed Bush administration officials.

It is hard to imagine any of these three mechanisms working on their own, but once arrayed in synthesis they generated major institutional change: new legal doctrines could be pushed through on the basis of powerful support and seemingly helpful innovation in means. Similarly, the rapid proliferation of CIA detention and interrogation sites, along with the internal normalisation of interrogation methods and training, was possible only due to the continued potency of the same kind of combination of causal processes. As the SSCI Report (2014) notes, Mitchell and Jessen continued to be directly involved in promoting the use of EITs and in overseeing interrogations as psychological advisers, while the independence of the CIA from their military counterparts in both Afghanistan and Iraq was secured on an exclusive legal basis, and by placing facilities under the command of personnel chosen for loyalty rather than experience. This interaction dynamic, which is hard to uncover through analytical lenses fixated exclusively

---

[47] As the SSCI Report describes this state of affairs: 'The Renditions Group's leadership considered the waterboard, which Chief of Interrogations [Redacted] was not certified to use, as "life threatening," and complained to the OIG that some CIA officers in the Directorate of Operations believed that, as a result, the Renditions Group was "running a 'sissified' interrogation program." At the same time, CIA CTC personnel criticized the Renditions Group and [Redacted] for their use of painful stress positions, as well as for the conditions at DETENTION SITE COBALT' (SSCI 2014, 65).

on single-mechanism explanations, clearly plays a central causal role once this case is studied as an interaction of all three.

5.4.3 The End of EITs and the Re-affirmation of a Prohibition on Torture

Despite the diffusion and rapid institutionalisation of EITs, opposition to them gained power and pace through a combination of government investigations and media-informed public pressures. Key legal authorisations were rescinded or overturned, while scepticism amongst security officials mounted over the efficacy of the techniques. The normative momentum around their use declined and, eventually, reversed. The cause of this, in analytical terms, lies in the eventual breakdown of one of the mechanisms, the collapse of which deprived the remaining two of their operative conditions. Specifically, increasing scepticism in the efficacy of EITs eroded the potency of the technological revision behind their use. Once the technological basis for the transformation in interrogation practice was undermined, internal legal opposition gained traction, and politically influential figures in the security bureaucracy and the broader partisan/legislative playing field – informed by internal audits, public leaks, and media exposures – began to agitate for an end to the CIA's detention and interrogation programme in general. In other words, the normative transformation was not yet fully institutionalised, and, without the harmonious operation of all three mechanisms, the normative configuration surrounding torture returned to something close to its original form.

The CIA's Office of the Inspector General (OIG) began investigating the detention and interrogation programme in mid-2003, gathering testimonies from agents involved in it and reviewing memos and cables. Their investigation was triggered by a request from the deputy director of operations to follow up on reports of unauthorised use of EITs and by separate information that 'some employees were concerned that certain covert Agency activities at an overseas detention and interrogation site might involve violations of human rights' (quoted in SSCI 2014, 121). In interviews with the OIG, numerous CIA personnel claimed the Agency had been unprepared for the detention and interrogation of Abu Zubaydah, questioned the analytical assumptions underpinning the Agency's interrogation practices, complained that interrogators lacked pertinent linguistic and cultural knowledge, and, most damningly, recounted pressure from CIA Headquarters to use EITs, which they attributed to flawed assumptions about how much detained persons actually knew (SSCI 2014, 121–2). The SSCI Report quotes testimony to this effect:

CTC does not know a lot about al-Qaʿida and as a result, Headquarters analysts have constructed 'models' of what al-Qaʿida represents to them. [Redacted] noted that the Agency does not have the linguists or subject matter experts it needs. The questions sent from CTC/Usama bin Laden (UBL) to the interrogators are based on SIGINT [signals intelligence] and other intelligence that often times is incomplete or wrong. When the detainee does not respond to the question, the assumption at Headquarters is that the detainee is holding back and 'knows' more, and consequently, Headquarters recommends resumption of EITs. This difference of opinion between the interrogators and Headquarters as to whether the detainee is 'compliant' is the type of ongoing pressure the interrogation team is exposed to. [Redacted] believes the waterboard was used 'recklessly' – 'too many times' on Abu Zubaydah at [DETENTION SITE GREEN], based in part on faulty intelligence. (SSCI 2014, 122)

When the OIG's final report was released, it did not at all conclude that the EITs were ineffective; despite documented scepticism from many personnel as to the use of EITs, based on Directorate of Operations disclosures, the OIG found the programme and its methods to be a major intelligence success. Yet the report nevertheless recommended that the CIA cease detentions and interrogations:

The Directorate of Operations (DO) should not be in the business of running prisons or 'temporary detention facilities'. The DO should focus on its core mission: clandestine intelligence operations. Accordingly, the DO should continue to hunt, capture, and render targets, and then exploit them for intelligence and ops leads once in custody. The management of their incarceration and interrogation should be conducted by appropriately experienced U.S. law enforcement officers, because that is their charter and they have the training and experience. (quoted in SSCI 2014, 125)

In other words, and crucially important for recognising the normative dimension to this case, the OIG recommended ending the CIA's detention and interrogation practices *not because the EITs didn't work* – despite having some basis for questioning their effectiveness – but because *the circumstances of their use was inappropriate* for the CIA's organisational mandate and orientation.

This does not show that resistance to EITs was in general traceable to any 'logic of appropriateness', but it does firmly establish that something beyond a consequentialist calculus of intelligence gain and loss was at play in contestation over interrogation practices, even within the CIA, and even after the detention and interrogation programme was well under way. Just as the supposed effectiveness of the EITs was foundational to their emergence and institutionalisation, the supposed impropriety of their use was a central pillar of mounting opposition to them. This again illustrates how the technical dimension of the normative transformation here feeds into the bureaucratic and discursive dimensions, with instrumental efficacy serving as a condition for successful overcoming of institutional opposition.

In addition to the OIG's report, there also emerged significant legal opposition to EITs and their institutionalisation both from within the CIA and from without. Early legal resistance had achieved little but set both precedent and tone for confrontations between the lawyers close to Rumsfeld and Cheney – the administration's driving force behind the use of EITs – and high-ranking counsels in the military and civil services.[48] Later in 2003 and 2004, Jack Goldsmith, director of the Office of Legal Counsel of the Department of Justice, advised that John Yoo's two 'torture memos' were based on flawed interpretations of the legal definition of torture and that Geneva Convention protections applied to all Iraqi detainees (Mayer 2008). Goldsmith's successor, Dan Levin, on 30 December 2004 posted a memo to the Justice Department's website offering new official guidelines on torture that

---

[48] In mid-December 2002, General Counsel of the United States Navy Alberto Mora was approached by David Brant, director of the Naval Criminal Investigative Service, with allegations that detainees at GTMO were being subjected to illegal forms of abuse with approval from the top echelons of the Bush administration (Mayer 2008). After a second meeting with Brant, Mora then enlisted the assistance of Steven Morello, the general counsel of the Army, to further investigate. Morello showed Mora a package of legal memos signed by Secretary of Defense Rumsfeld, on the formal recommendation of his legal counsel, Jim Haynes, approving a range of coercive interrogation methods discussed earlier in this chapter (Mayer 2008). Mora confronted Haynes with concerns that the approved coercive methods would, if combined, reach the level of torture. Haynes appointed a working group, in which he included Mora, but then stalled its findings, while working with John Yoo to produce a memo refuting every one of Mora's legal arguments. After a brief suspension, coercive interrogations continued at US military detention sites, while Mora and his fellow working group members were kept in the dark throughout 2003 (Mayer 2008).

overturned most of Yoo's (secret) justifications for the CIA.[49] When these guidelines were themselves abrogated by Levin's successor, Steven Bradbury, who in a 10 May 2005 memo in fact expanded the CIA's latitude for coercive interrogation techniques, within the CIA, the OIG quickly responded with strong disagreement:

On May 26, 2005, the CIA inspector general, who had been provided with [Bradbury's] memoranda, wrote a memo to the CIA director recommending that the CIA seek additional legal guidance on whether the CIA's enhanced interrogation techniques and conditions of confinement met the standard under Article 16 of the Convention Against Torture. The inspector general noted that 'a strong case can be made that the Agency's authorized interrogation techniques are the kinds of actions that Article 16 undertakes to prevent', adding that the use of the waterboard may be 'cruel' and 'extended detention with no clothing would be considered "degrading" in most cultures, particularly Muslim'. The inspector general further urged that the analysis of conditions was equally important, noting that the inspector general's staff had 'found a number of instances of detainee treatment which arguably violate the prohibition on cruel, inhuman, and/or degrading treatment'. (SSCI 2014, 145)

Internal dissent to EITs also came from outside the OIG: in October 2006 a panel of CIA interrogators concluded that four EITs – the abdominal slap, cramped confinement, forced nudity, and the waterboard – should no longer be used (SSCI 2014), though there is no information available on how this influenced CIA interrogation practices. Meanwhile, the Supreme Court in July 2008 recognised GTMO detainees' right to challenge their detention.[50] Faced with this ruling against a key brick in the administration's policies on detention and interrogation, with episodes of major pushback from within the Department of Justice, and with potent resistance from the OIG within the CIA, EIT defenders were seeing their legal footing erode.

Finally, public exposures of the brutal conditions of both CIA and military detention and interrogation programmes made it harder to sustain them, in terms of domestic opinion and of diplomatic fallout.

---

[49] Available courtesy of the American Civil Liberties Union at www.aclu.org/files/ torturefoia/released/082409/olcremand/2004olc96.pdf; accessed 18 April 2017.
[50] The full ruling, titled 'BOUMEDIENE ET AL. v. BUSH, PRESIDENT OF THE UNITED STATES, ET AL.', may be found at www.scotusblog.com/wp-content /uploads/2008/06/06-1195.pdf; accessed 18 April 2017.

Abroad, the result of this media attention was that fewer allied governments were willing to permit CIA 'black sites' on their soil, fearing major public relations damage should the sites be revealed to their constituencies. As the SSCI Report notes:

In March 2005, talking points prepared for the CIA director for a discussion with the National Security Council Principals Committee stated that it was: 'only a matter of time before our remaining handful of current blacksite hosts concludes that [US government] policy on [detainees] lacks direction and . . . [the blacksite hosts] ask us to depart from their soil . . . . Continuation of status quo will exacerbate tensions in these very valuable relationships and cause them to withdraw their critical support and cooperation with the [US government]. (SSCI 2014, 151)

Several US allies did indeed withdraw their willingness to host CIA detainees over the following year and a half (SSCI 2014), and on 6 September 2006 President Bush, in response to domestic agitation, publicly acknowledged that the CIA had been detaining and interrogating suspected terrorists using an 'alternative set of procedures'.[51] The Bush administration subsequently faced increasing legislative hostility to its detention and interrogation practices, culminating in a 2007/8 bill – the Intelligence Authorization Act for Fiscal Year 2008 – to prohibit all coercive interrogation practices and oblige all future US government interrogations to be conducted in accordance with the Army Field Manual on Human Intelligence Collector Operations.[52] President Bush vetoed the bill on 8 March 2008, reaffirming the intelligence-gathering effectiveness of EITs and claiming the relative ineffectiveness of the Army Field Manual,[53] and an 11 March 2008 vote by the House of Representatives failed to overturn the veto by an approximately 10 per cent margin.[54]

---

[51] See the transcript published in 'President Bush Delivers Remarks on Terrorism', *Washington Post*, 6 September 2006, available at www.washingtonpost.com/wp-dyn/content/article/2006/09/06/AR2006090601425.html; accessed 18 April 2017.

[52] The Intelligence Authorization Act for Fiscal Year 2008 passed the House of Representatives on 13 December 2007, 222 votes to 197, and passed the Senate on 13 February 2008, by 51 votes to 45 (SSCI 2014, 170).

[53] 'Text: Bush on Veto of Intelligence Bill', *New York Times*, 8 March 2008, available at www.nytimes.com/2008/03/08/washington/08cnd-ptext.html, accessed 18 April 2017.

[54] See Steven Lee Myers, 'Veto of Bill on C.I.A. Tactics Affirms Bush's Legacy', *New York Times*, 9 March 2008, available at www.nytimes.com/2008/03/09/washington/09policy.html; accessed 18 April 2017.

Yet by this point the CIA had already ceased further detentions and interrogations (SSCI 2014) – suggesting that the demise of EITs was in fact driven first and foremost by bureaucratic dynamics and only then cemented by broader legislative opposition. Executive Order 13491, signed by President Obama on 22 January 2009, directed the CIA to 'close as expeditiously as possible any detention facilities that it currently operates and [never to] operate any such detention facility in the future', while requiring US government employees to use only those interrogation methods authorised in the Army Field Manual on Human Intelligence Collector Operations.[55]

All this raises a question: what does the unravelling of these violent interrogation practices, and the return to a normative configuration broadly prohibiting torture, imply about the normative transformation that took place? While significant institutional and normative changes occurred, they were technologically, legally, and bureaucratically insecure enough to be robust in the face of attempts by opposing actors to revise and reform them.

I argue that the transformation 'back' to the status quo ante can be understood with reference to the same three causal mechanisms that led the United States to use torture in the first place. This process does not as clearly show what happens when they operate effectively and synthetically, but it does show what happens when they *fail*. One major explanation for their failure appears to be that technological revision in this case was not robust or evident enough to support convention reorientation and network synthesis, meaning that as it began to fail, so did the other two mechanisms. As scepticism within the US security apparatus mounted over the effectiveness of EITs, and as specific EITs were restricted or prohibited for legal reasons, the process of technological revision underlying their development began to slow or even reverse. The new capacities EITs supposedly provided either were perceived to fail to materialise or were taken off the table for normative reasons, and more 'traditional' interrogation methods returned to prominence. In the end, the new science of interrogation on which EITs rested did not actually produce the promised increase in intelligence-gathering capacity that made it possible for proponents

---

[55] Text of the executive order may be found at www.gpo.gov/fdsys/pkg/CFR-20 10-title3-vol1/pdf/CFR-2010-title3-vol1-eo13491.pdf; accessed 18 April 2017.

to argue their use was anything more sophisticated than doing violence to people until they yielded their secrets.

In addition to the significant technological failings of EITs, the US government lost access to spaces where it could continue to employ them within their established legal and institutional framework, as foreign countries began to refuse to host CIA detention sites. These spaces were essential because they were circumscribed by convention and authority to permit actions that would, in the United States itself, still be prohibited. Without those material conditions, the legal arguments and executive support comprising the conventional and bureaucratic forces for normative transformation here lost their power. Though the detention facilities at Guantanamo Bay and in the war zones of Afghanistan and Iraq could still serve this purpose, they were increasingly subject to public scrutiny and required greater partnership with military institutions – which in turn meant greater legal scrutiny as well.

Together, these factors turned the tide on executive support for EITs, which suffered increasing bureaucratic and public-relations costs. As the putative necessity and effectiveness of EITs is what gave institutional impetus for their use, the mounting concerns over their usefulness as intelligence-gathering instruments limited the normative resources their proponents had to argue for a permissive attitude in evaluating the legal basis for their use. That legal basis, in turn, was subject to persistent criticism by high-ranking legal officials in the civil service, impeding the power of pro-EIT memos, authored by a small group of lawyers close to the Bush administration, to establish a lasting reorientation in how the US government understood conventions against torture and abusive treatment during detention and interrogation.

While the involvement of a small and involved network of executive power brokers allowed for these legal criticisms to be overruled, it was not enough to permanently alter the bureaucratic and legal environment for the US government's treatment of detained enemy combatants. Network synthesis in this case was effective enough to lead to major institutional changes in the short term but was not broad enough to encompass the Supreme Court and a broader, bipartisan community of legislators and political elites. Hence by the time President Obama took office the CIA's detention and interrogation programme was already defunct, and it was bureaucratically, legally, and politically uncontroversial for him to formally end the use of EITs by fiat.

5.5 Summary

As also discussed in the preceding chapter, this case shows the transformative power produced by the *interaction* of all three causal mechanisms. While the strategic pressures of the War on Terror incentivised new practices and new technological developments in interrogation just as they did with targeting, EITs never ceased to be controversial on normative grounds. Indeed, the clear role of technical and scientific innovation in their development is in part a response to the impropriety of simply declaring that the new method was to inflict severe pain until detainees disclosed information. Moreover, while there was, and still is, a singular set of formalised, operative prohibitions on torture to be changed or overcome, in practice EITs nevertheless emerged on the basis of transformations in a complex set of normative imperatives and orientations, ranging from concerns over use of military force in general to the specific authorities held by each institution within the US security apparatus. This shows that EIT proponents were not just a collection of (misguided) strategic actors looking for a way to circumvent normative obstacles to employ what they thought to be more efficient means of gathering information. As in the previous case, they were preoccupied with questions of authority, of technology, and of managing competing normative commitments under pressure.

EITs came to be, and then ceased to be, in ways that established theories of norm change, whether focused on the life cycle of specific norms (Finnemore and Sikkink 1998), discursive contention (Wiener 2008), or rational choice (Morrow 2014), do not completely grasp. As with the case of the US targeted killing programme, the evidence suggests that torture continued to be prohibited even as violent interrogation practices emerged and became institutionalised. Again, this is not the same as 'norm' erosion or 'death' (Percy 2007a; 2007b; McKeown 2009; Panke and Petersohn 2011), nor local interpretation (Acharya 2004). More so than in the targeted killing case, significant dimensions of transformation relate not to redefining abusive treatment but to simply denying that protections against it existed for a given class of persons, which can be approached as a case of contestation (Wiener 2008). Yet the roles of technology and the establishment of new networks within the security apparatus is key to understanding *how* the legal and discursive efforts of EIT proponents proceeded. Their focus on distinguishing coercive interrogation practices – even those the US government considered to be unambiguous torture in the past – from EITs relied on the putatively advanced psychological science and on the production of a new community of interrogators without the normative 'baggage' of existing law enforcement and military ones. The eventual abandonment of EITs in turn was propelled by the absence of demonstrated benefits to them, which was instrumental in facilitating the reassertion of the prohibition and a transformation back towards the earlier status quo.

6 | Case 3

Private Military and Security Companies and the Prohibition on Mercenaries

I wish the US Congress would ask [Erik Prince] why they killed my innocent son, who called himself Allawi. Do you think that this child was a threat to your company? This giant company that has the biggest weapons, the heaviest weapons, the planes, and this boy was a threat to them? . . . I want Americans to know that this was a child that died for nothing

Mohammad Kinani, on the death of his nine-year-old son in the 16 September 2007 killings of seventeen Iraqi civilians by Blackwater Security Consulting[1]

6.1 Introduction

Since the 1990s, private military and security contractors (PMSCs) have increasingly participated in the military missions of a range of states, big and small, in ways that have led many to question whether the international prohibition on mercenarism still exists. The claim that PMSCs are mercenaries has been forcefully asserted by senior UN figures such as Ballesteros (2003) and journalists such as Scahill (2007); scholars such as Petersohn (2014) and Singer (2008) fall short of making this claim but do assert that the prevalence of these contractors indicate a major shift in international norms defining and prohibiting mercenaries. However, other scholars engaged in the study of the private military and security industry deny these claims, finding that the prohibition remains strong and is not contravened by the activities of the largest firms recently engaged by major governments (Avant 2016). In other words, the evolution of the mercenarism prohibition is another case of indistinct or complex normative transformation similar to the previous two cases I cover in this book.

[1] Quoted in Jeremy Scahill, 'Blackwater's Youngest Victim', *The Nation*, 28 January, available at www.thenation.com/article/blackwaters-youngest-victim/; accessed 9 May 2017.

The mercenarism prohibition has been deeply institutionalised within the international community for well over a century, and since the 1960s it has been affirmed in a range of UN resolutions and treaties. However, by now many thousands of contractors have been deployed all over the world in roles that require them to be armed like soldiers and to carry the risk of violent engagement with a similarly armed enemy. While many states are engaged in this practice,[2] the United States, especially in its campaigns in Afghanistan and Iraq, has by far been the primary employer of PMSCs over the past two decades. In 2012, for example, the total number of contractor personnel in Afghanistan exceeded 117,000, a sizeable portion of which were employed to provide security and military services (GAO 2016). These contractors are not identical to the mercenaries of previous eras – they do not mass, join battle, and capture enemy territory[3] – but their prevalence nevertheless represents a contentious change in the nature of the agents and institutions that governments employ to fight wars. A significant normative transformation has taken place: what was once extraordinary and illegitimate is now ordinary and acceptable, but only under certain conditions and not without ongoing contestation. This chapter investigates the origins, extent, and causal processes responsible for it.

However, this case is also different in form from the previous two, and, in order to produce a somewhat comparable structure of analysis of it, the scope of my examination in this chapter is constrained in two ways. The difference lies in the scale of the practice. The USA's targeted killing and interrogation programmes were primarily created and run by a relatively small set of actors and institutions, working within a discrete collection of government organisations and pursuing relatively well-defined ends. The employment of PMSCs involves a great many countries and bureaucratic entities, with vastly disparate legal and institutional contexts, working in many different operational environments. For this reason, much recent scholarship on the normative dimensions of PMSCs approaches them as

---

[2] PMSCs have been hired and deployed by/in a wide range of countries and conflicts, in roles that vary from providing trainers to militaries to fielding full-scale battalion-size fighting forces, across a range of regions – notably sub-Saharan Africa, the Balkans, the Persian Gulf, and Asia-Pacific (in the case of Papua New Guinea).

[3] With the (in)famous exception of the now-defunct South African company Executive Outcomes, discussed in greater detail in Section 6.4 of this chapter.

a global phenomenon (see, for example, Avant 2005; Percy 2007a; 2007b; Singer 2008; Abrahamsen and Williams 2009; Carmola 2010). Moreover, many contractors working for military or security organisations handle various logistical tasks that support combat operations but do not directly contribute to them – for example, by working as cooks, drivers, or housekeeping staff on bases. Hence, I focus on contractors doing things that look a lot like 'combat' or otherwise are military in nature,[4] and I focus the bulk of my attention specifically on the ways the United States has employed PMSCs, most notably in Afghanistan (2001–) and Iraq (2003–).[5] To be clear, while the United States has employed PMSCs as both guards and trainers since the mid-1990s, this was at a much smaller scale than would become the case from the 2000s onwards. Hence these earlier instances of US employment of PMSCs, and the employment by other states of PMSCs during this era, are less salient to my case study, though they are still relevant enough to warrant some discussion of their role in establishing prior normative conditions.

As in the previous two chapters, I de-reify the prohibition, locate agency within the normative configuration that underlies it, and trace the processes of transformation that took place over the course of the case. I find that the prohibition on mercenarism still exists – and indeed exists with greater institutional clarity than before, in terms of its articulation in law and practice – but, as with the prohibitions on assassination and torture, it changed over the course of extensive integration of PMSCs and regular forces in the War on Terror. This change was impelled by needs-driven expansions in the use of PMSCs and the reorientation of military forces towards

---

[4] The ambiguity of this language, it should be noted, is deliberate, designed to recognise that the definitions of combat and of military tasks are contested and subject to change; they are part of this case and thus must be left open enough at the outset to avoid begging the very question under investigation. My more detailed definition here is something like *those individuals or firms carrying out jobs in which personnel are at high risk of military attack, and thus in which they carry weapons and have a high probability of using them* (such as protecting militarily significant convoys, persons, or buildings), *or that are tactically instrumental to making military operations possible* (such as through field intelligence support or, potentially, through training missions). More sustained and less ambiguous attempts to define PMSCs may be found in Avant (2005), O'Brien (2007), Singer (2008), and Carmola (2010), among others.

[5] Note that, at the time of writing, the United States still has significant troop commitments in these countries, and thus while the USA's major expeditions to Afghanistan and Iraq have ended, the conflicts there have not.

offensive operations and away from passive protection activities, innovations in communications technology, and close cooperation between government officials and professional organisations to improve self-regulation.

6.2 De-reification: The Prohibition on Mercenaries and the Rise of the Modern PMSC

The international prohibition on mercenaries, in formal and informal conventions, has a long history, and from early modernity until the first emergence of modern PMSCs during the 1990s, it was relatively stable. It is entangled with the rise of the nation state and the monopolisation of organised military forces as components of the governments thereof. In addition to this slower and broader process of institutional transformation in who fights wars, there is more recent context to the prohibition on mercenaries as well – one stemming from the desire to limit coup-plotters from accessing powerful private forces capable of rapidly multiplying their capacity for disrupting or toppling regimes. I here separate them for the sake of analytical convenience. This identifies the normative tensions that have arisen along with changes in how states and their societies wage war, and thus where transformative mechanisms had the opportunity to exert an influence.

6.2.1 *Mercenaries and the Monopolisation of Military Force*

The international prohibition on mercenaries has its roots in the fitful but eventual consolidation and monopolisation of military power by European sovereign states, spanning the twelfth to the nineteenth centuries. Initially there were two reasons for this desire to eliminate mercenary companies. First, when fighting stopped, such as due to extended truces, unemployed mercenaries often engaged in banditry and preyed upon local populations; and second, the prevalence of individuals fighting for reasons of private gain rather than public duty clashed with the civic ethos that European regimes increasingly sought to establish amongst their citizens (Thompson 1994; Ortiz 2007; Percy 2007a; 2007b).[6] In the aftermath of the French Revolution, and with the

---

[6] Percy (2007b), in a thorough historical investigation of the prohibition on mercenaries, traces the predations of mercenaries-cum-bandit 'Free Companies'

emergence of vast citizen-armies and of new, totalising forms of warfare, that latter reason became increasingly significant. As militaries grew larger, recruitment gained in political salience, and by the early 1800s, for reasons of exigency (Posen 1993; Thompson 1994), ideology (Avant 2005), and institutional path dependence (Percy 2007a; 2007b), military service as citizen obligation had become normatively and practically entrenched. States no longer hired regiments of foreigners to fight their battles and typically prohibited their own citizens from serving in others' armies. While the prohibition on mercenaries was only weakly formalised, with limited legal articulation culminating in the denial of combatant privileges to mercenaries under the Geneva Conventions,[7] European states nevertheless adhered to it in their wars with one another. The normative combatant was one who fought for the country of which they were a citizen, in official military organisations, and ideally out of patriotism or loyalty to their community rather than for personal gain.

Yet European states did feature exceptions to this: chartered trade companies and their standing armed forces. Unlike privateers, who were simply granted autonomy to lawfully prey upon ships flying enemy flags, chartered trading companies such as the British East India Company possessed complex and extensive armies and navies and deployed them to protect national assets as well as private ones such as trading posts or routes – they even, at times, were used to put down colonial revolts (Thomson 1994; Singer 2008). Chartered trading companies were permitted to openly recruit enlisted troops and to commission officers from the same pools as did the official armed forces of their respective states (Thomson 1994). Moreover, they did not exclusively serve the states whose charter they carried and would in some instances provide military services and training to foreign sovereigns for both direct compensation and for favourable trade relationships (Ortiz 2007). These companies thus engaged in military activities sometimes, similar to those of the increasingly proscribed mercenary groups of Europe, but with several noteworthy differences. First, they were bureaucratised, long-term

---

during the Hundred Years War, the poor reputation of Swiss and (foreigner-comprised) Italian mercenary companies from the fourteenth to sixteenth centuries due to prominent incidents of atrocity, duplicity, and avarice. A number of other scholars conduct similar historical surveys (Thompson 1994; Avant 2005), and thus for reasons of both space and redundancy, I do not attempt to reproduce their work here.

[7] The weaknesses and tensions of how the Geneva Conventions define 'mercenary' will be discussed in Section 6.2.2.

administrative entities using armed force to secure trade monopolies of great value to their sponsors; second, they plied their trade in the colonies and not in Europe itself; third, they did so under considerably greater state oversight and control (Ortiz 2007). Whether chartered trade companies constituted 'proto-PMSCs' and whether this implies weaknesses or internal tensions in contemporaneous prohibitions on mercenaries lies outside the historical remit of this chapter.

6.2.2 Prohibitions on Mercenaries in the Modern Context

The era after the Second World War featured the emergence of a different kind of prohibition on mercenaries – one driven not by concerns over banditry or ideological purity of service but over the power of small groups of private military experts to either overthrow legitimate governments or greatly multiply the repressive capacities of authoritarian states. In other words, the concern was that mercenaries would interfere with national self-determination, and this framing of the problem presented by mercenarism was affirmed in numerous UN General Assembly resolutions.[8]

Moreover, the focus of the prohibition was almost exclusively on sub-Saharan Africa. There, private fighting forces led by European officers had been instrumental in several attempted coups and several counter-insurgencies, such as in the Congo from 1960 to 1968, for both sides of the civil war, and in the 1967–70 Nigerian civil war, both on behalf of the separatists and for the government (Thomson 1994). As these examples imply, it would not be unusual to see something akin to an organisational arms race, whereby both sides of a conflict seek to acquire their own European military experts. As a result of regional perception that mercenaries thus constituted an 'African security dilemma' (Musah et al. 2000; see also O'Brien 2007), African states have been instrumental in driving stronger formal prohibitions on mercenary activities (Percy 2007a; 2007b). Though, as previously noted, mercenaries do not enjoy combatant privileges under the Geneva Conventions, they have not traditionally been subjected to strong condemnation or punishment; the Organization for African Unity Convention for the Elimination of Mercenarism in Africa, signed

---

[8] For examples, see indices of these resolutions in Doswald-Beck (2007) and Percy (2007a; 2007b).

on 3 July 1977 in Libreville, was an attempt to resolve this. Signatories committed to a domestic ban on mercenarism and to criminally pros-ecuting mercenaries within their territory.[9] African countries were also instrumental in strengthening prohibitions on mercenaries in Protocol Additional I to the 1949 Geneva Conventions (1977; see Article 47). During the 1960s and 1970s, numerous UN resolutions passed in the General Assembly condemning mercenaries, again focused on the African context.[10] The mercenary, in this new era of explicit and formal normative elucidation, was a vestige of colonial domination: white men taking African money to crush local aspirations and prop up illegitimate regimes.

In the last two decades of the twentieth century, a more robust set of international legal instruments prohibiting mercenaries emerged. By the 1980s, Western states had more explicitly and firmly signed on to what had earlier mostly been a preoccupation of the postcolonial world. In 1980, the General Assembly established the Ad Hoc Committee on the Drafting of an International Convention against the Recruitment, Use, Financing and Training of Mercenaries; on 4 November 1989, it passed resolution 44/34, adopting the draft convention prepared by the com-mittee and opened for signatures, ratification, and accession the International Convention against the Recruitment Use, Financing and Training of Mercenaries.[11] It is worth noting, however, that while the United States had assisted Nigeria in the mid-1970s in drafting the OAC convention (Percy 2007b) and voted to pass a 1977 Security Council resolution condemning mercenarism in Benin,[12] it did not sign the International Convention. Nor did, among others, the United Kingdom, China, Russia, and – despite having assisted in the production of the treaty – France.[13] Moreover, even as the Convention accumulated signatures, by the mid-1990s Angola and Sierra Leone, both signatories, had employed private companies of foreign military experts in direct combat against rebel movements. While backlash against both

[9] The text of the convention may be found at http://hrlibrary.umn.edu/instree/m ercenaryconvention.html; accessed 8 April 2017.
[10] See O'Brien (2007) for details.
[11] Full information on the committee and convention may be found at http://legal .un.org/avl/ha/icruftm/icruftm.html; accessed 8 April 2017.
[12] Text of the resolution and record of its passing may be found at www.un.org/ga/ search/view_doc.asp?symbol=S/RES/405(1977); accessed 8 April 2017.
[13] For details and records, see http://legal.un.org/avl/ha/icruftm/icruftm.html; accessed 8 April 2017.

companies led to their demise, their emergence marked the beginning of a new era of private military and security contracting – and the historical starting-point of the analysis of normative transformation in this chapter of the book.

6.3 Attributing Agency: Technological and Ethical Potential for Change

In this case, by comparison to the previous ones, the level or scale of action makes it harder to find specific *actors* of special influence, and thus a reminder of how I define agency may be helpful. Agency is the potential for generating change that lies in an unfolding arrangement of action. To attribute agency is to find where, in such an arrangement, the particular transactions that comprise it are most likely to encounter disruption and where the resolution of disruption is most likely to have a powerful effect in driving a broader transformation. Hence when I talk about agency, I mean something that lies in a situation, rather than something possessed by a given actor or agent. This collapses the more familiar co-constitutive dichotomy of structures and agents into ongoing relations of mutual adjustment among people and their worlds – a single-layered ontology rather than a stratified one.[14] In the previous two cases, I still found a close association between agency and the actions of a delimited collection of individual persons, but in this case, because it spans a much larger array of people and places, attributing agency (and, after, tracing transactions) directs attention at wide-ranging organisational processes.

I find that the potential for a rapid growth in PMSC presence and deployment in the major US expeditions in Afghanistan and Iraq lay in the confluence of three historical conditions: organisational changes in the US military, limitations of legal prohibitions that might restrict PMSCs, and the institutional composition of US operations. Together these conditions established a situation in which all three causal mechanisms were able to operate; in other words, these conditions generated agency for effecting normative transformation.

The first condition was a shift towards a smaller, highly professionalised, and more operationally focused military, driven by factors of cost and of enabling technology. During the 1990s, the US military

---

[14] For extensive discussion of this, see Chapter 2; see also Depélteau (2013).

downsized; without the Soviet Union, there was diminished strategic need and value in maintaining such a large force. At the same time, the types of operations and conflicts the United States found itself fighting also transformed. Rather than fight a large-scale ground war in Europe against a powerful rival superpower, troops could instead expect to be deployed into existing war zones as peacekeepers, such as in the former Yugoslavia, or used as rapid reaction forces to intervene in foreign conflicts, such as in the Gulf War. Finally, as military technology increased in sophistication and cost, budget cuts led to the prioritisation of expensive weapons systems over staging expeditions.

This organisational shift not only led to a smaller military but required a more professionalised one, as personnel could expect to face complex political circumstances, requiring great discrimination or restraint in use of force. The result was a shortage of manpower for certain jobs – most saliently guard duties (O'Brien 2007) but also management of increasingly sophisticated high technology (Singer 2008) – that PMSCs could resolve (Avant 2005; Isenberg 2007; Singer 2008; Carmola 2010; Kruck 2013).[15] Moreover, the new emphasis on multilateral operations created jurisdictional issues that private actors could evade as a consequence of not being an official arm of any particular state (Avant 2007). Finally, the result of downsizing was also to establish a pool of unemployed military experts who could sell their skills to states looking to upgrade their capabilities (Avant 2005; 2007). The outcome of these changes was an organisational transformation in the military – driven adaption to new strategic and operational environments – that created both demand and supply for PMSCs.

The second condition for normative transformation was the definitional specificity of formal prohibitions on mercenarism, which made it difficult to argue for the illegality of most PMSCs and easier to draw a clear distinction between PMSCs and mercenaries in legal and public discourses. This is a key dimension of what made/makes the prohibition

---

[15] One Pentagon official heavily involved in establishing and regulating PMSCs in Iraq, Col. (ret.) Christopher Mayer, emphasised to me in both an interview with him and a subsequent email exchange, however, that historically contractors have often taken on these duties. Confining them to official military personnel should be associated with the excess manpower available to twentieth-century armies. Nevertheless, recent or not, it was a normative feature of conflict that soldiers should guard and escort in conflict zones.

on mercenaries a 'strong norm, weak law', to quote Percy's article by that title in *International Organization* (2007a). Article 47 of the Protocol Additional I to the 1949 Geneva Conventions (1977), which denies combatant rights and prisoner-of-war protections to mercenaries, offers the following definition:

A mercenary is any person who: (a) is specially recruited locally or abroad in order to fight in an armed conflict; (b) does, in fact, take a direct part in the hostilities; (c) is motivated to take part in the hostilities essentially by the desire for private gain and, in fact, is promised, by or on behalf of a Party to the conflict, material compensation substantially in excess of that promised or paid to combatants of similar ranks and functions in the armed forces of that Party; (d) is neither a national of a Party to the conflict nor a resident of territory controlled by a Party to the conflict; (e) is not a member of the armed forces of a Party to the conflict; and (f) has not been sent by a State which is not a Party to the conflict on official duty as a member of its armed forces.

This definition leaves a wide scope for PMSCs to avoid classification as mercenaries, particularly when they are indigenous to the states hiring them, which virtually ensures that they will not fall under criterion (d). Moreover, by declaring ideological goals alongside profit-seeking ones, PMSCs can avoid falling under criterion (c) – and indeed, this was part of the (relatively unsuccessful) self-portrayal argued by the CEO of the now-defunct company Sandline, in defence of their operations in Sierra Leone.[16] Finally, by claiming to use force only in self-defence, such as by claiming that guard duties do not constitute fighting in an armed conflict, PMSCs can avoid falling under criterion (a). For example, as Petersohn (2014) notes, attempts by Eeben Barlow, CEO of Executive Outcomes, to frame his company's operations in this light enjoyed limited success due to their employees' participation in staging operations to capture rebel-held territories and facilities in Angola but have since become standard arguments from those seeking to differentiate PMSCs from mercenaries. The International Convention does not significantly alter this definition to make it any more inclusive.[17]

---

[16] See Petersohn (2014).
[17] It adds only the following:

A mercenary is also any person who, in any other situation: (a) Is specially recruited locally or abroad for the purpose of participating in a concerted act of violence aimed at: (i) Overthrowing a Government or otherwise undermining the constitutional order of a State; or (ii) Undermining the territorial integrity of a State; (b) Is motivated to take part therein essentially by the desire for

Though formal definitions are often more restrictive than informal or popular ones, legal prohibitions on mercenaries in international law nevertheless offered PMSCs and their sponsors multiple avenues to claim not that mercenarism should be permissible but simply that they are not engaging in it.[18]

The third condition making it possible for PMSCs to become normal and common in US military expeditions was the large number of private firms and government organisations working in operational spaces, coupled with a general interest in privatisation when possible. A consequence of the longer-term, stability-oriented operations that the United States and its partners now engaged in, this established the institutional conditions for a diverse array of contractors, rather than relying upon government personnel for force protection or other military tasks (O'Brien 2007; Isenberg 2007). For example, from the beginning of the war in Iraq, 'national military forces involved in the conflict refused outright to provide [guarding services for corporate and civilian assets], concentrating wholly on combating their enemies while attempting to establish and train a new national military in-country' (O'Brien 2007, 32). Meanwhile, though a greater number of Department of Defense employees and sites typically received military protection than did those of the Department of State, both were free to choose private options, and the latter depended especially heavily on PMSC security (Lovewine 2012). Last but certainly not least, as these institutions and agencies were operating – and still are – in a broader governmental environment in which privatisation is understood to be more efficient and therefore more desirable, institutional practices and cultures were already organised around a search for market solutions whenever possible (Avant 2005).

Taken together, these three conditions did not make it inevitable that the United States would come to rely so heavily on PMSCs for the sorts

---

significant private gain and is prompted by the promise or payment of material compensation; (c) Is neither a national nor a resident of the State against which such an act is directed; (d) Has not been sent by a State on official duty; and (e) Is not a member of the armed forces of the State on whose territory the act is undertaken.

The full text is available at www.un.org/documents/ga/res/44/a44r034.htm; accessed 8 April 2017.

[18] This is reminiscent of statements in the previous two cases, where actors did not attempt to defend assassination or torture as justifiable or good but instead sought to refute or deny claims that they were engaging in these activities.

of dangerous, combat-like jobs that have prompted concerns over the demise of the prohibition on mercenarism. Rather, they made it *possible* for a normative transformation to occur, establishing an environment in which the use of PMSCs was strategically valuable and potentially legitimate, while investing particular actors with the authority and capacity to hire them. In this sense, they were jointly necessary but not sufficient; it is difficult to imagine the explosion of the PMSC industry without strategic need, legal clearance, and institutional disposition to meet needs with market solutions, but to see how and where these conditions led to that outcome it is necessary to examine the operation of subsequent causal mechanisms.

6.4 Tracing Transactions: The Three Mechanisms at Work

In this section, I provide an account of the causal mechanisms that generated the emergence of the PMSC industry servicing the wars in Afghanistan and Iraq (and, more recently, beyond) and of the normative transformation it involved. Specifically, I show how the synthetic operation of the three causal mechanisms – convention re-orientation, technological revision, and network synthesis – explains how PMSCs became a fixture of these conflicts, carrying and using weapons in military engagements in ways that imply significant changes in the kinds of actors invested with the legitimacy to fight. For analytical clarity, I divide the account into three sub-sections. First, I examine the emergence of a PMSC industry during the 1990s, as well as responses by PMSCs to critics labelling them mercenaries. Second, I look at the extensive employment of PMSCs during post-invasion occupation and reconstruction efforts in Afghanistan and Iraq, in particular how the position of PMSCs transformed over time through situated institutional innovation. Third, I discuss the international normative directions the PMSC industry has taken above and beyond the conflict zones of Iraq and Afghanistan, indicating its longer-term trajectory.

6.4.1 *PMSCs and the Emerging Market for Force*

Most discussions of private military and security contracting during the 1990s focus on the (in)famous activities of the two large 'operational providers' – companies providing forces capable of mounting military operations – Executive Outcomes and Sandline International. Executive Outcomes (EO), formed in 1989 by former South African Defence Forces (SADF) Lieutenant-Colonel Eeben Barlow and primarily comprising demobilised SADF special forces personnel, played a pivotal role in civil wars in Angola and Sierra Leone. Barlow and his employees offered military training and advisory services in contracts with a range of states in Africa, Asia, and Latin America but are primarily known for embedding with government troops in Angola in 1993, to capture two oil-industry installations from UNITA rebels, and with government troops in Sierra Leone from 1995 to 1997, where it provided ground, air, and intelligence support to facilitate major victories against the RUF.[19] Founded by retired colonel Timothy Spicer, formerly of the United Kingdom's Scots Guards, Sandline provided training, materiel, and tactical assistance to the government of Papua New Guinea in 1996 and to the ousted Sierra Leonian government in 1997–8, assisting the latter in retaking the country from military putschists and RUF forces but contributing inadvertently to the downfall of the former (De Nevers 2009). EO found few contracts following its withdrawal from Sierra Leone in 1997 – though its employees found work as subcontractors, including to Sandline – and permanently disbanded on 31 December 1998 after South Africa passed a law restricting PMSC activities by its citizens (Singer 2008). Meanwhile, after parliamentary investigations for violating UN arms embargos by shipping weapons to Sierra Leone,[20] Sandline International closed its offices on 16 April 2004.[21]

EO and Sandline employed different legitimation strategies to justify their activities when faced with accusations of mercenarism. Sandline claimed it worked for governments to restore order, in some cases with official deputization; in Papua New Guinea, Sandline's personnel were obliged by contract to join the state's military as special constables, though it is unclear if this was ever formally fulfilled in practice (Singer

---

[19] The 'story of EO' may be found in virtually every prominent book-length treatment of the PMSC industry (see, inter alia, Avant 2005; Kinsey 2006; Percy 2007b; several chapters in the volume edited by Chesterman and Lehnhard 2007; Singer 2008; Cameron and Chetail 2013).

[20] Sandline's arms shipments, which took place in 1998, were found to be in violation of UK and international law (See 'Spicer calls Sierra Leone affair "ethical"', BBC News, 5 November 1998, available at news.bbc.co.uk/2/hi/special_report/1998/05/98/arms_to_africa_row/207586.stm; accessed 8 April 2017.)

[21] As was noted on its company website (www.sandline.com/).

2008). On this basis, Sandline was able to claim that its use of force was as a sovereign agent and thus that their employees were not mercenaries. EO claimed that their employees used force only in personal self-defence and thus were not contracted specifically to fight (Petersohn 2014). As Petersohn (2014) notes, neither of these defences were especially successful: working for governments did little to diminish public impressions (and legal realities) of Sandline as guns for hire, while EO's crucial and proactive leadership in mounting operations to storm and capture rebel-held locations in Angola and Sierra Leone would seem to contradict its claims to use force exclusively in self-defence. In other words, while the rise of these two companies is frequently detailed in examinations of the possible erosion of the international prohibition on mercenarism, the fall of both, and the failure of their legitimation strategies, strongly implies the prohibition still carried weight during their operations.

During this time, however, the United States also hosted (and employed) another prominent PMSC: Military Professional Resources Incorporated (MPRI). Founded by former US army officers in 1987 and still currently a major player in the PMSC industry, it offered a wide range of non-combat services to both US and allied military forces throughout the 1990s. These include contracts for training and materiel acquisition of Croatian forces in Bosnia in 1995 (discussed presently) and training of the Equatorial Guinea coast guard in 1998 – both with the guidance and approval of the US government, on the grounds that these contracts served US interests while saving US taxpayers from the costs of a military deployment (Avant 2007, 426). The majority of MPRI's employees comprise retired US military officials, often of high rank, and the company maintains a close relationship with contacts in the departments of Defence and State (Binder 2007). In addition to outsourcing training of its own personnel to MPRI, the US government also arranged a contract for the firm to advise, equip, and (unofficially) train the Croatian military.[22] This was a delicate strategic move: the Clinton administration wanted to avoid explicitly and significantly intervening in the mounting crisis in the Balkans, and thus it hoped that a strengthened Croatia would create a military balance of power that would bring warring parties to the bargaining table (Binder 2007). In other words, MPRI was not merely

---

[22] While MPRI has officially denied that it offered direct training to Croatian troops (Singer 2008), this denial strains credulity.

a private actor taking advantage of a market but a policy option that the US government pursued in lieu of committing its uniformed forces.

This was a highly influential action. On 4 August 1995, approximately 130,000 Croatian troops began a large offensive and over a span of four days recaptured almost all Serbian-held portions of Krajian territory (Binder 2007). Though MPRI had spent only a few months 'advising' Croatian forces, observers described their operation as a 'U.S.-style attack' (Zarate 1998, 107) that 'bore many hallmarks of U.S. Army doctrine' (per a journalist quoted in Singer 2008, 5) for its combination of simultaneous air raids, artillery bombardments, and rapid infantry manoeuvres. Contributing to this surprising operational success likely was the high-level assistance MPRI offered to Croatia in its planning: CEO and retired US general Carl Vuono met several times the top-ranked Croatian military officials in command of the offensive (Binder 2007). Thus while MPRI did not provide the sort of direct tactical support offered by EO and Sandline – and that would later be offered by US-employed PMSCs like Blackwater – it nevertheless offered critical military services to a government during a war.

The rise and fall of EO and Sandline, and the more enduring success of MPRI, show the synthetic interaction of all three mechanisms. Network synthesis is perhaps the clearest of the three: these organisations – and in the case of EO and Sandline, the local breakaway firms they left in their wake – formed out of existing networks of military personnel, then traded their services in an international market where their experience and connections made them invaluable as force multipliers. This mechanism was triggered by major military downsizing and diplomatic shifts following the end of the Cold War and provided the two PMSCs with access to both clients and, via military and government connections, the human and material resources required to offer a high-quality product.

But the evidence also shows additional interaction with the other two mechanisms, and this fills in the rest of the story. First, convention reorientation transformed the diplomatic and international legal environment in ways that made PMSCs appear more legitimate and other military options less so. Without superpower competition, 'weak' states facing local insurgencies could no longer rely on military support from patrons, while the United States no longer had a mandate to commit significant official resources to intervene, directly or indirectly (such as though training and materiel), in propping up beleaguered foreign allies. This created normative space for private actors to claim to be picking up the slack (Petersohn 2014). Second, technological revision in practices of warfighting transformed the kinds of military means and skills governments needed for their security apparatuses. In this sense, technological revision involved skills more than it did materiel: while 'high-tech' weapons and communications systems imposed operational needs that PMCSs were in a position to provide, in many places the practices of warfare shifted as well, and PMSCs knew how to adapt, or teach others to adapt, to their exigencies. The focus of armed conflict had shifted from large-scale conventional war or superpower-backed counterinsurgency to managing (and winning) ethnic or internecine civil wars while sparing civilians as much harm as possible. PMSCs took advantage of this shift by adapting existing military skills for the private market for force.

This process shows how the three mechanisms worked in jointly and mutually reinforcing ways, and not just as independent, additive contributions to an ongoing change in practices. The PMSCs of the post–Cold War decade were able to recruit personnel through social networks of retired soldiers and officers and had services in particular demand because of the rise of so-called new wars – factional and often internecine struggles with no clear military solution that blur the lines of war and peace, civilian and combatant (Kaldor 1999; see also Kinsey 2006). In these conflicts, PMSCs provided the right set of tools for the strategic environment and could seek legitimacy within a growing quasi-private market for force, amidst a broader global trend towards market solutions. It is difficult to imagine PMSCs attaining significant prominence as market actors without all of these conditions obtaining. As noted earlier, this process also reveals a key difference in the PMSC case compared to the previous two: the scale or locus of the mechanisms is bigger and broader, working across a wide range of states and settings, rather than a small set of bureaucracies and amongst a small set of actors. Agency is harder to pin down to a specific set of people and their activities, and it instead emerges out of more complex transinstitutional processes.

However, by this point a major normative transformation had yet to take place – or was, at least, in an early and widely contested phase. In 1998, the UN special rapporteur on mercenarism, Enrique Bernales Ballesteros, submitted a report that summarised and exemplified scepticism of the legitimacy of PMSCs (Bernales Ballesteros 1998). The report, which made direct reference to EO and Sandline International (see especially paragraphs 77–9), offered a number of indictments of the PMSC industry: that 'firms providing consulting services, military training and private security ... present a more modern and efficient image and engage in activities which are apparently legal, but in fact they work with mercenaries and represent a danger to the economies, democracy and self-determination of peoples' (paragraph 25); that 'modern private security companies ... are covers for former professional soldiers and mercenaries who ... today represent the biggest and most sophisticated threat to the peace, sovereignty and self-determination of the peoples of many countries' (paragraph 28); and, perhaps most summarily, that

having observed how they operate, the Special Rapporteur suggests that private companies offering international security represent a new operational model that is more up to date and effective and with a relatively adequate legal cover, but nevertheless linked to mercenary activities, as they intervene militarily and for pay, in activities which it was more prudent to entrust to State authorities than to abandon to the vagaries of free-market competition. (Bernales Ballesteros 1998, paragraph 68)

The strength of this rejection of the legitimacy of PMSCs, primarily informal in language but nevertheless making extensive reference to principles of sovereignty and state control over instruments of political violence, heavily indicate that the industry still sat on the margins of legitimacy for the international community. While the conditions for a new kind of marketised, privatised force emerged in the 1990s, the international normative environment still restricted the legitimacy of PMSCs, with their operations either confined to 'behind the scenes' support missions, as in the case of MPRI, or facing major censure from national and supranational governments, as in the case of EO and Sandline. During this phase, the scope of agency for generating normative transformation was thus still narrow, even though it was clearly present in the form of some operation of the three mechanisms.

Nevertheless, the processes of strategic and normative change responsible for growth of a PMSC industry did not cease with the shuttering of EO and Sandline. The success of MPRI in developing Croat military capabilities showed the political efficacy and expediency offered by a private market for force – and set precedents that defence policymakers and politicians would remember. With the advent of the

US 'Global War on Terror' and its campaigns in Afghanistan and Iraq, these processes resulted in clearer and firmer normative transformation. It is to this second phase that I now turn.

6.4.2 *PMSCs and the Wars in Afghanistan and Iraq*

The prominent role PMSCs have played in Afghanistan and Iraq over the past two decades garnered the private military and security industry notoriety and made the activities of armed contractors a matter of general public knowledge and controversy. Moreover, it is in the US-led invasions and counter-insurgencies in these two countries that the greatest market expansion and normative transformation in the industry took place. PMSCs certainly were active in other places during this time, ranging from recruitment and training of the Liberian military in 2005 to extensive employment in maritime security duties in the Gulf of Aden (McFate 2014). Focusing on Iraq and Afghanistan allows for a fine-grained analysis of the period's most influential process of normative transformation, but it certainly is not the only example available. In both, early military success gave way to long-term instability and a campaign of militarised public security and institution-building. The United States (and its allies), faced with manpower shortages, became major clients of the PMSC industry, meaning that the latter increasingly integrated into the highly bureaucratised and regulated institutions of the US security apparatus. In other words, in Afghanistan and Iraq, PMSCs eventually became institutionalised parts of the US force structure. While the United States can, as a global hegemon, get away with doing what African states cannot, its entrance into the market for force changed that market's environment – and, in turn, created the conditions for convention reorientation, technological revision, and network synthesis to generate a more enduring normative transformation.

The United States and its allies employed, from 2001 to 2009, approximately 28,000 armed civilian contractors in Afghanistan and approximately 65,000 armed civilian contractors in Iraq.[23] The primary job of these PMSCs was to provide security for Department of Defense and Department of State operations (Lovewine 2012), as well as for certain UN and local government activities. A rough distinction can thus be made, for functional and regulatory purposes, amongst contractors

---

[23] See the compilation of several sources offered in Lovewine (2012).

working directly for the DoD, those working for other US government agents such as the Department of State or USAID, and those working for NGOs or private companies (Petersohn 2011).[24] PMSCs were not thus specifically tasked with fighting these wars in the conventional sense of seeking out and engaging an enemy force. This established from the outset a different position, in law and in discursive framing, for PMSCs in Afghanistan and Iraq compared to that of Executive Outcomes and Sandline, which unequivocally engaged in military action.

However, it quickly became apparent that guard duty could also be combat duty, entailing frequent pitched battles with opposing forces. In Afghanistan, ISAF-employed security guards for convoys on the road between Kabul and Kandahar repeatedly engaged with as many as 200 fighters and involved similar numbers of guards. Company reports referred to such incidents to as 'enemy actions' producing 'battle damage' (Krahman 2013, 63). In Iraq, a 2007 congressional investigation found that Blackwater employees alone had 'fired their weapons 195 times since early 2005 and in a vast majority of incidents used their weapons before taking any hostile fire'.[25] In one mid-2004 episode, Blackwater guards engaged in an hours-long gun battle with a Shī'ī militants to defend the headquarters of Coalition Provisional Authority in Iraq.[26] This shows that while the market for force may have offered ways around the resource limits of US and allied forces, it introduced unforeseen normative and operational tensions, primarily around guarding and escort duties. Moreover, PMSCs were also tasked with training government security forces, both police and military, in Afghanistan (GAO 2013) and Iraq (Elsea et al. 2008). In other words, PMSCs were a key part of the US and ISAF/Coalition campaigns, performing essential functions that would otherwise be performed by uniformed forces, and were assigned combat-like duties.

Though PMSCs stopped gaps in manpower shortages, their increasing prevalence in Afghanistan and Iraq presented two major dilemmas

[24] An extended index of these PMSCs and the tasks for which they were employed is offered in Lovewine (2012).

[25] See John M. Broder, 'Chief of Blackwater Defends His Employees', *New York Times*, 3 October 2007, available at www.nytimes.com/2007/10/03/washington/03blackwater.html; accessed 10 May 2017.

[26] See Dana Priest, 'Private Guards Repel Attack on U.S. Headquarters', *Washington Post*, 6 April 2004, available at www.washingtonpost.com/archive/politics/2004/04/06/private-guards-repel-attack-on-us-headquarters/fe2e4dd8-b6d2-4478-b92a-b269f8d7fb9b/; accessed 10 May 2017.

with normative and strategic significance: coordination and regulation. These dilemmas went hand-in-hand, as poor communication between military forces and contractors, discrepancies in operational procedures, and uncertainty over the laws to which contractors were subject all reinforced one another, resulting in mutual antagonism. While government officials and agencies encountered little resistance in hiring PMSCs, they encountered considerable problems in actually deploying or using them in ways that added value to its operations.

These problems of coordination and regulation are well documented. In Afghanistan until 2008, many locally employed PMSC personnel were found to be employees of local warlords with connections to organised crime and in some cases to the Taliban itself (SASC 2010), suggesting low vetting standards and minimal integration of these personnel into broader military command and information structures. Meanwhile, in a 2005 report by the US Government Accountability Office containing interviews focusing on the role of PMSCs in Iraq, one contractor reported that 'the company is routinely involved in friendly fire incidents at check points and when encountering U.S. military convoys', that 'no standard procedures [exist] for dealing with U.S. military either at check points or when encountering a military convoy', and that 'U.S. troops lack "trigger discipline" particularly when troops first come into country'.[27] Another contractor reported that 'P[M]SCs are not communicating with each other or the military' and complained that requests for military support during emergencies had been ignored.[28] Meanwhile, one officer interviewed summarised the PMSC presence as

an enormous amount of contract security that roam the Green Zone with seemingly limited adult supervision [creating] an image of a pseudo mercenary army in the green zone. Soldiers have little regard for them bordering on contempt for their lack of standards and discipline.[29]

---

[27] Interview by Steve Sternlieb and Carole Coffey, Government Accountability Office (GAO), of a name-redacted contractor, 7 April 2005. See page 70 of a compilation of GAO interviews available online at https://fas.org/sgp/gao/psc-iraq.pdf; accessed 10 May 2017.

[28] Interview by Steve Sternlieb et al., GAO, of a name-redacted contractor, 27 July 2004. See page 4 of a compilation of GAO interviews available online at https://fas.org/sgp/gao/psc-iraq.pdf; accessed 10 May 2017.

[29] Interview by Carole Coffey, GAO, and name-redacted others, of a name-redacted US military officer, 26 April 2005. See page 101 of a compilation of GAO interviews available online at https://fas.org/sgp/gao/psc-iraq.pdf; accessed 10 May 2017.

The officer complained about a lack of

[s]tandards of conduct that apply to all contractors that clearly define lines of communication and authority. Specifically, we continually had problems with contractors carrying loaded weapons on secure military compounds and in our dining facilities.

Another interviewee discussed her difficulties working for the military judge advocate general on issues relating to PMSCs, explaining that her headquarters initially held the position that 'arming contractors was a violation of the rules of war as was having contractors provide security, including for convoy', and more broadly that '[i]t was unclear as to what laws covered contractors. There was no martial law in Iraq before the transition.' She is described by the authors of the report as having

had numerous conversations on the applicability of the law of occupation, which she did not believe was developed for the modern battlefield. The law of occupation mostly deals with obligations to the civilian population, not contractors. In many ways they were in unchartered territory in Iraq.[30]

In other words, bringing PMSCs into broader military command and control structures, to avoid accidental exchanges between troops and to keep contractors abreast of any urgent threat intelligence, required defining and standardising their practices and their position under the law.

Practitioner attempts to solve these problems shows the operation of the three causal mechanisms, and tracing those mechanisms helps locate when the normative transformation truly entered its second phase, with the end result being that PMSCs become normatively stable part of broader US (and allied) operations. This is best documented as it took place in Iraq and in domestic US law-making.[31] Formal convention reorientation involved clarifying the legal and operational position of

[30] Interview by Steve Sternlieb, GAO, of a name-redacted JAG officer, 9 December 2004. See page 49 of a compilation of GAO interviews available online at https://fas.org/sgp/gao/psc-iraq.pdf; accessed 10 May 2017.
[31] In Afghanistan, regulation and coordination with PMSCs took longer and was complicated by the significant numbers of local personnel recruited from local militias (see, for example, SASC 2010). Government agencies employing contractors eventually developed better oversight and training standards (GAO 2013; see also a 2016 report by the DoD, available at www.acq.osd.mil/log/ps/.CENTCOM_reports.html/5A_July_2016_Final.pdf; accessed 10 May 2017). However, there is less of a paper trail accounting for their origins and implementation. For this reason, I am here focusing more on Iraq, where the evidence permits a finer-grained analysis of the three mechanisms at work.

PMSCs when deployed. Initially, PMSCs were first exempt from local laws, and all coalition personnel were to be subject to the exclusive jurisdiction of their 'parent states'.[32] On 26 June 2004, the CPA issued Memorandum 17, which subjected all PMSCs to Iraqi trade laws and licensing regimes.[33] Yet this did little to address core issues in defining PMSC status under international humanitarian law and criminal law. On 4 October 2007, Congress passed the MEJA Expansion and Enforcement Act, enlarging upon the Military Extraterritorial Jurisdiction Act (MEJA) of 2000, providing that 'persons ... employed under a federal agency contract in, or in close proximity to, an area where the Armed Forces are conducting a contingency operation' under US jurisdiction for criminal offences.[34] In 2007, Congress also amended the Uniform Code of Military Justice (USMJ) to provide that '[i]n time of declared war or a contingency operation, persons serving with or accompanying an armed force in the field' can be tried and punished for violations of the UCMJ', effectively placing all civilian employees of the US government, whether contractor or not, under its military laws.[35] In practice, the function (and purpose) of these legal measures were to close the gap between PMSCs and uniformed military personnel, defining PMSC obligations and status in ways increasingly similar to those of troops.

Alongside these laws, which comprise the first formal phases of convention reorientation, were informal processes that linked together changes in applicable conventions with network synthesis and technological revision. As noted, military and PMSC personnel lacked explicit and codified procedures of interaction, and the need to build those

[32] See 'COALITION PROVISIONAL AUTHORITY ORDER NUMBER 17: STATUS OF THE COALITION, FOREIGN LIAISON MISSIONS, THEIR PERSONNEL AND CONTRACTORS', available at www.usace.army.mil/Portals/2/docs/COALITION_PROVISIONAL.pdf; accessed 10 May 2017.

[33] See 'COALITION PROVISIONAL AUTHORITY MEMORANDUM NUMBER 17: REGISTRATION REQUIREMENTS FOR PRIVATE SECURITY COMPANIES (PSC)', available at www-tc.pbs.org/wgbh/pages/frontline/shows/warriors/faqs/cpamemo.pdf; accessed 10 May 2017.

[34] Text of the bill available at www.congress.gov/bill/110th-congress/house-bill/2740; accessed 10 May 2017. Though despite this, as discussed in de Nevers (2009), lawyers representing the Blackwater contractors responsible for the Nisour Square shootings of Iraqi civilians were able to argue that, because the employer was DoS rather than DoD, MEJA didn't apply.

[35] For full text of the legislation, see digitalcommons.wcl.american.edu/cgi/viewcontent.cgi?article=1088&context=nslb; accessed 10 May 2017.

procedures, coupled with the absence of standardised and common radio and other communications infrastructure between the two, incentivised social networking as an ad hoc solution. Contractors and military officers developed regular points of contact to exchange information and coordinate the activities, resulting in the basis for institutionalised arrangements in the future, even if not in the present. This began relatively early, with interviewees for the GAO's 2005 report describing coordination and intelligence-sharing through mobile phone or in-person arrival of contractors to units' tactical operations centres, while in some cases contractors loaned radios to military teams they were working with to ensure reliable communications.[36] While these ad hoc initiatives did not amount to much on their own, they did presage more significant investment: a contract totalling almost $300 million to Aegis Defence, one of the largest UK-based PMSC firms, to coordinate PMSC activities and allow the US military to track where contractor security details actually were operating.[37]

Beginning in October 2004, Aegis Defence began running the Reconstruction Operations Center (ROC) 'to improve coordination between contractors and the major subordinate [and serve] as the interface between the military and the contractors in Iraq' (GAO 2005, 23). The ROC provided services such as intelligence sharing, calling in emergency military assistance from nearby military personnel, and location-specific contact information for contractors and military units sharing a given area (GAO 2005, 25–6). Here is where technological developments became key. One official, Col. (ret.) Christopher Mayer, spoke effusively of the role of new radio tracking systems, when asked about technological innovation that took place to make better regulation of PMSCs during this time possible:

This was awesome, okay? We knew that the military had Blue-Force Tracker for a while. And what happened was that Aegis did research for it and came

---

[36] 'We had established relationships with these organizations that knew how to contact us at our operations center by cell phone or by coming to the TOC' (interview by Carole Coffey, GAO, and name-redacted others, of a name-redacted US military officer, 26 April 2005. See pages 98–9 of a compilation of GAO interviews available at https://fas.org/sgp/gao/psc-iraq.pdf; accessed 10 May 2017.

[37] Ironically, and as Isenberg (2007) notes, that this task was itself contracted out indicates the US military had neither the capacity nor the inclination to perform this task internally.

up and found that there was this system called Tapestry which essentially was a civilian version or Blue-Force Tracker. Blue-Force Tracker could read all of the Tapestry movements. But of course people who were running Tapestry could not see the Blue-Force Tracker, so they couldn't see the military movements but we could see the civilian movements.[38]

The establishment of an institutional and technical basis for coordinating PMSC activities with military operations and oversight is a concrete demonstration of how network synthesis and technological revision interacted in this case. Yet the ROC still had limited effect, as participation was voluntary and not all contractors participated. It excluded those companies not employed by the Deparment of Defense, such as Blackwater, DynCorp, and Triple Canopy, who instead used the Department of State's independent coordination system (in which a security officer relayed information on PMSC positions to the military), and did not resolve the problems of horizontal communication between deployed contractors and military units by way of often-unreliable mobile phones (Petersohn 2011; see also GAO 2005).

However, the continued interaction of network synthesis and technological revision resolved some of these problems. At the beginning of 2008, the US military and its partners set up six Contractor Operations Cells (CONOC) to coordinate US government-hired PMSC activities with military forces, in which participation was mandatory for all contractors hired by both departments and through which all contractors would need to submit and receive approval for movement requests (SIGIR 2009). The cells also more widely issued radio communications equipment to participating PMSCs that would ensure standardised, horizontal communication through a stable medium (Petersohn 2011). This meant military leaders could both track and direct PMSCs in ways that could resolve many of the failures of oversight and communication that lead to the perception of PMSCs as uncontrollable. A GAO report enumerated the ways this led to more seamless integration of PMSCs within the US military force structure:

According to [DoD] officials, the Contractor Operations Cells provide a better mechanism for coordination than did the Reconstruction Operations Center, for several reasons. First, ... the Contractor Operations

---

[38] Christopher Mayer, interview with author, 19 May 2017.

Cells are co-located with the tactical units responsible for the battle space, making coordination easier. Second, commanders have improved situational awareness because information related to P[M]SCs is now viewed in context with other battle space activities. For example, the State Department provides the Contractor Operations Cells with U.S. Embassy PSC movement information that can be tracked by battlefield commanders using the same system as is used to track military vehicles. This movement information was never provided to the Reconstruction Operations Center when it was responsible for tracking DOD's P[M]SC movements. Third, battle space commanders now control the movement of DOD P[M]SCs in Iraq. (GAO 2008, 21)

Meanwhile, the Department of Defense also incorporated PMSC management and interactions into its predeployment programme for officers and staff at multiple levels of command, albeit with limited incorporation of organisational changes such as the creation of the CONOCs (GAO 2008, 17–18), and the Department of State had begun transmitting intelligence on route security to its PMSC guards (GAO 2008, 20). By late 2008 and 2009, US military officers on the ground were reporting no significant problems or tensions with PMSCs – a major shift from the state of affairs a few years prior.

Essentially, the Department of Defence and eventually the Department of State brought PMSCs into the structure of military bureaucracy, with its approach to delegating authorities, issuing directions, and managing operational procedures. By restricting PMSCs through the imposition of regulations and curtailing some of their more contentious and problematic practices, the US conferred legitimacy on PMSC operations *within* an authorised scope. This began with ad hoc, horizontal networking by deployed contractors and local military units, but then, expanded to encompass the rules, technologies, and formal organisational structures of broader military command and control. While convention reorientation occurred through executive-level Coalition Provisional Authority orders and through legislative action in the United States, the integration of PMSCs into a coordinated, military-led operational infrastructure also owed to increasingly strict and universal standards for use of force, which obliged contractors to comport themselves with greater professionalism and which made possible better operational coordination with military forces. The introduction of tracking systems that allowed a military-led command centre to maintain an operational picture of PMSC positions, and then of a radio system that allowed PMSCs and military forces to share common channels, introduced the technological capacities needed for close and ongoing, multi-level cooperation. The establishment of hubs for managing intelligence sharing and authorisation constituted network interchanges linking together disparate PMSCs with one another and with the military, regularising and diversifying the interactions of these actors. By the end of this process, PMSCs were integrated into the military's force structure in unprecedented ways, neither as independent battalions nor as individual soldiers of fortune – which may explain why it is possible to talk about a persistent prohibition on mercenarism even as the war efforts in Afghanistan and Iraq rested so heavily on armed contractors.

In this account, I have noted the interaction of mechanisms, but the way each one worked as a necessary condition for the others warrants more focused explication. Without the increased regulation and professionalization of convention reorientation, it is difficult to imagine a close working relationship between PMSC personnel and military forces, as early 'cowboy' behaviour from the former generated antagonism from the latter. The success of the Contractor Operations Cells in integrating and coordinating PMSC activities with military command and control clearly depended on both regulatory mandates and on the simple presence of reliable communications channels through standardised radio kit. Of the three mechanisms, it is perhaps possible to imagine convention reorientation working absent the other two, but the outcome would have been significantly different, without the same transformation in what constituted a normal array of actors and practices in the operational environment of the US campaigns.

Yet these changes still comprise only part of the process leading to the current state of affairs. While precedent-establishing, they were primarily confined mainly to Iraq, and to a lesser extent to Afghanistan, and bound up with temporary institutions set up to deal with operational challenges that have decreased in salience now that the US campaigns in these places have (mostly) ended. They comprised actors less interested in generating enduring normative change, compared to those in the cases of targeted killing and coercive interrogation, and more interested in resolving shorter-term, pressing regulatory and organisational dilemmas thrust upon them by messy conflict environments and manpower needs. In a sense, this phase featured a sort of 'normative transformation by default', where PMSCs had become a common and crucial component of US military efforts, and actors in a range of institutions learned to cope with their presence.

In other words, the account offered in this section covers essential institutional developments in establishing normative configurations specific to the wars in Afghanistan and Iraq. The integration of PMSC personnel into military force structures was a process of conflict-specific adaptation and thus was relatively restricted in social and physical time and place. One of the ways this case differs from the previous two, though, is that it involves both 'on the ground' changes and a broader set of international ones. In the next section, I discuss the ways the PMSC industry and its state patrons consolidated their local institutional achievements and attained a greater degree of legitimacy at the global level. With these concurrent and subsequent international processes of network formation and largely self-directed regulation and professionalisation by PMSCs themselves, in partnership with prominent government and NGO stakeholders, a more robust and expansive normative transformation took shape.

6.4.3 *PMSCs and the International Normative Environment*

During the early-to-middle phases of the wars in Afghanistan and Iraq, when PMSCs were becoming increasingly normal and authorised participants in those conflicts, they still faced broad international condemnation as mercenaries. Ballesteros, in a 2007 address to the UN General Assembly, referred to contractors as the 'new modalities of mercenarism', while the International Consortium of Investigative Journalists similarly labelled private contractors 'euphemisms for mercenaries' that same year (both quoted in Petersohn 2014, 476). In response to the 2008 release of the Montreux Document, a non-binding compilation of international legal obligations and best practices for PMSCs to follow on a voluntary basis, Jose Luis Gomez del Prado, chair of the UN Working Group on the Use of Mercenaries, complained about the legitimacy it conferred upon 'this new industry and the military and security services it provides' (del Prado 2008, 444). Thus, while PMSCs had become a normal and normative fixture of the conflict zones of Afghanistan and Iraq from the perspective of their primarily American employers there, and while they featured in conflicts elsewhere in ways that did not invite categorical UN and NGO disapproval, they were not yet an unproblematic fixture of war in general, under the conventions of the international community.

This began to change in the first decade of the new millennium, however, with early shifts at the international level happening concurrently with those taking place in Afghanistan and Iraq. The Montreux Document itself was part of that process, establishing both professional standards and a basis for firms to organise, as part of an ongoing, internalised interaction of convention reorientation and network synthesis. In 2005, the Swiss government and the International Committee of the Red Cross (ICRC) set out to develop a better-defined regulatory apparatus for PMSCs, beginning with consultations with industry experts in January 2006, with follow-up meetings in November 2006 and April 2008. The 'Swiss Initiative' gathered diverse stakeholders together to produce an index of *existing regulations* while focusing discussion on IHL and human rights concerns. As one representative of the ICRC explained, the Montreux Document

reaffirms States' primary responsibility and restates existing rules of international law and recognized 'good practices' for the implementation of these. The focus is thus on ensuring the faithful implementation of existing law by all those involved. [It] is not an international treaty and it does not create new legal obligations – it reaffirms and clarifies existing obligations of States under international law.[39]

Their goals and accomplishments were thus modest: beyond supplying a set of categories for describing government–PMSC relations and redirecting the conversation from mercenarism to IHL conformance, the only novel legal material introduced by the process was the development of an agreeable definition for what actually constituted a PMSC.[40]

Nevertheless, the performative reaffirmation of a human-rights- and IHL-oriented framework for PMSC operations was significant, with involved states indicating commitments to holding PMSCs accountable for their activities and acknowledging that state responsibilities cannot be transferred to private actors via contract (DeWinter-Schmitt 2013). Moreover, as one official indicated, the process also served to document and consolidate specific regulatory practices learned in Iraq:

We were very enthusiastic and very supportive of the first initial meeting, that they had a series of seminars, but there was a pre-meeting where they got

---

[39] Personal correspondence with Tilman Rodenhäuser, legal adviser, International Committee of the Red Cross (ICRC), via email, dated 16 May 2017.

[40] See the website of the Geneva Centre for the Democratic Control of Armed Forces, an international NGO focused on security sector governance, available at www.dcaf.ch/private-security-regulation-montreux-document; accessed 10 May 2017.

a group of experts together to decide – to formulate – what it was they actually wanted to do, and we wrote a big part of that, not just myself but the OG officer – Officer General Counsel representative – is part, was part, of that from the very beginning. We had good regulations; by that time, the time that the first one kicked off, we had the first series of regulations that were derived from what we had learned in 2004, were already published in 2005.[41]

This is normative novelty of a different sort – one in which innovations in the *institutionalisation* of conventions, in an applied sense, could be disseminated and made more robust. It also illustrates one of the advantages to understanding normative transformation in terms of the position of regulations or standards within a community of practice or within a network of practitioners: the same substantive statements or commitments can play different roles in action depending on how they are institutionalised or where they are placed within a broader normative configuration.

At least as important as the substance of the agreements the meetings in Montreux produced, however, was the simple fact of their occur-rence, which was designed to showcase to the United States the possi-bility of self-regulation within the PMSC industry.[42] The UN too began to change its framework for approaching PMSCs, directing its Working Group, in 2008, to treat PMSCs not as mercenaries but as legitimate companies in need of better regulation (Avant 2016). The ICRC's position was that the document allowed for PMSCs to be approached as a present feature of conflicts without legitimating their use,[43] and civil society groups such as Amnesty International followed in their footsteps by endorsing the document.[44] When the UN's Working Group released, in July 2009, the Draft International Convention on the Regulation, Oversight and Monitoring of Private Military and Security Companies, it built upon the basic categories and definitions codified in the Montreux Document and cemented its approach as the trajectory for firmer transnational regulation of

---

[41] Mayer, interview with author, 19 May 2017.
[42] Indeed, as one US defence official remarked, the Swiss Initiative proved 'responsive to needs' (Col. Christopher Meyer (ret.) in Avant 2016, 7).
[43] Correspondence with Tilman Rodenhauser, 16 May 2017.
[44] See Amnesty International's 14 October 2008 statement on the Montreux Document, available at www.amnesty.org/en/documents/IOR30/010/2008/en/; accessed 15 May 2017.

PMSCs. Since 2008, it has garnered endorsements from fifty-three states, including the United States, the United Kingdom, and France,[45] and constitutes a major touchstone for tracking where and how PMSCs are regulated.

Tracing the reciprocal operation of convention reorientation and network synthesis explains the production of the Montreux Document and its role in practice – how it came to exist and why it had an effect on the normative status of PMSCs for much of the international community. Initial scepticism of the legitimacy of PMSCs by NGO figures, along with scepticism on the part of industry and government figures as to the desirability and effectiveness of transnational regulation, limited the extent of convention reorientation to mere clarification of definitions. Yet this small element of novelty nevertheless was significant, as it not only changed the content of the normative environment for the market for force but also signified the possibility and potency of bringing together diverse PMSC stakeholders to solve regulatory problems. Crucially, it allowed organisations unwilling to legitimate PMSCs to participate in their regulation without endorsing any new legal instruments or passing judgement on the adequacy of current ones – in other words, without taking a position on the adequacy of existing or new conventions. Without network synthesis, it would not have amounted to much practical change in the regulatory environment; without convention reorientation, it would have been a more limited achievement as an index of existing regulations.

This process did not end here, either. Building on the Montreux Document, a range of stakeholders in the PMSC industry, a range of civil society organisations, and a number of states including the United States[46] came together to produce two major regulatory institutions: a new set of professional conventions set out in the International Code of Conduct for Private Security Service Providers (ICoC);[47] and an agency to monitor and manage conformance with them, the International Code

---

[45] See the list of participants on the Montreux Document Forum's website, available at www.mdforum.ch/en/participants/; accessed 20 May 2017.

[46] Quoting interviews with numerous US defence officials, Avant (2016) describes how an initial hesitation on the part of the US government to support the ICoC gave way to more enthusiastic involvement as officials in the departments of Defense and State realised the benefits to an industry-led regulatory regime going beyond only those PMSCs employed by the US government.

[47] Full text of the code available at www.icoca.ch/en/the_icoc/; accessed 20 May 2017.

of Conduct Association (ICoCA). Finished in October 2010 and initially garnering fifty-eight PMSC signatories,[48] the ICoC explicitly and clearly endorses a human-rights-based normative framework in the first few paragraphs of its preamble;[49] restricts the use of weapons to self-defence only (para. 31) or, if a company is deputised for law enforcement duties, requires that the use of force 'comply with all national and international obligations applicable to regular law enforcement officials of that state' (para. 32); establishes strict vetting standards for employees (paras. 45–51); and requires that signatory companies document all use-of-weapons incidents in a transparent manner (para. 63). By September 2013, 708 companies had signed on to it, although, with the establishment of ICoCA that month, active membership in the association became best standard of compliance.[50] Membership as of January 2017 sits at 116, ninety-one of which are PMSCs, seven of which are states, and eighteen of which are civil society organisations primarily focused on human rights issues.[51]

The ICoC and ICoCA are still imperfect regulatory instruments. It is notable that far fewer companies are current members of the association than signed the Code. Mayer offers some insight into why this might be:

One of the problems is that the ICoCA is not fully up and running yet . . . A lot of companies may be holding on to say, 'Well, let's see what actually this organization is like once it really is certifying membership, once it is doing active monitoring, once it's processing complaints, then we can decide whether that's something we want to do'. But in the meantime, we can say that we are in fact committed to the commitments, the general principles, that are described in the ICoC.[52]

Hence signing the ICoC is a signal of normative commitment and good corporate citizenship, even if companies are hesitant to join the association. While Mayer details some struggles by the association to attract members, he also affirms its role in institutionalising market-based self-regulation initiatives, going beyond the focus on states characteristic of

---

[48] See www.dcaf.ch/Project/International-Code-of-Conduct-for-Private-Security-Service-Providers/.
[49] See especially paragraphs 2 and 3; full text of the code available at www.icoca.ch/en/the_icoc/; accessed 20 May 2017.
[50] Christopher Mayer, interview with author, 19 May 2017.
[51] See the website of the ICoCA, available at www.icoca.ch/en/membership/; accessed 20 May 2017.
[52] Interview with author, 19 May 2017.

the Montreux Document and of previous international debates over the prohibition on mercenarism.

Perhaps the best evidence that the ICoC, in substance and in process, signified a new normative state of affairs is that the United States was willing to orient its own regulation of PMSCs around it. The National Defense Authorization Act for Fiscal Year 2011, in a deceptively short clause,[53] required the Secretary of Defense to define 'sustainable practices in the procurement of products and services'. Rather than focus on domestic laws and interests alone, those responsible in the DoD instead looked to the Montreux Document and the ICoC

to (i) enhance the legitimacy of US policy in transnational eyes, (ii) boost the potential for uptake of standards based on the ICoC by putting US purchasing behind it, and (iii) allow more latitude for executive agencies to hire more qualified (rather than only least costly) companies. US officials explicitly describe this as an effort to encourage a wider array of PMSCs to behave in a way consistent with the Montreux Document and the ICoC – and thus support US interests. The logic of delegation was thus shaped by the reimagined US interests that resulted from the Montreux/ICoC process. And the delegation used congressional demand to develop standards based on a transnational process. (Avant 2016, 9)

The Department of State has since described the ICoC as a precedent-setting integration of US interests within multi-party commitments (Avant 2016), while the ICoC's standards have become required and enforceable components of PMSC contracts with major US government clients.

As with the initial interactions that produced the Montreux Document, the process behind the production of the ICoC and the ICoCA clearly attests to the synthetic interaction of convention reorientation and network synthesis – the evidence is inconsistent with one or the other playing a primary role. The development of a relatively settled and institutionalised normative configuration is the outcome of an authoritative network establishing a robust conventional position for PMSCs that positions them outside of 'mercenarism' so long as they follow professional standards. This is especially well-established in Avant's (2016) extensive interviewing and contemporaneous participant

---

[53] See the text of the National Defense Authorization Act for Fiscal Year 2011, available at www.gpo.gov/fdsys/pkg/CRPT-111hrpt491/pdf/CRPT-111hrp t491.pdf; accessed 20 May 2017.

observation showing the importance of the personal connections that formed across stakeholder groups. These connections were key factors in sustaining engagement through problem periods and for building trust enough to overcome parties' scepticisms of one another (Avant 2016, 10). Moreover, the existence of an established regulatory regime involving a ranging network of stakeholders influenced the normative content of US convention setting, offering an international, industry-driven approach to defining the professional roles and standards of PMSC operations. Conversely, the continued involvement of previously sceptical UN and civil society actors rests on the readiness of industry and government stakeholders' clear support for a human-rights-oriented regulatory approach – showing how normative content has played a role in bringing those actors fully on board.

Noticeably absent in this international process, however, is any clear operation of the technological revision mechanism, even given the broad conception of technology I use here. The emergence of a regulatory regime out of the Montreux process and the development of the ICoC did not require significant changes in the types of channels or instruments through which human beings influence their worlds; familiar diplomatic skills and the coincidence of interests fuelled a process of networking and normative clarification. This does not mean that technology is irrelevant to the international regulation of PMSCs, however. The practices of communications and monitoring established in Afghanistan and Iraq, which were highly reliant upon the introduction of new physical media of action, are sustained in institutional memory and official documentation. They provide part of the enabling context for the more recent international process detailed in this section – a section delineated not by ontological distinctiveness but by analytical convenience. Nevertheless, the fact that a discussion of technology diminishes in salience for this part of the explanation is noteworthy, as it shows that the role of technology in normative transformation, which is clear in a broad examination of this case, can fade from view when analysis is focused on more specific historical processes.

6.5 Summary

The normative transformations surrounding the prohibition on mercenarism studied in this chapter may differ in scale and range of actors, compared to those surrounding the prohibitions on assassination and torture, but they do not differ in kind. Explanations focusing purely on strategic exigency or on ethical contestation will miss the way these things interacted; the answer must focus on problem-solving in the face of challenges of both a moral and an instrumental nature. The end of the Cold War established supply-and-demand conditions for a market for force, and initially PMSCs within that market looked and acted in ways that appeared to many to fit the definition of mercenarism. With the emergence of the wars in Afghanistan and Iraq, PMSCs continued to offer recognisably military services, albeit without fielding entire fighting forces in the manner of EO and Sandline International. However, driven by convention reorientation, technological revision, and network synthesis, PMSCs in these war zones integrated with US military force structures and agencies in ways that regulated and normalised their operations, establishing them as legitimate actors *rather than mercenaries*, at least on the understanding of the actors involved. While technological revision was not notably salient to the most recent, international process of regulating PMSCs beyond those conflict zones, the other two mechanisms, convention reorientation and network synthesis, explain how the industry was able to more fully leave behind its mercenary connotations in the eyes of remaining sceptics.

This final phase of normative transformation shows how the prohibition on mercenaries persists but no longer encompasses the activities of PMSCs, even when those activities involve the performance of armed and 'combat-esque' duties formerly the sole province of official military forces. The unregulated, 'cowboy-like' image of PMSCs has faded as leading industry figures successfully established professional standards enforced through a multi-party, government-backed regulatory regime. Thus regulated, PMSCs no longer suffer from the stigma of the mercenary label, even if the previously contentious features of their work remain. Like in the cases of targeted killing and enhanced interrogation, proponent practitioners asserted that the prohibition they are accused of violating still exists and still carries legitimacy, but they were also able to convince detractors that their activities were not what it prohibited – in this case, with greater and clearly more enduring success than in the case of the CIA's interrogation programme, and perhaps more so also than in the case of targeted killing.

Nevertheless, my findings show that the strategic 'headache' of unregulated PMSCs was also a normative challenge. While practitioners were primarily preoccupied with organisational management, their consistent concerns with professionalism and the propriety of contractors' roles is clear. This case may be contrasted to the previous two in both scope and outcome, requiring different analytical resolution, but it nevertheless shows the distinctive and essential interaction of all three mechanisms of normative transformation. In the next, and final, chapter, I will flesh out this comparison and draw several others.

7 | *Conclusion*

Normative Transformation, International Politics, and the World beyond Counterterrorism

7.1 Introduction

Normative transformation is often a complex institutional process, but it is a key part of the evolution of new practices of counterterrorism and warfare in the United States. To investigate changing understandings of assassination, torture, and mercenarism in the US security apparatus, I described three mechanisms of change – convention reorientation, technological revision, and network synthesis – and traced how these mechanisms produced new normative horizons of value, identity, and permissibility. This process changed the orientations, dispositions, and regulatory structures of US institutions.

Central to this explanation is a theory of *innovation*, whereby normative transformation is the result of creative problem-solving actions knitting together ethical and strategic factors, along with new technologies. It focuses on change 'from below' – from within bureaucracies and amongst practitioners, rather as a result of executive orders and external pressures. I developed this approach a way of explaining the peculiar dynamics of three specific cases and to critically examine existing scholarly accounts. However, as I will discuss, the approach is more broadly applicable and can offer scholars of international politics a set of analytical instruments applicable to a wide range of investigations.

In this concluding chapter, I take up several tasks. First, I close my arguments on the three cases: what they show about their similarities and differences, about possible cases of the same type, and about investigations of other transformations in the use and regulation of state-directed violence. This clarifies the contributions of my work to the literature on norms and state security policies and practices. Second, I consider the ways in which my approach addresses other ways of studying institutions and of conceptualising the relationships between technology and ethics. I also suggest some other kinds of normative transformation that could be similarly studied, in other issue areas than security, or in other kinds of entities than state institutions. Third, I explore the critical and normative implications of both my theoretical approach and my empirical findings. I finish with some brief remarks as to where my work stands in relation to the field more broadly.

7.2 Broader Lessons on Norms and the USA's Targeted Killing, Torture, and Contractors

This book addressed the apparent demise or erosion of prohibitions on assassination, torture, and mercenarism, which appear to be violated or overridden by the USA's targeted killings, use of torture, and use of PMSCs in its national security activities. I am not the first IR scholar to consider this puzzle, but I differ from other perspectives by showing that a debate over erosion or demise is largely misguided. The people I studied have forcefully expressed commitments to the very prohibitions they have supposedly contravened, and these prohibitions remained institutionalised throughout the cases in question. My empirical findings show that practitioners are relatively utilitarian, and this may, at first glance, support an explanation that focuses rational calculations of strategic benefit, rather than normative calculations of right and wrong. However, these actors were still preoccupied with the delegation of authority and the law. This preoccupation may be instrumental or cynical in nature – nobody wants to get sacked or, worse, to get charged with a crime – but the outcome of it is nevertheless normative at the institutional level. What actually took place is a change in the shape of prohibition institutionalisation, indicating a normative transformation rather than normative deterioration or 'norm death'.

This difference can be hard to see using existing theories of norm change in IR but is clarified when normativity is treated as the outcome of a broader constellation of institutions and conventions and by granting agency to the *situation* of interactions between actors and their environments, defined by technological and cultural resources and pressures. I do this in Chapter 2, by critically reconstructing social theories of norms and action into the concept of 'normative configurations', and in Chapter 3, by methodologically applying that concept to propose a set of causal mechanisms. This yielded a picture of how socio-material circumstances interweave and how prohibitions are embedded and embodied in practice. Applied to the three cases, it shows how, by navigating ethical and strategic challenges, security practitioners reformed their own normative environment even as they were reshaped by it, producing an evolution in security policies and practices (see Table 7.1).

Beyond this primary finding, however, other findings emerge in considering the evidence and analyses presented in my case studies, spanning Chapters 4, 5, and 6. They come from three comparisons. The first two are comparisons across my cases; while all three are examples of recent and contentious transformations in US security and counterterrorism practices, some finer-grained commonalities and differences between them imply additional insights. The third is to compare my approach to those others have taken on the same cases. In this section I discuss each in turn.

7.2.1 Comparing and Contrasting Case Studies: Targeted Killing and Torture

There are two 'paired comparisons' (Tarrow 2007) one can examine in looking at how my three cases differ from one another in their trajectories and outcomes. The first is to compare the enduring normative transformation associated with the targeted killing programme and the relatively non-enduring normative transformations associated with EITs and the detention and interrogation programme. These cases share some significant similarities that make their difference in outcomes intriguing:

- they both involve the same primary institution (the CIA);
- they both turn on innovative legal interpretations offered by lawyers in the executive branch;
- they are both part of the rapid expansion and militarisation of the CIA, and the CTC in particular, following from the aftermath of the 9/11 attacks; and
- they both proceed through major overhauls in the technologies, broadly defined, employed in the practice of counterterrorism.

These similarities establish a kind of commonality in 'scope conditions', making it reasonable to focus on differences in process as important for explaining differences in outcome. Specifically, these two cases have three major divergences:

1 Advocates of EIT confronted a much more clearly defined and more formally institutionalised prohibition on torture, meaning their legal

Table 7.1 *Summary of key case traits and findings*

Cases	Targeted killing	Enhanced interrogation	PMSCs
Prohibition	Assassination	Torture	Mercenarism
Key institution	CIA	CIA	Military/NGOs
Normative form at outset	Aversion to 'pre-Church' paramilitary operations in the CIA	Interrogation handled by law enforcement according to strict legal limits	Military tasks restricted to military personnel
Key practical dilemma	Risk of bystander and mistaken deaths	Torture elicits unreliable intelligence, evokes disgust	Regulation and oversight difficult
Institutional and practical change	Legal framework for targeting, restructuring for paramilitary actions	Legal framework for use of 'EITs', in-house detention, and interrogation centres. established.	PMSCs under command/control, firms self-regulate
Robustness of transformation	Robust; targeted killing continues, is a stable and staple part of US counterterrorism operations	Fleeting; torture programme ended, was widely perceived as unhelpful/destructive to the CIA and US interests	Semi-robust; fewer PMSCs as deployments end, but practice will likely continue
Key technology	Drones	New interrogation 'science'	Communications technology

or conventional position required more work to secure and was easier for opponents to attack. Put differently, while the overarching 'instrumental variable' in both cases is practitioner-driven 'intra-institutional insurgency', the normative *status quo ante* differed between them.

2 Advocates of EITs had a less secure technological basis for their innovative practices: targeted killing used new means of delivering selective violence with obviously greater accuracy than earlier means, rendering concerns about discrimination and proportionality less salient, while the 'science' behind EIT did not yield obvious improvements on previous methods in gathering information from detainees.

3 Advocates of EIT had a smaller executive and organisational support base, meaning that they faced sustained governmental opposition from key institutions, whereas those same institutions were either ambivalent towards, or supportive of, targeted killing. This means not only that the torture prohibition was better institutionalised in a conventional or legal sense but also that those who sought to transform it faced more powerful opposition.

Corresponding roughly to each of the three mechanisms, these differences show that the causal pathways through which normative transformation proceeds were, in the case of torture and EITs, narrower and filled with more obstacles, compared to the case of assassination and targeted killing. Effectively, these causal pathways reversed direction after the normative configuration in question failed to travel far enough down them.

In looking closely at my empirical findings, however, one divergence stands out as especially salient: the disparity in technological efficacy. Executive opposition to targeted killing, as opposed to internal organisational opposition due to institutional culture and convention, was mostly based on the absence of a satisfying method. Cruise missiles risked killing many civilians, in violation of principles of discrimination in the use of military force, while a commando raid risked a bloodbath and an unacceptable number of American casualties. Armed UAVs risked neither and moreover showed steady improvement over time, as they gained better cameras, greater flight times, and larger payloads. They delivered results in the form of a formally covert but nevertheless widely reported series of successful operations to kill al-Qa'ida commanders. While opponents argued against the programme on the grounds that it was inappropriate for an intelligence agency to be so militarised, ultimately they were confronting an administration looking for easy 'wins' and in possession of an instrument that dealt with some of the most pressing normative problems of killing in war. Reformed as an organisation and eventually equipped with a legally and bureaucratically standardised set of conventions regulating the practice, targeted killing became part of the normative configuration, and the transformation was complete.

Conversely, EIT proponents were not able to benefit from a clear boost in intelligence and counterterrorism effectiveness because of their technological revision. Initially buoyed by the seemingly authoritative scientific basis for a new approach, and by a new set of methods in hand, proponents argued that ethical and legal concerns over whether EITs constituted torture were overruled by the valuable intelligence that they might gain from detained terrorists concealing knowledge of plans for terrible attacks. The spectre of a 'ticking time bomb' held normative force: who would complain about rough questioning – which proponents went to lengths to distinguish from 'real' torture – of certain villains if it would save innocent lives? However, over time the absence of demonstrated technical advantages to EITs meant that many professional interrogators and intelligence officers were unpersuaded of its necessity, and legal or ethical concerns rose in salience and potency. While the tenuousness of the legal defences offered for EITs and the diminishing number of executive and legislative actors willing to defend them also played a role, the apparent technological failure of the approach still provided a centre of gravity to the opposition. EITs were not technically distinguishable from torture and did not deliver their promised outcomes.

The lesson here is that normative transformation has a major technological component that should be analytically distinguished from contestation over framing, bureaucratic politics, and the law but included as a causal factor in explanations of change. While this lesson is already found in existing IR scholarship on norms, in most of this work the role of technology is not given an independent place in theories of change. The comparison of the targeted killing and torture cases demonstrates the explanatory value of doing so.

7.2.2 Comparing and Contrasting Case Studies: Targeted Killing and PMSCs

The second fruitful comparison to draw is between the two cases of relatively enduring normative transformations – those with similar outcomes – but with salient differences in how those transformations proceeded. The cases of targeted killing and PMSCs have some similarities in this respect:

- both show enduring changes in the entities authorised to employ violence in pursuit of security objectives, with the CIA becoming militarised and key military duties in conflict zones becoming privatised;
- both were propelled by advances in technology, not just in a broad sense that might involve new scientific ideas but also in a narrow sense of involving material devices – though the PMSC case is still much less reliant on this than the targeted killing one; and
- both show early developments of a lightly regulated and somewhat ad hoc practice that later become routinised though increasing legal and bureaucratic convention.

Yet they diverge in one, especially major way: while the development of the US targeted killing programme can be traced to a small set of persons, agencies, executive functions, and technologies, the proliferation of PMSCs as legitimate components of US military operations has no such 'central cast of characters'. This normative transformation is a result of large structural trends in the economics of manpower and logistics, changes in conflict environments, and diplomatic challenges or initiatives encompassing many different actors. While this may suggest that the approach I develop is ill-suited to analysing the PMSC case, I nevertheless found it clarified the causal processes responsible.

This shows a benefit to my approach beyond simple analytical flexibility or portability: agency detection in cases where it is hard to pin down who the 'agents' are as such. When there are many actors, large social or economic structures, and multiple contexts of action all coming together with diverse interests, my approach offers a way of identifying and foregrounding agency. This comes from the relational understanding of agency I discuss at length in Chapter 2: by allowing for agency to exist without being attached to a specific, discrete 'agent', complex and ad hoc processes of adjustment by multiple actors in multiple places can be foregrounded in an explanation of broader transformation, even if causing such a transformation was not their intention. Put differently, this is a solution to the inability to delineate structure and agency in cases where the two are merged in especially inseparable ways. The solution is to treat agency as an arrangement of local problem-solving processes enacted by people whose practical horizons are temporally and institutionally smaller than those of the big transformations they have collectively generated. Scholars can use this understanding of agency to identify causal mechanisms in cases that would otherwise look like a tangled mess of overlapping situations and relationships.

7.2.3 Comparing and Contrasting Approaches: Mine and Others

The third fruitful comparison is to consider my methodological or analytical (rather than just theoretical) approach in relation to other ways of studying normative and strategic transformations in how national security apparatuses direct and regulate violence.[1] In the Introduction and Chapters 1 and 2 on theory I reviewed IR scholarship on norms at length, so (rather than repeat this discussion) it would be more helpful to highlight here similarities and differences in an applied or methodological sense – as pertaining to the data that matter in my analysis and in the way I use them to make my claims. I joined with other scholars studying norms in several practical ways:

- my analyses largely revolve around tracing the course of legal and rhetorical contestation;
- actor identities were prominent focal points of debate, and studying their implications in the eyes of research subjects was key to learning what the normative environment actually was, 'before and after'; and
- while de-reification may be an analytical manoeuvre in my case analyses, I conclude those analyses by, effectively, 're-concretising' normative arrangements by showing how they have crystallised into institutionalised, authoritative forms, such as might be described as 'norms'.

---

[1] Of the three possible dyads, the comparison between the torture case and the PMSC case is simply not fruitful as a paired comparison, as there is dissimilarity in both institutional outset conditions and in outcome. However, as a significant component of this book has been to establish the theoretical significance of a pragmatist and process-relational approach to norms and normative change, it is worth comparing how I approach my cases versus how other scholars have approached the same ones through more familiar means.

In other words, my investigation has still examined discourses and identities as sites and bases for actors to generate 'norm change'. However, my analyses contained four premises that are less often part of scholarship in the norms research programme:

1 I granted considerable analytical space for technological changes as drivers (though not necessarily determinants) of normative transformation, on the basis of a materialist social ontology;
2 I oriented analysis around practices rather than norms as such, which allowed me to avoid specifying or defining *a priori* which specific norms were present or salient in a situation except as a minimum hypothesis;
3 I defined the relevant causal mechanisms as processual outcomes of problem-solving and innovation, meaning that the key condition of possibility for normative transformation to take place, in an overall ontological sense, is situated in *creativity* – defined as the capacity to imagine and produce novel, world-altering changes to action; and
4 I defined agency as the outcome of situations rather than something possessed by agents, which moves sharply away from the structure-agency dichotomy and its resolutions as commonly understood in conventional constructivist scholarship.

These premises make sense given my theoretical commitments, which accord ontological priority to practices and which are specifically designed to knit together strategic, technical, and cultural/normative factors, but investigators can study these things without committing to pragmatist and relational metatheory. However, it is harder to study them consistently and coherently without the vocabulary I adopt.

This is why I am revisiting my approach after having shown what it can do: in line with a pragmatist epistemology (as opposed to ontology), I ultimately justify theory on the basis of its use as a conceptual and cognitive ordering device. As I have argued throughout this book, cases such as the ones I study here are confusing unless investigated in ways that support both the inclusion of technological and strategic pressures and the avoidance of overly predefined views about what 'norms' are present. Moreover, the emphasis I place on creativity is especially crucial to understanding how it is that ad hoc modifications or innovations by practitioners can 'scale up' to broad and extensive transformations in normative configurations and thus in the shapes of international orders. Norms scholars have already shown that they can study normative transformation while still subscribing to ontological dualism, actor-centric theories of agency, and the structure–agency binary, as well as by reifying normativity. They have already done so for all three of the cases I examine here, as noted in the respective chapters. I have hopefully shown, however, that adopting alternatives to these commitments yields more complete and satisfying accounts of these cases' history and outcomes.

This is especially clear with the relational understanding of agency I use. In the first two cases, a delimited number of people intentionally generated institutional change through various uses of argumentative, technical, and bureaucratic resources. In the third case, while the scale of analysis is much wider, it is still possible to conceive of the normative transformation in question as the outcome of aggregates of intentional actions, preserving the coherence of an actor-centric view of agency. Undeniably, scholars attached to the actor-centric view will still be able to explain much of what happened. However, the relational understanding adds something that would otherwise be missing. By understanding agency as situational in these causes, technology gains importance not just as a resource but as a dispositional part of practice, playing a role in constituting practitioners. What it means to carry out targeted killings, to be an interrogator, or to be part of the broader US broader military apparatus is defined by relationships between people and technology. Granting analytical priority to actors underappreciates the role of technology, just as granting priority to technology would be deterministic. Moreover, by attributing agency to situations rather than actors, it becomes easier to appreciate the unintended consequences of mechanisms working in concert and the failure of some attempts at forcing change – notably visible in the reversal of the normative transformation discussed in case of EITs and the prohibition on torture. Finally, and perhaps most significantly, since normativity can emerge from situations in which actors are cynics, attributing agency to those situations, rather than those actors, avoids ontological reductionism.

This opens the door to treating as 'normative transformations' a broader range of cases than just those that imply an obvious change in a relatively clearly understood way of regulating and directing state action in the realm of national and international security. Primarily I have defined my theoretical contributions with reference to the literature on norms, arguing for an approach to bringing out strategic and technological dimensions to cases, but my approach also brings out the *normative* dimension of strategic and technological change. Even if cases do not appear to involve a challenge to a specific norm, they must feature normative configurations, and if there is any degree of contestation or controversy within an institution over emerging trans-formations of practices, it should be explicable through tracing the operations of convention reorientation, technological revision, and network synthesis.

7.3 Broader Horizons of Normative Transformation and the Three Mechanisms

The pragmatist and relational approach I developed here has implica-tions beyond just theorising changes in prohibitions. First and foremost, it contributes to the developing 'practice turn' in IR scholarship, linking practice theory – and practice theorists – to the study of norms and normative transformations. This developing meta-approach in the field focuses on practices and performances as the basic media through which social life is embodied, agency and structure knitted together, and through which knowledge forms and transforms (Adler and Pouliot 2011; see also Adler 2019). Yet so far, scholarship associated with the practice turn in IR has not focused on norms, preferring more granular and relational objects of analysis such as fields, pecking orders, emo-tions, and communities of practice (Adler and Greve 2009; Bigo 2011; Mérand and Pouliot 2013; Pouliot 2016). This produces a silo-like division of past constructivist work oriented around norms and practice-oriented work that, as McCourt (2016) has recently argued, constitutes a progressive broadening of constructivism's own narrowing ontological lens. By de-reifying norms into practices and relations, I better connect constructivism's past with its future, making norms scholarship legible and tractable within practice-theoretic and relational approaches.

I accomplish this through a synthesis of major perspectives in prac-tice theory, pragmatist social theory, and relational sociology. Characteristic of all three is a focus on practitioners, processes of transformation in single cases, and configurational analysis (Jackson and Nexon 1999; Friedrichs and Kratochwil 2009; Adler and Pouliot 2011; Adler-Nissen 2013; Büger and Gadinger 2015; see also Elias 1994; Depélteau 2013), and scholars working from these premises have been critical of more mainstream research on norms (Jackson et al. 2004). The three mechanisms I trace in my cases are sensitive to dynamics of contestation and agency, in large part because they proceed from an understanding of practice based in pragmatism, rather than Bourdieu's more structuralist account.[2] McCourt (2016) suggests that these approaches are in opposition to dominant constructivist scholarship, but my work begins with case-identification and puzzle-specification similar to mainstream constructivist scholars of norm change. I discuss how the practical, complex, and often multivalent normative character of contentious actions are obscured or idealised when encapsulated within the conceptual container of 'norm', but this does not oppose the norms research programme in intent and outcome.

By taking this approach, I clarify the role of creativity and innovation 'from below' as key drivers of institutional and normative change. To some degree, the cases I study show evidence of *bricolage* – the recombination of resources at hand, in ad hoc and tactical ways, to solve pressing problems rather than to serve some grand institutional project (Levi-Strauss 1962). Key actors, especially in the chaotic environments of Afghanistan and Iraq as covered in Chapter 6 on PMSCs, reformed normative configurations by recombining the techno-social resources at hand. But the understanding of creativity I develop here is also more transactional and less bound to psychological or agency-centric conceptions than many other views in the field. I try to show empirically what Joas (1996) argues at the level of social theory and philosophy: creativity is a property of actions rather than actors, and to study how it operates scholars must look at a broad arrangement of relations, environmental conditions, and communal repertoires of action. Finally, I offer both theoretical and empirical reasons to view creativity as a morally neutral force for social change; while creativity is often thought of as a good, allowing humans to overcome their problems, I show that creativity can also allow actors to undermine, revise, or bypass regulations we may think of as legitimate to do things we may think of as wrong. Herein lies a key contribution to practice theory, which, in its more pragmatist forms, adopts a transactional view of action (Bueger and Gadinger 2014), but which in IR scholarship has been used mainly to study the maintenance or tactical adjustment of social orders rather than their novel reformation.

---

[2] In this, I deviate from the bulk of existing 'practice turn' literature in the field, which takes its cues more from Bourdieu (Bueger and Gadinger 2015).

Moreover, by focusing on the role of technology in normative trans-formation, I approached it not just as a source of moral and strategic problems and solutions but also as a force for actors to remake themselves, entangled with broader processes of normative and institutional reforma-tion. New technology alters identities and authorities in ways that may not change *which* normative configurations define a practice, but it does change *how* regulations and principles are applied in action. Technology is part of existing accounts of norm change – one cannot talk about weapons taboos, for example, without talking about weapons – but its role in interpretation and contestation is especially important in the approach I take, given the emphasis practice theory and pragmatism place on the materiality of cognition and social interaction. Granting a broader role to technology also links with existing scholarship from other bodies of work already attentive to it. Studies into liberalism and its attendant mode of warfare, for example, explicitly trace the history of drones and targeted killing (Shaw 2013; Carvin and Williams 2014; Grayson 2016) and consider the cultural implications of their use (Holmqvist 2013; Wilcox 2017). Carvin and Williams (2014) examine the broad historical transformation of warfare, and the others focus on the normative implications of technology rather than the causal origins of its evolution and institutionalisation. My approach shares their sensitivity to these things but operationalises the normative dimension through a mechanism-based aetiology, applied to more institutionally and tempor-ally delimited cases.

Finally, I foregrounded the reciprocal relationship between ends and means – between the normative and the strategic – by showing how perceptions of appropriate or legitimate conduct change in concert with political and practical problem-solving.[3] This illustrates the trans-formational potential lying even in local and immediate situations of social interaction – a subject of ongoing creative meta-theorising (Adler 2019) and political critique (Cochran 2012). Studying the reciprocity of normativity and strategy also links to recent attempts by scholars to revisit classical realism and critically evaluate the direction of main-stream constructivist research (Barkin 2003; Levine 2012). While these themes exist in more mainstream norms, scholarship to a limited degree (see, for example, Schmidt 2014; Wiener 2014; Hofferberth and Weber

---

[3] This contrasts with a strict separation of action theory into contrasting logics of appropriateness and consequences (March and Olsen 1998).

2015), they do so from theoretical first premises. In starting with a concrete historical problem, as I have done, scholars working in these critical traditions can contribute to mainstream research programmes as a whole. The result should be a plurality of progressive approaches and a livelier conversation on the facets of the problems to which they may be applied, new or enduring.

The approach I developed can thus illuminate international processes and dynamics beyond changes to the way states regulate the use of force or prohibit specific military practices. It offers a way to analyse transformations in non-security-related international practices and in non-state entities or institutions. This potential lies especially in the role *technological revision* plays in facilitating the discursive, legal, and bureaucratic processes associated with *convention reorientation* and *network synthesis*. By incorporating the ways material means both facilitate and limit action into a sociological model of contestation and change, it is easier to see how power operates. This is true even for forms of governance and international life without much influence over the coercive instruments of the state. Crucially, the mechanisms I develop and employ here do not require 'uptake' of a new standard by any specific entity and instead focus on processes and relations of discursive and bureaucratic manoeuvring. As a result, they are portable enough to be used to study governance without governments, regimes without regents, or rules without rulers.

One example of this is a discussion of emerging forms of global governance that are oriented around voluntary projects by non-state actors. Normative transformations can affect transnational institutional arrangements primarily comprising non-state actors. One salient domain where this has recently occurred is in global non-state governance – where regulation, information, and steerage is primarily provided by associations of actors and organisations from outside of state apparatuses. This is already visible in the PMSC case, where non-state global governance constitutes the final shift towards the stable (self-)normalisation of PMSC roles and practices in present-date national security and military operations. Global governance, whether or not led by states, requires communicative and organisational capacities to create and manage public, civil, and bureaucratic spheres above, beyond, and beside the systems of authority constituted by state borders (Castells 2008). Not only does this require physical technologies like internet access, but it also requires conventional arrangements granting non-state or multi-/supra-national entities legitimacy and networks with sources or nodes of power. When global or transnational governance rests with private actors, these requirements pose a particularly salient normative and institutional problem (Risse 2006; Börzel and Risse 2010). It also becomes harder, with non-state global governance, to evaluate and recognise effectiveness, as both the mechanisms and definitions of success can differ from those of state governments (Beisheim and Dingwerth 2008). Hence IR research on norms may not offer much traction here.

However, the three mechanisms I trace in my case studies are also useful for making sense of normative transformations in non-state global governance. While limitations of space prevent me from demonstrating this with another case study, it is worth discussing in a more limited way how my approach might be of value to scholars studying this subject. First, tracing the interaction of the three mechanisms gives explicit theoretical space for the material and technological conditions of global governance, linking them to the role of networks and of discursive or legal innovations establishing new regulations as legitimate or authoritative. Second, these mechanisms do not require something like 'norm uptake' by states; the international institutional dynamics to which they refer can exist in private organisations as well. Third, they provide explicit indications for how to measure governmental or regulatory success, since, from a pragmatist understanding of action, normativity is oriented around successful resolution of practical and ethical problems, flexibly defined. Fourth and finally, if a theory of normative transformation can be productively applied to topics in global governance, there is also the added benefit of cross-fertilisation in bridging two distinct research programmes, by better establishing an overlap in the objects and mechanisms particular to the domains of each.

A good illustration of this lies in analysing the trajectory of climate governance – an area where non-state actors and initiatives have been able to accomplish regulatory achievements that states have not. Private firms, especially in the energy and transport sectors, have provided expert knowledge, lobbying, and technologies and developed a range of investment and corporate social responsibility strategies oriented around emissions reduction, leading to the development of a robust carbon governance regime (Bulkeley and Newell 2015). By organising amongst themselves to trade emissions and carbon credits, market actors have voluntarily embraced and achieved reductions beyond the regulatory minimum (Bernstein et al. 2010). This is the outcome of a broader 'experiment' in global climate governance, where the frustrations of multilateral treaty negotiations have led to a devolution of lower-level partnerships, summits, and cooperative projects that, less constrained by raison d'etat, facilitate a robust emissions reduction regime (Hoffmann 2011). These initiatives are often located at the level of urban municipalities, where there is greater governmental autonomy and thus greater flexibility for interactions with state institutions (Bulkeley 2010). Overall, the result is a normative transformation affecting practices in ways less dependent upon state-level treaties and domestic regulations.

The trajectory of climate governance is easier to understand if viewed as the outcome of convention reorientation, technological revision, and network synthesis. Market actors are particularly well equipped to mobilise new technologies, as they are already invested in the research, development, and use of emissions-producing devices. They are thus able to rest a new regime on practices in ways state bodies cannot. Moreover, by incorporating lower-level governmental partners along with private firms, the networks and authorities comprising the regime gain local flexibility and can incorporate market leaders to serve as examples or trendsetters. Finally, adopting a market-driven approach shifts climate governance into the conventions of neoliberal and corporate incentive structures, casting them not as governmental interference but as supportive public–private partnerships directed at industrial efficiency and broader horizons of trade. None of these suggests my approach is necessary to understand global climate governance in this way, but it does show enough analytical flexibility to be helpful to scholars studying different kinds of normative transformations than those occurring within or across state bureaucracies.

Another possible area of study where my approach may add value concerns transformation in precarious or marginalised transnational communities that are often understood to be conventionally weak but are nevertheless robust in the face of challenges to ontological and physical security. Transnational entities such as diasporas, nomads, and newly emerging social movements – even, in previous eras, pirates – often extend through borders, cross great physical distances, and act within multiple cultural contexts (Agnew 1994; MacKay et al. 2014; Adamson 2016). They exist in social arrangements outside of many of the normative and institutional configurations designed to protect, regulate, and steer international politics. As such, their security concerns are hard to grasp with a state-centric analytical framework (Adamson 2016), pose challenges to existing institutions of governance, and occupy a different horizon of possible supra- or non-national polities (Abraham and Abramson 2017). The approach I develop here aides scholars trying to navigate those analytical problems in studying these precarious communities. In particular, my approach makes it easier to investigate one particular dimension of normative transformation: self-reformation.

The dynamics of identity and integration in diaspora communities are frequently implicated in trade, war and peace, migration, and foreign policy. Their presence predicts outbreaks of conflict, their 'ethnic lobbies' influence domestic politics, and their simultaneous role as local citizenry and foreign 'others' challenges traditional conceptions of state sovereignty and national identity (Shain and Barth 2003). As a concept, 'diaspora' offers an analytical framework to explore the links among territory, identity, governance, and transnational flows of information and people (Wahlbeck 2002; Adamson and Demetriou 2007; Ragazzi 2007). By taking a pragmatist and relational view of social life, and by investigating normative transformations as outcomes of the three mechanisms I discuss, scholars can see how diasporas possess greater strength than one would assume based purely on their access to instruments of policy making. This reaffirms the importance of diasporas to the constitution of major actors and settings of importance to international politics today, by connecting their dynamics and trajectories to other ongoing IR research programmes in the study of norms and state power.

This brief discussion of diasporas is only to show how the interaction of discursive, organisational, and technological factors is apparent in very different kinds of normative transformations than the ones most commonly examined in the norms research programme in IR. It shows that the universe of cases to which my approach can be applied is broader than it may seem at first glance and suggests that my theory 'has legs' to walk in different directions than just the analysis of national security issues. However, the fact that it *can* be so broadly applied does not establish that it *should be*; in the next section of this chapter, I therefore discuss the critical and normative implications of

studying normative transformations (of any sort) through the processual, relational, and pragmatist lens employed throughout this book.

7.4 Normative Implications of a Pragmatist Theory of Normative Transformation

The final contribution of this book is normative. It offers answers to
questions of how best to navigate the ethical challenges of contemporary counterterrorism, as well as how to make use of explanations *of*
change in proposals *for* change. This book is not a piece of political or
critical theory, and I do not purport to offer a major addition to
scholarship in these areas. However, there are still political and critical
lessons to be found in it, largely because pragmatist philosophy – the
ontological and epistemological centre of gravity in my approach – is
specifically aimed at bridging fact and value, or description and prescription. I divide this section into two parts. In the first, I discuss how –
by tracing the causal processes responsible, the rise of targeted killing,
the emergence (and disappearance) of institutionalised torture, and the
shift to PMSCs in the US security apparatus – the book can inform
ongoing debates over the legitimacy and trajectory of these normative
transformations. In the second, I discuss the broader normative and
critical benefits of employing a pragmatist, processual, and relational
approach to explanations of international politics.

7.4.1 The Ethics of Counterterrorism and the Three Mechanisms of Normative Transformation

Ethical concerns over all three cases examined in this book converge on
worries about the ways counterterrorism involves the use of force
outside of the boundaries of transparent, liberal statecraft. Critics of
targeted killing argue that it is a violation of due process and constitutes
a form of extrajudicial execution – or, at the very least, may violate the
moral innocence of combatants, a central normative premise in just
war theory and international humanitarian law (Kretzmer 2005;
Melzer 2008). Meanwhile, critics of targeted killing are distressed by
the increasing automation that has accompanied its escalation in use, as
unmanned aerial vehicles are the primary platform used. Their concerns culminate in the accusation that the US targeted killing programme will lead to an unaccountable and roboticised assassination

apparatus (Krishnan 2009). Meanwhile, critics of the CIA's use of torture worry that the demise of 'enhanced interrogation' is not firm enough and that the backlash against its associated practices has not been sufficiently severe to deter their use in the future.[4] Moreover, these critics note that the CIA continues to obstruct investigations into the programme and its victims, while its primary architects continue to publicly defend their actions and face no prospect of legal repercussions.[5] Finally, critics of widespread use of PMSCs express concerns about inadequate training, oversight, accountability, and intentions, compared with official and uniformed armed forces personnel.[6] Again, the thread tying these together is that they prioritise a certain 'liberal way of war' characterised by respect for international humanitarian law and 'clean' use of force (Carvin and Williams 2014), with deviations in the technological and institutional instruments of it seen as ethically problematic.

My work do not resolve these concerns, but they may clarify them. One way in which they do owes to my empirical findings: the facts I uncover provide insight into the powers and limits of liberal criticism of US counterterrorism policies and practices. The USA's targeted killing programme is firmly rooted in the conventional logic of armed conflict, meaning that practitioners are not selecting targets to punish them for past crimes but as combatants whose death degrades an enemy military organisation. Moreover, as the programme has become legally normalised and increasingly shifted from the CIA to military control,[7] requests for accountability and transparency can be articulated in similar terms as those pertinent to any military action; the special secrecy enjoyed by civilian intelligence agencies, while

---

[4] See Erin M. Kearns, 'Torture Doesn't Work, So Why Are We Still Discussing It?', *Political Violence @ a Glance*, 2 February 2017, available at http://politicalvio lenceataglance.org/2017/02/02/torture-doesnt-work-so-why-are-we-still-discussing-it/; accessed 15 May 2017.

[5] See James Risen, Sheri Fink, and Charlie Savage. 'State Secrets Privilege Invoked to Block Testimony in C.I.A. Torture Case', *New York Times*, 8 March 2017, available at www.nytimes.com/2017/03/08/us/justice-department-cia-psychologists-interrogation-program.html, accessed 15 May 2017.

[6] These are reviewed at length in Chapter 6.

[7] This shift, which came near the end of Obama's tenure, does appear to be rolled back under Trump. See Gordon Lubold and Shane Harris. 'Trump Broadens CIA Powers, Allows Deadly Drone Strikes', *Wall Street Journal*, 13 March 2017, available at www.wsj.com/articles/trump-gave-cia-power-to-launch-drone-strikes-1489444374/; accessed 15 May 2017.

institutionalised, is less salient. Meanwhile, though it may be frustrating for critics of the CIA's detention and interrogation programme that those responsible for setting it up and running it escape legal penalty, the key technological driver of the programme has been completely deflated of credibility as an effective means of inducing useful cooperation. Even if the legislative and bureaucratic fallout from the programme were successfully overturned, the practice of 'enhanced interrogation' has lost its instrumental foundation. Finally, as PMSCs have voluntarily developed regulatory mechanisms and have better institutionalised their involvement in, and relationship to, larger US and allied military expeditions, their conduct has increasingly shifted away from practices likely to be seen as mercenarism. Simply put, the trajectory of all three cases suggests that rumours of the demise of normatively liberal warfare – with its attendant discourses of transparency, accountability, precision, and respect for noncombatant rights – are premature.

Another way my findings speak to these concerns, however, is in showing when they would, in fact, be justified. By looking at the way the three cases unfolded and focusing on the interaction of the three mechanisms, the counterfactual possibilities that might produce much broader normative shifts in how states use force become clearer. First, a major crisis would generate a strong impetus amongst politicians and security practitioners to look for innovative ways of dealing with its ensuing new challenges. Then, actors would mobilise new technological solutions, through engineering and the acquisition of new skills, offering an appealing boost in efficiency that could come with lower ethical 'costs' or avoid ethical problems present in previously available means. Yet, as technological innovations always carry a wide range of possible implementations and regulations, their normative horizons emerge within existing institutional structures modified to include new means without losing coherence.[8] Existing normative arrangements are the context for any evolution in practice. This suggests that the true demise of liberal principles in how states use force or pursue security goals would require a significant overhaul of applicable laws – especially or primarily domestic – and a purge of security institutions that would eliminate or marginalise practitioners whose

---

[8] I elsewhere develop this relational conception of ontological security in institutional settings further (see Pratt 2016).

expertise and ethical commitments are too firmly based on liberal values. This did not take place in the United States, despite movements towards it, but it may yet happen.

In turn, my work suggests several lessons for activists interested in maintaining and strengthening normative liberalism within the US security apparatus. First, technology is important not just for reasons of instrumental efficiency but also because it may offer ways around existing ethical dilemmas that make existing means unacceptable for some uses. Therefore, to resist an undesirable normative transformation, contest both the instrumental benefits of that technology ('it won't be efficient') and its possible integration within foreseeable existing institutions ('using this would require undesirable institutional change'). Contesting efficiency alone neglects institutional or ethical dimensions and depends too much on the limits of human engineering. Contesting laws and legitimacy alone concedes most of the argument. The interaction effect linking technological revision to the other mechanisms of normative transformation should be a focal point for contentious politics.

A second lesson is that the law is flexible. As was both asserted in interviews and demonstrated in practice by actors in the three cases I examine, legal arguments can be crafted to support a wide range of actions, including counternormative ones, and even if these arguments eventually face powerful challenges, it may take time before they are judicially overturned. For those opposed to brutal state security practices, legal discourse, and its attendant regulatory mechanisms are not enough to restrain or reinforce 'right conduct'. Legal contestation should also be informed by a deep knowledge of institutional context and culture – by an understanding of the technical/technological and bureaucratic arrangements. In other words, while the US security apparatus has a heavily embedded legalism, and this gives the law influence upon its normative composition, other factors have a strong impact upon how the law is interpreted and followed in practice. Critics should press for judicial and legislative measures that are designed with this interaction effect in mind.

These empirically grounded findings do not exhaust the normative implications of my work here, however; there is also a set of broader ontological and epistemological implications to my approach that pertain to the relationship between facts and values. I describe these in the next and final section.

7.4.2 From Facts to Values in a Theory of Normative Transformation

Existing norms scholarship in IR tends to presume that knowing the facts of a case does not, on its own, provide insight into what is good or bad about it. Mainstream constructivist IR scholars accept the fact–value distinction as a central premise of social science theorising. This is despite some attempts to cross that divide. Price (2008) argues that, as the conceptual architecture of constructivist theorising is devoted to the study of how values are produced and contended, it is also especially well-suited to studying cultural horizons of transformative possibility, shedding light on 'moral limit and possibility'. Along a similar vein, Hoffmann (2009) enquires into the ethical implications of methodologically sound constructivist scholarship. In conversation with critical constructivism, Hoffmann concludes that, as constructivism entails continual exposure to, and explanation of, greatly varying and diverse moral arrangements, the ethic of a 'good' constructivist is one of 'humility and self-reflexivity' (Hoffmann 2009, 243). Yet Price, as others have observed (Inayatullah and Blaney 2012; Weber 2014), constrains moral discourse within reified cultural horizons-in-view, resulting in a status quo bias. Meanwhile, Hoffmann appears to assert Moore's naturalistic fallacy by claiming that the fact of cultural variance is sufficient to entail ethical consequences, and his arguments are reminiscent of well-litigated defences of moral relativism on sociological and anthropological grounds (Gowans 2015), despite his protestations to the contrary. These philosophical problems suggest that few normative implications can be derived from research conducted per dominant approaches to studying the causal implications of normativity, identity, learning, and other major themes of constructivist enquiry in the field.

However, the approach I use offers a way around this problem, when applied not just to the actors and institutions under investigation but to the investigator as well. A pragmatist approach implies that there are normative reasons for investigating normative transformations and that the innovative, problem-solving interplay of values, facts, and strategies of action produces and orients theorising about the world. In a broad sense, a pragmatist philosophical ethos requires that scholarship 'aid human communities precisely in the improvement of their possibilities of collective action, and [further] the solidarity of a community of human beings who collectively recognize and discuss their earthly problems and creatively solve them' (Joas 1993, 257). These democratic ends to theory require the existence of a functional 'public' as their social condition of possibility: a 'circle of citizens who, on the basis of a jointly experienced concern, share the conviction that they have to turn to the rest of society for the purposes of administratively controlling the relevant interaction' (Honneth 1998, 774). The kinds of processes that lead to the generation of publics is an empirical matter for debate, but within IR, efforts to examine the possibility of a 'global public' point to participatory governance and the opening of closed, 'expert' discourses to include parties normally only treated as consumers, rather than producers, of knowledge (Abraham and Abramson 2017). In other words, the creation of publics can provide an end around which scholarship may be oriented, and if there is a need to prioritise one methodological approach over others, scholars should do so according to how best to achieve that end.

In the field of security studies, this can bring together largely disparate mainstream and critical literatures. Once the main preserve of 'realists', who sought to portray the world as it is rather than as one might hope it should be, security studies has expanded to include elements of critical theorising as well. Some of these has emerged out of a return to classical realist thinkers who urged students of IR to engage with the ethical dimensions of theory rather than to sanitise scholarship of them (Barkin 2003; Levine 2012; cf. Levine 2013) More broadly, however, the sensitivities and methods of critical theorising illuminate features of security and defence that are politically important. These include the epistemic and rhetorical processes by which communities come to see certain things as security threats (Buzan et al. 1998), the imperial origins, premises, and implications of humanitarianism (Orford 1999), and the ways institutional practices and public discourses on security sustain gendered and racialised categories (Youngs 2006; Razack 2008; Mahmood 2009) – to name only a few examples. Critical theorising supplies challenge to dominant perspectives and practices that emerge as communities make their decisions, uncovering in them forms of ethical inconsistency,[9] unrecognised interests or power-relations,[10] or processes of cultural production,[11] to introduce to political discourses alternative

---

[9] Such as in attempting to wage a 'war' against terrorism (Crawford 2003).
[10] Such as in showing the chauvinist underpinnings of cosmopolitan humanitarianism (Crawford 2002).
[11] Such as in the popular tropes and stereotypes underpinning the US 'War on Terror' (Croft 2006).

views of victims, perpetrators, heroes, uninvolved bystanders, winners, and losers.

The benefits of pragmatist ontological and epistemological premises for critical scholarship on security are best illustrated through two examples. First, in the broader debate over targeted killing, metrics for assessing outcomes and categorising casualties as enemies or bystanders are topics of major interest (Kessler and Werner 2008; Jordan 2009; Carvin 2012; Grayson 2012; Johnston 2012; Pugliese 2013), ranging from concerns over the consequences of 'gamefied' war (Gregory 2011; see also Kilcullen and Exum 2009) to the biopolitics of algorithmic targeting (Allinson 2015). Resolving this debate requires not only that stakeholders receive better information on whether targeted killing 'works' or is 'precise' but also extensive and ongoing reflection over what that would even mean. As I show in this book, a pragmatist study of targeted killing can incorporate a wide range of factors and implications, including those often overlooked, without overloading scholarly observers with detail. It makes visible overlooked terrain and context, granting epistemic force to ethical challenges while ensuring that they are addressed with the appropriate information.

Second, and more simply, pragmatism offers a vision for critical scholarship in security studies that does not necessarily position critique at, or from, the margins of the discipline, opposed to or sceptical of the scholarly ends of a supposed mainstream. Critical security scholars have a long (and arguably justified) history of suspicion of mainstream or 'positivist' security studies, because of its historical relationship with defence policy-making (Krause 1998; Jones 1999; Browning and McDonald 2013). A pragmatist understanding of theory and of the world of study, however, gives those seeking to describe the world as it is some much-needed tools for potent immanent critique. Meanwhile, if critical scholars similarly adopt a pragmatist sensibility, they gain the rhetorical and institutional resources for speaking to an audience amongst segments of the IR community traditionally less open to hearing what they have to say.

7.5 Final Remarks

Normativity suffuses the relations and processes of international politics. The norms research programme may focus on the origins and changes of specific prohibitions, taboos, and conventions as they travel throughout the international system, but theories about these things should not be isolated from new ways of thinking about social change. In this book, by engaging with social theory and philosophy, by investigating three significant cases, and through the remarks in this concluding chapter, I have shown that normative transformations bring together a range of mechanisms and occur in a range of institutional spaces in ways that scholars of norms have often ignored for analytical convenience. Bringing pragmatism, relational sociology, and practice theory to a discussion of normative transformation, I contribute to the empirical and conceptual study of security, norms, and practices.

As I continued this project, the question I asked at the start, about the apparent erosion of prohibitions, quickly became a question on the *evolution* of them, once it was clear that these prohibitions were revised through innovative, practitioner-led problem-solving. Innovation is often imagined to be an essential good, but it has led, as I show, to practices and policies of considerable moral concern for informed observers and stakeholders. Moreover, when prohibitions or conventions persist in name but are changed in content or practical form, the term 'norm' can become a source of confusion rather than clarity, because any given rule dissolves into a constellation of interwoven principles and practices – into normative configurations, as I have called them. The need to dismantle 'norms' and look at their moving parts is driven by the particular analytical problems of my three cases, but there is something deeper, and more fundamental, to my approach that obliges this. Pragmatism obliges scientists to continually revise the contents of their theories in the face of new challenges, but moreover a processual and relational understanding of social causality shifts analytical attention from entities to their constitutive processes and relations.

The approach I take in this book does not explode or undermine existing scholarship on norms in international politics but does identify its limits. There is nothing wrong with building a research programme on top of a convenient set of terms, concepts, or objects, but doing so always entails a set horizon of explanatory or theoretical possibility. Studies of norms lie at the heart of the constructivist turn in IR, comprising its early and most successful attempts to go beyond the narrowly populated theoretical world of rationalism and investigate the causal role of identity, morality, and culture. But as the field has opened its sociological mind, research into norms has gained an increasingly diverse set of theoretical and analytical instruments, which puts great stress on the original terms out of which the research programme has been constructed even as it expands the range of explainable phenomena. Rather than amplify that stress to the point at which it becomes shattering or reduce it through meta-theoretical interventions that recognise new forces without substantively revising theories of norms in an applied sense, I have taken a middle ground: I have linked reification (and de-reification) of 'norms' to specific empirical puzzles, affirming existing scholarship while expanding its possible extensions or progressions.

Particularly for security studies, scholarship on norms and normativity itself carries significant normative implications. For any engaged citizen, it is imperative to know how the use of violence by state security apparatuses can be effectively and robustly controlled, and this is fundamental to the legitimacy of any state that kills on behalf of its constituencies. This means developing theories that identify when and how those controls change in practice, as well as ensuring that the language we use for talking about the security challenges states confront is suitable for ethical analysis. Security scholars need to help citizens recognise the dialectic, for lack of a better term, of realism and idealism that permeates all levels of statecraft – and which, by necessity and design, should stimulate public conversation. While not a work of critical security scholarship, this book has embraced many of its central preoccupations: it criticises reification, focuses on processes of normative change, and connects change to the relationships between discourse, technology, and bureaucracy. I have adopted a broad political and ethical orientation to solve a problem that matters for publics, rather than one immanent to a scientific research programme. Herein lies the normative status I claim for my work: *polity relevance*.

References

Abbott, Andrew. 1995. 'Things of Boundaries'. *Social Research* 62(4): 857–62.

Abraham, Kavi Joseph, and Yehonatan Abramson. 2015. 'A Pragmatist Vocation for International Relations: The (Global) Public and Its Problems'. *European Journal of International Relations* 23(1): 26.

Abrahamsen, Rita, and Michael C. Williams. 2009. 'Security Beyond the State: Global Security Assemblages in International Politics'. *International Political Sociology* 3(1): 1–17. doi:10.1111/j.1749-5687.2008.00060.x.

Acharya, Amitav. 2004. 'How Ideas Spread: Whose Norms Matter? Norm Localization and Institutional Change in Asian Regionalism'. *International Organization* 58(2): 239–75. doi:10.1017/S0020818304 582024.

Ackerman, Spencer. 2014. 'Torture Victims Will Bear Psychological Scars Long after CIA Report Scandal Fades'. *The Guardian*, 13 December. www.theguardian.com/law/2014/dec/13/learned-helplessness-enduring -effects-torture-haunt-victims.

Acuto, Michele, and Simon Curtis. 2014. 'Assemblage Thinking and International Relations'. In *Reassembling International Theory*, edited by Michele Acuto and Simon Curtis, pp. 1–15. Basingstoke: Palgrave Macmillan.

Adamson, Fiona B. 2016. 'Spaces of Global Security: Beyond Methodological Nationalism'. *Journal of Global Security Studies* 1(1): 19–35.

Adamson, Fiona B., and Madeleine Demetriou. 2007. 'Remapping the Boundaries of "State" and "National Identity": Incorporating Diasporas into IR Theorizing'. *European Journal of International Relations* 13(4): 489–526. doi: 10.1177/1354066107083145.

Adler, Emanuel. 2019. *World Ordering: A Social Theory of Cognitive Evolution*. Cambridge: Cambridge University Press.

Adler, Emanuel, and Patricia Greve. 2009. 'When Security Community Meets Balance of Power: Overlapping Regional Mechanisms of Security Governance'. *Review of International Studies* 35(S1): 59–84.

Adler, Emanuel, and Vincent Pouliot. 2011. 'International Practices'. *International Theory* 3(1): 1–36. doi:10.1017/S175297191000031X.

Adler-Nissen, Rebecca, ed. 2013. *Bourdieu in International Relations: Rethinking Key Concepts in IR*. Oxford: Routledge.

2014. 'Stigma Management in International Relations: Transgressive Identities, Norms, and Order in International Society'. *International Organization* 68(1): 143–76.

Agnew, John. 1994. 'The Territorial Trap: The Geographical Assumptions of International Relations Theory'. *Review of International Political Economy* 1(1): 53–80.

Alexander, Thomas M. 1987. *John Dewey's Theory of Art, Experience, and Nature*. Albany, NY: State University of New York Press.

Allinson, Jamie. 2015. 'The Necropolitics of Drones'. *International Political Sociology* 9(2): 113–27.

Allison, Graham T. 1971. *The Essence of Decision: Explaining the Cuban Missile Crisis*. Boston, MA: Little, Brown, and Company.

Allison, Graham T., and Morton H. Halperin. 1972. 'Bureaucratic Politics: A Paradigm and Some Policy Implications'. *World Politics* 24(1): 40–79.

Archer, Margaret S. 1982. 'Morphogenesis versus Structuration: On Combining Structure and Action'. *British Journal of Sociology* 33(4): 455–83.

1995. *Realist Social Theory: The Morphogenetic Approach*. Cambridge: Cambridge University Press.

Arkin, Ronald. 2009. *Governing Lethal Behavior in Autonomous Robots*. Boca Raton, FL: CRC Press.

Avant, Deborah D. 2005. *The Market for Force: The Consequences of Privatizing Security*. Cambridge: Cambridge University Press.

2007. 'Selling Security: Trade-Offs in State Regulation of the Private Security Industry'. In *Private Military and Security Companies: Chances, Problems, Pitfalls and Prospects*, edited by Thomas Jäger and Gerhard Kümmel, pp. 419–42. Wiesbaden: VS Verlag für Sozialwissenschaften.

2016. 'Pragmatic Networks and Transnational Governance of Private Military and Security Services'. *International Studies Quarterly* 60(2): 330–42.

Axelrod, Robert. 1986. 'An Evolutionary Approach to Norms'. *American Political Science Review* 80(4): 1095–111.

Banka, Andris, and Adam Quinn. 2018. 'Killing Norms Softly: US Targeted Killing, Quasi-Secrecy and the Assassination Ban'. *Security Studies* 27 (4): 665–703.

Banks, William C., and Peter Raven-Hansen. 2003. 'Targeted Killing and Assassination: The US Legal Framework'. *University of Richmond Law Review* 37: 667–749.

Barkin, J. Samuel. 2003. 'Realist Constructivism'. *International Studies Review* 5(3): 325–42.

Barkin, J. Samuel, and Bruce Cronin. 1994. 'The State and the Nation: Changing Norms and the Rules of Sovereignty in International Relations'. *International Organization* 48(1): 107. doi:10.1017/S0020818300000837.

Barnett, Michael. 2005. 'Humanitarianism Transformed'. *Perspectives on Politics* 3(4): 723–40. doi:10.1017/S1537592705050401.

Baynes, Kenneth. 2004. 'The Transcendental Turn: Habermas' "Kantian Pragmatism"'. In *The Cambridge Companion to Critical Theory*, edited by Fred Rush, pp. 194–218. Cambridge: Cambridge University Press.

Beisheim, Marianne, and Klaus Dingwerth. 2008. 'Procedural Legitimacy and Private Transnational Governance: Are the Good Ones Doing Better?'. SFB-Governance Working Paper Series, no. 11. Berlin.

Bennett, Andrew, and Jeffrey T. Checkel. 2015. 'Process Tracing: From Philosophical Roots to Best Practices'. In *Process Tracing: From Metaphor to Analytic Tool*, edited by Andrew Bennett and Jeffrey T. Checkel, pp. 3–37. Cambridge: Cambridge University Press. doi:http://dx.doi.org/10.1017/CBO9781139858472.

Beres, Louis R. 1991. 'The Permissibility of State-Sponsored Assassination During Peace and War'. *Temple International & Comparative Law Journal* 5: 231.

Bernales Ballesteros, Enrique. 1998. 'Report on the Question of the Use of Mercenaries as a Means of Violating Human Rights and Impeding the Exercise of the Rights of Peoples to Self-Determination'. Geneva: UN Commission on Human Rights, 55th Session.

 2003. 'Report on the Question of the Use of Mercenaries as a Means of Violating Human Rights and Impeding the Exercise of the Right of Peoples to Self-Determination'. Geneva: UN Commission on Human Rights, 60th Session. https://digitallibrary.un.org/record/515408.

Bernstein, Steven. 2001. *The Compromise of Liberal Environmentalism*. New York: Columbia University Press.

Bernstein, Steven, Michele Betsill, Matthew Hoffmann, and Matthew Paterson. 2010. 'A Tale of Two Copenhagens: Carbon Markets and Climate Governance'. *Millennium: Journal of International Studies* 39(1): 161–73.

Bernstein, Steven, R. N. Lebow, J. G. Stein, and S. Weber. 2000. 'God Gave Physics the Easy Problems: Adapting Social Science to an Unpredictable World'. *European Journal of International Relations* 7(1): 43–76. https://doi.org/10.1177/1354066100006001003.

Bhaskar, Roy. 1998. *The Possibility of Naturalism: A Philosophical Critique of the Contemporary Human Sciences*. Oxford: Routledge.

Bicchieri, Cristina. 2005. *The Grammar of Society: The Nature and Dynamics of Social Norms.* Cambridge: Cambridge University Press.

Bigo, Didier. 2011. 'Pierre Bourdieu and International Relations: Power of Practices, Practices of Power'. *International Political Sociology* 5: 225–58. doi:10.1111/j.1749-5687.2011.00132.x.

Binder, Martin. 2007. 'Norms versus Rationality: Why Democracies Use Private Military Companies in Civil Wars'. In *Private Military and Security Companies: Chances, Problems, Pitfalls and Prospects*, edited by Thomas Jäger and Gerhard Kümmel, pp. 307–20. Wiesbaden: VS Verlag für Sozialwissenschaften.

Blum, Gabriella, and Philip Heymann. 2010. 'Law and Policy of Targeted Killing'. *Harvard National Security Journal* 1(1): 145–70.

Bohman, James. 1999. 'Practical Reason and Cultural Constraint: Agency in Bourdieu's Theory of Practice'. In *Bourdieu: A Critical Reader*, edited by Richard Shusterman, 129–52. Oxford: Blackwell.

Boltanski, Luc. 2012. *Love and Justice as Competences: Three Essays on the Sociology of Action.* Cambridge: Polity.

Boltanski, Luc, and Laurent Thévenot. 2006. *On Justification: Economies of Worth.* Princeton, NJ: Princeton University Press.

Börzel, Tanja A, and Thomas Risse. 2010. 'Governance without a State: Can It Work?' *Regulation & Governance* 4(2): 113–34.

Boudon, Raymond. 1998. 'Limitations of Rational Choice Theory 1'. *American Journal of Sociology* 104(3): 817–28.

Bourdieu, Pierre. 1977. *Outline of a Theory of Practice.* Cambridge: Cambridge University Press.

   1984. *Distinction: A Social Critique of the Judgement of Taste.* Cambridge, MA: Harvard University Press.

   1993. *The Field of Cultural Production.* New York: Columbia University Press.

Bousquet, Antoine. 2008. 'Chaoplexic Warfare or the Future of Military Organization'. *International Affairs* 84(5): 915–29.

Browning, Christopher S., and Matt McDonald. 2013. 'The Future of Critical Security Studies: Ethics and the Politics of Security'. *European Journal of International Relations* 19(2): 235–55.

Brunnée, Jutta, and Stephen J. Toope. 2011. 'Interactional International Law: An Introduction'. *International Theory* 3(2): 307–18.

Bucher, Bernd. 2014. 'Acting Abstractions: Metaphors, Narrative Structures, and the Eclipse of Agency'. *European Journal of International Relations* 20(3): 742–65. doi:10.1177/1354066113503481.

Bueger, Christian, and Frank Gadinger. 2014. *International Practice Theory: New Perspectives.* London: Palgrave.

2015. 'The Play of International Practice'. *International Studies Quarterly* 59(3): 449–60.

Bulkeley, Harriet. 2010. 'Cities and the Governing of Climate Change'. *Annual Review of Environment and Resources* 35: 229–53.

Bulkeley, Harriet, and Peter Newell. 2015. *Governing Climate Change*. London: Routledge.

Buzan, Barry, Ole Wæver, and Jaap De Wilde. 1998. *Security: A New Framework for Analysis*. Boulder, CO: Lynne Rienner Publishers.

Byrne, David. 1998. *Complexity Theory and the Social Sciences*. New York: Routledge.

Calhoun, Craig. 1998. 'Explanation in Historical Sociology: Narrative, General Theory, and Historically Specific Theory'. *American Journal of Sociology* 104(3): 846–71.

Cameron, Lindsey, and Vincent Chetail. 2013. *Privatizing War: Private Military and Security Companies under Public International Law*. Cambridge: Cambridge University Press.

Cancian, Francesca M. 1975. *What Are Norms? A Study of Beliefs and Action in a Maya Community*. Cambridge: Cambridge University Press.

Carmola, Kateri. 2010. *Private Security Contractors and New Wars: Risk, Law, and Ethics*. Oxford: Routledge.

Carvin, Stephanie. 2012. 'The Trouble with Targeted Killing'. *Security Studies* 21(3): 529–55.

2015. 'Getting Drones Wrong'. *International Journal of Human Rights* 19 (2): 127–41.

Carvin, Stephanie, and Michael John Williams. 2015. *Law, Science, Liberalism, and the American Way of Warfare*. Cambridge: Cambridge University Press.

'Case of Ireland v. The United Kingdom'. 1978. European Court of Human Rights. http://hudoc.echr.coe.int/eng#%7B%22itemid%22:%5B%22 001-57506%22%5D%7D.

Castells, Manuel. 2008. 'The New Public Sphere: Global Civil Society, Communication Networks, and Global Governance'. *Annals of the American Academy of Political and Social Science* 616(1): 78–93.

2009. *Communication Power*. Oxford: Oxford University Press.

Checkel, Jeffrey T. 1997. 'International Norms and Domestic Politics: Bridging the Rationalist-Constructivist Divide'. *European Journal of International Relations* 3(4): 473–95.

Chesterman, Simon, and Chia Lehnardt, eds. 2007. *From Mercenaries to Market: The Rise and Regulation of Private Military Companies*. Oxford: Oxford University Press.

Clarke, Richard A. 2004. *Against All Enemies: Inside America's War on Terror*. New York: Free Press.

Clarke, Simon. 2006. 'Theory and Practice: Psychoanalytic Sociology as Psycho-Social Studies'. *Sociology* 40(6): 1153–69. doi:10.1177/0038038506069855.

Cochran, Molly. 2012. 'Pragmatism and International Relations: A Story of Closure and Opening'. *European Journal of Pragmatism and American Philosophy* 6(1):138–58.

Coll, Stephen. 2004. *Ghost Wars: The Secret History of the CIA, Afghanistan and Bin Laden, from the Soviet Invasion to September 10, 2001*. London: Penguin Press.

2014. 'The Unblinking Stare'. *The New Yorker*, November 24. www .newyorker.com/magazine/2014/11/24/unblinking-stare.

Committee on Armed Services, United States Senate. 2008. *Inquiry Into the Treatment of Detainees in U.S. Custody, Volume 4.*

'Convention against Torture and Other Cruel, Inhuman or Degrading Treatment or Punishment'. 1984. UN General Assembly.

Coole, Diana. 2013. 'Agentic Capacities and Capacious Historical Materialism: Thinking with New Materialisms in the Political Sciences'. *Millennium: Journal of International Studies* 41(3): 451–69.

Cortell, Andrew P., and James W. Davis. 1996. 'How Do International Institutions Matter? The Domestic Impact of International Rules and Norms'. *International Studies Quarterly* 40(4): 451–78.

2005. 'When Norms Clash: International Norms, Domestic Practices, and Japan's Internalisation of the GATT/WTO'. *Review of International Studies* 31(1): 3–25. doi:10.1017/S0260210505006273.

Craib, Ian. 1990. *Psychoanalysis and Social Theory*. Amhurst: University of Massachusetts Press.

Crawford, Neta. 2002. *Argument and Change in World Politics: Ethics, Decolonization, and Humanitarian Intervention*. Cambridge: Cambridge University Press.

2003. 'Just War Theory and the Iraq War'. *Perspectives on Politics* 1(1): 5–25.

Croft, Stuart. 2006. *Culture, Crisis and America's War on Terror*. Cambridge: Cambridge University Press.

2012. 'Constructing Ontological Insecurity: The Insecuritization of Britain's Muslims'. *Contemporary Security Policy* 33(2): 219–35.

De Goede, Marieke. 2008. 'Beyond Risk: Premediation and the Post-9/11 Security Imagination'. *Security Dialogue* 39(2–3): 155–76.

De Nevers, Renee. 2009. '(Self) Regulating War? Voluntary Regulation and the Private Security'. *Security Studies* 18: 479–516. doi:10.1080/09636410903132854.

del Prado, José L. Gómez. 2008. 'Private Military and Security Companies and the UN Working Group on the Use of Mercenaries'. *Journal of Conflict and Security Law* 13(3): 429–50.

Department of Justice. 2012. 'Lawfulness of a Lethal Operation Directed against a U.S. Citizen Who Is a Senior Operational Leader of Al-Qa'ida or an Associated Force'. White paper. http://msnbcmedia.msn.com/i/m snbc/sections/news/020413_DOJ_White_Paper.pdf.

Depélteau, François. 2013. 'What Is the Direction of the "Relational Turn?"'. In *Conceptualizing Relational Sociology*, edited by Christopher Powell and François Dépelteau, pp. 163–86. New York: Palgrave Macmillan.

Deudney, Daniel. 2000. 'Geopolitics as Theory: Historical Security Materialism'. *European Journal of International Relations* 6(1): 77–107.

Dewey, John. 1978. *The Middle Works of John Dewey, 1899–1924, Volume 6: 1910–1911, Journal Articles, Book Reviews, Miscellany in the 1910–11 Period, and How We Think*. Edited by Jo Ann Boydston. Carbondale: Southern Illinois University Press.

1983. *The Middle Works of John Dewey, 1899–1924, Volume 14: 1922, Human Nature and Conduct*. Edited by Jo Ann Boydston. Carbondale: Southern Illinois University Press.

1987. *The Later Works of John Dewey, 1925–1953, Volume 10: 1934, Art as Experience*. Edited by Jo Ann Boydston. Carbondale: Southern Illinois University Press.

Dewey, John, and Arthur Bentley. 1949. *Knowing and the Known*. Boston, MA: Beacon Press.

DeWinter-Schmitt, Rebecca. 2013. 'Montreux Five Years On: A Analysis of State Efforts to Implement Montreux Document Legal Obligations and Good Practices'. Washington College of Law and NOVACT, Washington, DC. www.wcl.american.edu/index.cfm?LinkServID=B1 E626D9-095E-4A28-94A94551CEA3488E.

Dittmer, Jason. 2017. *Diplomatic Material: Affect, Assemblage, and Foreign Policy*. Durham, NC: Duke University Press.

Doswald-Beck, Louise. 2007. 'Private Military Companies under International Humanitarian Law'. In *From Mercenaries to Market: The Rise and Regulation of Private Military Companies*, edited by Simon Chesterman and Sophia Lehnardt, pp. 115–38. Oxford: Oxford University Press.

Dubois, Nicole. 2003. 'Introduction: The Concept of Norm'. In *A Sociocognitive Approach to Social Norms*, edited by Nicole Dubois, 1–16. London: Routledge.

Elias, Norbert. 1978. *What Is Sociology.* New York: Columbia University Press.
   1994. *The Civilizing Process: Sociogenetic and Psychogenetic Investigations.* Oxford: Blackwell Publishers.
Elliott, Anthony. 2014. *Routledge Handbook of Social and Cultural Theory.* Oxford: Routledge.
Elsea, Jennifer K., Moshe Schwartz, and Kennon H. Nakamura. 2008. *Private Security Contractors in Iraq: Background, Legal Status, and Other Issues.* Washington, DC.: Congressional Research Service. www.everycrsreport.com/reports/RL32419.html.
Elster, Jon. 1989a. *Nuts and Bolts for the Social Sciences.* Cambridge: Cambridge University Press.
   1989b. 'Social Norms and Economic Theory'. *Journal of Economic Perspectives* 3(4): 99–117.
   2008. *Reason and Rationality.* Princeton, NJ: Princeton University Press.
Emirbayer, Mustafa. 1997. 'Manifesto for a Relational Sociology'. *American Journal of Sociology* 103(2): 281–317.
Emirbayer, Mustafa, and Ann Mische. 1998. 'What Is Agency?' *American Journal of Sociology* 103(4): 962–1023.
Epstein, Charlotte. 2008. *The Power of Words in International Relations: Birth of an Anti-Whaling Discourse.* Cambridge: Cambridge University Press.
   2013. 'Norms'. In *Bourdieu in International Relations: Rethinking Key Concepts in IR*, edited by Rebecca Adler-Nissen, pp. 165–78. Oxford: Routledge.
Evers, Miles. 2017. 'On Transgression'. *International Studies Quarterly* 61 (4): 786–94.
Fearon, James, and Alexander Wendt. 2002. 'Rationalism v. Constructivism: A Skeptical View'. In *Handbook of International Relations*, edited by Walter Carlsnaes, Thomas Risse, and Beth A. Simmons, 52–72. London: Sage.
Finnemore, Martha. 1996a. 'Constructing Norms of Humanitarian Intervention'. In *The Culture of National Security: Norms and Identity in World Politics*, edited by Peter J. Katzenstein, pp. 153–85. New York: Columbia University Press.
   1996b. 'Norms, Culture, and World Politics: Insights from Sociology's Institutionalism'. *International Organization* 50(2): 325–47.
   2003. *The Purpose of Intervention: Changing Beliefs about the Use of Force.* Ithaca, NY: Cornell University Press.
Finnemore, Martha, and Kathryn Sikkink. 1998. 'International Norm Dynamics and Political Change'. *International Organization* 52(4): 887–917.
Fligstein, Neil, and Doug McAdam. 2012. *A Theory of Fields.* Oxford: Oxford University Press. doi:10.1093/acprof.

Florini, Ann. 1996. 'The Evolution of International Norms'. *International Studies Quarterly* 40(3): 363–89. doi:10.2307/2600716.

'FM 31-15 Operations against Irregular Forces'. 1961. Washington, DC: Headquarters, Department of the Army. https://wikispooks.com/w/images/6/62/FM_31-15.pdf.

Foot, R. 2006. 'Torture: The Struggle over a Peremptory Norm in a Counter-Terrorist Era'. *International Relations* 20(2): 131–51. doi:10.1177/0047117806063844.

Foucault, Michel. 1980. *Power/Knowledge*. Edited by Colin Gordon. New York: Pantheon Books.

Freedman, Lawrence. 2000. *Kennedy's Wars: Berlin, Cuba, Laos, and Vietnam*. New York: Oxford University Press.

Friedrichs, Jörg, and Friedrich Kratochwil. 2009. 'On Acting and Knowing: How Pragmatism Can Advance International Relations Research and Methodology'. *International Organization* 63(Fall): 701–31.

Fuller, Christopher J. 2015. 'The Eagle Comes Home to Roost: The Historical Origins of the CIA's Lethal Drone Program'. *Intelligence and National Security* 30(6): 769–92. doi:10.1080/02684527.2014.895569.

2017. *See It/Shoot It: The Secret History of the CIA's Lethal Drone Program*. New Haven, CT: Yale University Press.

GAO. 2005. 'Rebuilding Iraq: Actions Needed to Improve Use of Private Security Providers'. Washington, DC. www.gao.gov/products/gao-05-737.

2008. 'DOD and State Department Have Improved Oversight and Coordination of Private Security Contractors in Iraq, but Further Actions Are Needed to Sustain Improvements'. Washington, DC: Government Accountability Office (GAO-08-966). www.gao.gov/new/items/d08966.pdf.

2013. 'Afghanistan: Key Oversight Issues'. Washington, DC. www.gao.gov/assets/660/652075.pdf.

2016. 'Observations on the Use of Force Management Levels in Afghanistan, Iraq, and Syria'. Washington, DC. www.gao.gov/assets/690/681336.pdf.

Gazit, Nir, and Robert J. Brym. 2011. 'State-Directed Political Assassination in Israel: A Political Hypothesis'. *International Sociology* 26(6): 862–77.

Gebhardt, James F. 2005. *The Road to Abu Ghraib: US Army Detainee Doctrine and Experience*. Fort Leavenworth, KS: Combat Studies Institute Press.

'Geneva Convention Relative to the Protection of Civilian Persons in Time of War (Fourth Geneva Convention)'. 1949. International Committee of the Red Cross (ICRC).

Giddens, Anthony. 1979. *Central Problems in Social Theory: Action, Structure, and Contradiction in Social Analysis*. Berkeley: University of California Press.

  1984. *The Constitution of Society: Outline of a Theory of Structuration*. Berkeley: University of California Press.

Go, Julian. 2008. 'Global Fields and Imperial Forms: Field Theory and the British and American Empires'. *Sociological Theory* 26(3): 201–29.

Goddard, Stacie E. 2006. 'Uncommon Ground: Indivisible Territory and the Politics of Legitimacy'. *International Organization* 60(1): 35–68.

  2009. 'Brokering Change: Networks and Entrepreneurs in International Politics'. *International Theory* 1(2): 249–81.

Goddard, Stacie E., and Ronald R. Krebs. 2015. 'Rhetoric, Legitimation, and Grand Strategy'. *Security Studies* 24(1): 5–36.

Goffman, Erving. 1959. *The Presentation of the Self in Everyday Life*. New York: Anchor Books.

  1969. *Strategic Interaction*. Philadelphia: University of Pennsylvania Press.

  1983. 'The Interaction Order: American Sociological Association, 1982 Presidential Address'. *American Sociological Review* 48(1): 1–17.

Gordon, Avishag. 2006. '"Purity of Arms," "Preemptive War," and "Selective Targeting" in the Context of Terrorism: General, Conceptual, and Legal Analyses'. *Studies in Conflict and Terrorism* 29(5): 493–508. doi: 10.1080/10576100600698501.

Gorski, Philip S. 2013. *Bourdieu and Historical Analysis*. Durham, NC: Duke University Press.

Gowans, Chris. 2015. 'Moral Relativism'. *Stanford Encyclopedia of Philosophy*. http://stanford.library.usyd.edu.au/archives/win2015/entries/moral-relativism/.

Grayson, Kyle. 2012. 'Six Theses on Targeted Killing'. *Politics* 32(2): 120–8.

  2016. *Cultural Politics of Targeted Killing*. London: Routledge.

Gregory, Derek. 2011. 'From a View to a Kill: Drones and Late Modern War'. *Theory, Culture & Society* 28(7–8): 188–215.

Großklaus, Mathias. 2017. 'Friction, Not Erosion: Assassination Norms at the Fault Line between Sovereignty and Liberal Values'. *Contemporary Security Policy* 38(2): 260–80. https://doi.org/10.1080/13523260.2017.1335135.

Gross, Neil. 2009. 'A Pragmatist Theory of Social Mechanisms'. *American Sociological Review* 74(3): 358–79. doi:10.1177/000312240907400302.

  2010. 'Charles Tilly and American Pragmatism'. *American Sociologist* 41 (4): 337–57.

Guillaume, Xavier, and Jef Huysmans. 2013. *Citizenship and Security: The Constitution of Political Being*. Oxford: Routledge.

Guzzini, Stefano. 2011. 'Securitization as a Causal Mechanism'. *Security Dialogue* 42(4–5): 329–41.

2013. *Power, Realism and Constructivism*. Oxford: Routledge.

Habermas, Jürgen. 1968. *Knowledge and Human Interests*. Boston, MA: Beacon Press.

1984. *The Theory of Communicative Action, Vol. 1*. Boston, MA: Beacon Press.

Hafner-Burton, Emilie M., Miles Kahler, and Alexander H. Montgomery. 2009. 'Network Analysis for International Relations'. *International Organization* 63(3): 559–92. doi:10.1017/S0020818309090195.

Hall, Peter A., ed. 1989. *The Political Power of Economic Ideas*. Princeton, NJ: Princeton University Press.

Halperin, Morton H., and Priscilla A. Clapp. 2006. *Bureaucratic Politics and Foreign Policy*. Washington, DC: Brookings Institution Press.

Harlow, Bill, ed. 2015. *Rebuttal: The CIA Responds to the Senate Intelligence Committee's Study of Its Detention and Interrogation Program*. Annapolis, MD: Naval Institute Press.

Hellmann, Gunther. 2009. 'Beliefs as Rules for Action: Pragmatism as a Theory of Thought and Action'. *International Studies Review* 11: 638–62. http://scholar.google.com/scholar?hl=en&btnG=Search&q=intitle:Beliefs+as+Rules+for+Action+:+Pragmatism+as+a+Theory+of+Thought+and+Action#0.

Hildebrand, David L. 2008. *Dewey: A Beginner's Guide*. Oxford: Oneworld Publications.

Hofferberth, Matthias, and Christian Weber. 2015. 'Lost in Translation: A Critique of Constructivist Norm Research'. *Journal of International Relations and Development* 18(1): 75–103. doi:10.1057/jird.2014.1.

Hoffmann, Matthew J. 2009. 'Is Constructivist Ethics an Oxymoron?' *International Studies Review* 11(2): 231–52. doi:10.1111/j.1468-2486.2009.00847.x.

2010. 'Norms and Social Constructivism in International Relations'. *International Studies Encyclopedia*. Blackwell Reference Online. www.isacompendium.com/subscriber/tocnode.html?id=g9781444336597_yr2013_chunk_g978144433659714_ss1-8.

2011. *Climate Governance at the Crossroads: Experimenting with a Global Response after Kyoto*. Oxford: Oxford University Press.

Holmqvist, Caroline. 2013. 'Undoing War: War Ontologies and the Materiality of Drone Warfare'. *Millennium: Journal of International Studies* 43(3):535–52.

Honneth, Axel. 1998. 'Democracy as Reflexive Cooperation John Dewey and the Theory of Democracy Today'. *Political Theory* 26(6): 763–83.

Hopf, Ted. 2010. 'The Logic of Habit in International Relations'. *European Journal of International Relations* 16(4): 539–61. doi:10.1177/ 1354066110363502.

Horne, Alistair. 2012. *A Savage War of Peace: Algeria 1954–1962.* Basingstoke, UK: Pan Macmillan.

'Human Resource Exploitation Training Manual'. 1983. Langley, DC: CIA. http://nsarchive.gwu.edu/NSAEBB/NSAEBB122/CIA%Human%Res %Exploit%A1-G11.pdf.

Humphreys, Macartan, and Alan M. Jacobs. 2015. 'Mixing Methods: A Bayesian Approach'. *American Political Science Review* 109(4): 653–73.

Hurd, Ian. 2017. 'Targeted Killing in International Relations Theory: Recursive Politics of Technology, Law, and Practice'. *Contemporary Security Policy* 38(2): 307–19.

Imseis, Ardi. 2001. 'Moderate Torture on Trial: Critical Reflections on the Israeli Supreme Court Judgement Concerning the Legality of General Security Service Interrogation Methods'. *Berkeley Journal of International Law* 19: 328.

Inayatullah, Naeem, and David L. Blaney. 2012. 'The Dark Heart of Kindness: The Social Construction of Deflection'. *International Studies Perspectives* 13(2): 164–75.

Isenberg, David. 2007. 'A Government in Search of Cover: Private Military Companies in Iraq'. In *From Mercenaries to Market: The Rise and Regulation of Private Military Companies,* edited by Simon Chesterman and Chia Lehnardt, pp. 82–93. Oxford: Oxford University Press.

Jackson, Patrick Thaddeus. 2004. 'Hegel's House, or "People Are States Too"'. *Review of International Studies* 30: 281–7. doi:10.1017/ S0260210504006072.

  2006. *Civilizing the Enemy: German Reconstruction and the Invention of the West.* Ann Arbor: University of Michigan Press.

  2012. "The Constructivism That Wasn't." Blog post. Duck of Minerva. www.duckofminerva.com/2012/04/constructivism-that-wasnt.html.

Jackson, Patrick Thaddeus, and Daniel H. Nexon. 1999. 'Relations before States: Substance, Process and the Study of World Politics'. *European Journal of International Relations* 5(3): 291–332.

Jenkins, Richard. 2002. *Pierre Bourdieu.* 2nd ed. Oxford: Routledge.

Jervis, Robert. 1997. *System Effects: Complexity in Political and Social Life.* Princeton, NJ: Princeton University Press.

Joas, Hans. 1993. *Pragmatism and Social Theory.* Chicago, IL: University of Chicago Press.

  1996. *The Creativity of Action.* Cambridge: Polity Press.

  2000. *The Genesis of Values.* Chicago, IL: University of Chicago Press.

Joas, Hans, and Jens Beckert. 2001. 'Action Theory'. In *Handbook of Sociological Theory*, edited by Jonathan H. Turner, pp. 269–86. New York: Springer.

Johnston, Patrick B. 2012. 'Does Decapitation Work? Assessing the Effectiveness of Leadership Targeting in Counterinsurgency Campaigns'. *International Security* 36(4): 47–79.

Jones, Richard Wyn. 1999. *Security, Strategy, and Critical Theory*. Boulder, CO: Lynne Rienner Publishers.

Jordan, Jenna. 2009. 'When Heads Roll: Assessing the Effectiveness of Leadership Decapitation'. *Security Studies* 18(4): 719–55.

Jose, Betcy. 2017a. 'Bin Laden's Targeted Killing and Emerging Norms'. *Critical Studies on Terrorism* 10(1): 44–66.

2017b. 'Not Completely the New Normal: How Human Rights Watch Tried to Suppress the Targeted Killing Norm'. *Contemporary Security Policy* 38(2): 237–59.

Kahneman, Daniel, and Dale T. Miller. 1986. 'Norm Theory: Comparing Reality to Its Alternatives'. *Psychological Review* 93(2): 136.

Kalberg, Stephen. 1980. 'Max Weber's Types of Rationality: Cornerstones for the Analysis of Rationalization Processes in History'. *American Journal of Sociology* 85(5): 1145–79.

Kaldor, Mary. 1999. *Old and New Wars: Organized Violence in a Global Era*. Cambridge: Polity Press.

Kasher, Asa, and Amos Yadlin. 2005. 'Assassination and Preventive Killing'. *SAIS Review of International Affairs* 25(1): 41–57. doi: 10.1353/sais.2005.0011.

Katzenstein, Peter J, ed. 1996. *The Culture of National Security: Norms and Identity in World Politics*. New Directions in World Politics. New York: Columbia University Press.

Kay, Sean. 2012. 'Ontological Security and Peace-Building in Northern Ireland'. *Contemporary Security Policy* 33(2): 236–63.

Keck, Margeret E., and Kathryn Sikkink. 1998. *Activists Beyond Borders*. Ithaca, NY: Cornell University Press.

Kessler, Oliver, and Wouter Werner. 2008. 'Extrajudicial Killing as Risk Management'. *Security Dialogue* 39(2–3): 289–308.

Kilcullen, David, and Andrew McDonald Exum. 2009. 'Death from Above, Outrage Down Below'. *New York Times*, May 16. www.nytimes.com /2009/05/17/opinion/17exum.html.

Kinnvall, Catarina. 2004. 'Globalization and Religious Nationalism: Self, Identity, and the Search for Ontological Security'. *Political Psychology* 25(5): 741–67. doi:10.1111/j.1467-9221.2004.00396.x.

2006. *Globalization and Religious Nationalism in India*. Oxford: Routledge.

Kinsey, Christopher. 2006. *Corperate Soldiers and International Security: The Rise of Private Military Companies*. London: Routledge.

Klotz, Audie. 'Norms Reconstituting Interests: Global Racial Equality and U.S. Sanctions against South Africa'. *International Organization* 49, no. 3 (1995): 451. https://doi.org/10.1017/S0020818300033348.

Kornprobst, Markus. 2007. 'Argumentation and Compromise: Ireland's Selection of the Territorial Status Quo Norm'. *International Organization* 61(1): 69–98. doi:10.1017/S0020818307070026.

2019. 'Framing, Resonance and War: Foregrounds and Backgrounds of Cultural Congruence'. *European Journal of International Relations* 25 (1): 61–85.

Krahmann, Elke. 2013. 'The United States, PMSCs and the State Monopoly on Violence: Leading the Way towards Norm Change'. *Security Dialogue* 44(1): 53–71.

Kratochwil, Friedrich. 1989. *Rules Norms and Decisions: On the Conditions of Practical and Legal Reasoning in International Relations and Domestic Affairs*. Cambridge: Cambridge University Press.

Kratochwil, Friedrich, and John Gerard Ruggie. 1986. 'A State of the Art on an Art of the State'. *International Organization* 40(4): 753–75.

Krause, Keith. 1998. 'Critical Theory and Security Studies: The Research Programme of Critical Security Studies'. *Cooperation and Conflict* 33 (3): 298–333.

Krebs, Ronald. R., and Patrick Thaddeus Jackson. 2007. 'Twisting Tongues and Twisting Arms: The Power of Political Rhetoric'. *European Journal of International Relations* 13(1): 35–66. doi:10.1177/1354066107074284.

Kretzmer, David. 2005. 'Targeted Killing of Suspected Terrorists: Extra-Judicial Executions or Legitimate Means of Defence?' *European Journal of International Law* 16(2): 171–212. doi:10.1093/ejil/chi114.

Krishnan, Armin. 2009. *Killer Robots: Legality and Ethicality of Autonomous Weapons*. Farnham, UK: Ashgate Publishing.

Krolikowski, Alanna. 2008. 'State Personhood in Ontological Security Theories of International Relations and Chinese Nationalism: A Sceptical View'. *Chinese Journal of International Politics* 2(1): 109–33.

Krook, M. L., and J. True. 2012. 'Rethinking the Life Cycles of International Norms: The United Nations and the Global Promotion of Gender Equality'. *European Journal of International Relations* 18(1): 103–27. doi:10.1177/1354066110380963.

Kruck, Andreas. 2013. 'Theorising the Use of Private Military and Security Companies: A Synthetic Perspective'. *Journal of International Relations and Development* 17(1): 112–41. doi:10.1057/jird.2013.4.

'KUBARK Counterintelligence Interrogation'. 1963. Langley, DC: CIA. http://nsarchive.gwu.edu/NSAEBB/NSAEBB122/Kubark 82-104.pdf.

Latour, Bruno. 2005. *Reassembling the Social: An Introduction to Actor-Network-Theory*. Oxford: Oxford University Press. doi:10.1163/156913308X336453.

Legro, Jeffrey W. 1996. 'Culture and Preferences in the International Culture Cooperation'. *American Political Science Review* 90(1): 118–37.

Levine, Daniel J. 2012. *Recovering International Relations: The Promise of Sustainable Critique*. New York: Oxford University Press.

2013. 'Why Hans Morgenthau Was Not a Critical Theorist (and Why Contemporary IR Realists Should Care)'. *International Relations* 27(1): 95–118.

Lévi-Strauss, Claude. *La pensée sauvage*. Paris: Plon, 1962.

Liivoja, Rain. 2015. 'Technological Change and the Evolution of the Law of War'. *International Review of the Red Cross* 97(900): 1157–77. https://doi.org/10.1017/S1816383116000424.

Linklater, Andrew. 2011. *The Problem of Harm in International Politics*. Cambridge: Cambridge University Press.

Lovewine, George C. 2012. *Outsourcing the Global War on Terrorism: Private Military Companies and American Intervention in Iraq and Afghanistan*. New York: Palgrave Macmillan.

Loyal, Steven. 2003. *The Sociology of Anthony Giddens*. London: Pluto Press.

Lukács, Georg. 1971. 'Reification and the Consciousness of the Proletariat'. In *History & Class Consciousness: Studies in Marxist Dialectics*. Talgarth: Merlin Press.

Mac Ginty, Roger. 2017. 'A Material Turn in International Relations: The 4x4, Intervention and Resistance'. *Review of International Studies* 43 (5): 855–74.

MacKay, Joseph. 2013. 'Pirate Nations'. *Social Science History* 37(4): 551–73.

MacKay, Joseph, and Jamie Levin. 2015. 'Hanging Out in International Politics: Two Kinds of Explanatory Political Ethnography for IR'. *International Studies Review* 17(2): 163–88.

MacKay, Joseph, Jamie Levin, Gustavo de Carvalho, Kristin Cavoukian, and Ross Cuthbert. 2014. 'Before and after Borders: The Nomadic Challenge to Sovereign Territoriality'. *International Politics* 51(1): 101–23.

Mahmood, Saba. 2009. 'Gendering Religion and Politics: Untangling Modernities'. In *Gendering Religion and Politics*, edited by Hanna Herzog and Ann Braude, 193–215. New York: Palgrave Macmillan US. doi:10.1057/9780230623378_9.

Mann, Michael. 1993. *The Sources of Social Power, Vol. II: The Rise of Classes and Nation-States, 1760–1914.* Cambridge: Cambridge University Press.

March, James G., and Johan P. Olsen. 1998. 'Institutional Dynamics of International Political Orders'. *International Organization* 52(4): 943–69.

Margolis, Joseph. 1999. 'Pierre Bourdieu: Habitus and the Logic of Practice'. In *Bourdieu: A Critical Reader*, edited by Richard Shusterman, 64–83. Oxford: Blackwell.

Massey, Garth. 2011. *Ways of Social Change: Making Sense of Modern Times.* Los Angeles, CA: Sage.

Mayer, Jane. 2008. *The Dark Side.* New York: Doubleday.

Mazzetti, Mark. 2013. *The Way of the Knife.* New York: Penguin Press.

McAdam, Doug, Sidney Tarrow, and Charles Tilly. 2001. *Dynamics of Contention: Social Science.* Cambridge: Cambridge University Press.

McCourt, David M. 2016. 'Practice Theory and Relationalism as the New Constructivism'. *International Studies Quarterly* 60(3): 475–85.

McFate, Sean. 2014. *The Modern Mercenary: Private Armies and What They Mean for World Order.* Oxford: Oxford University Press.

McKeown, Ryder. 2009. 'Norm Regress: US Revisionism and the Slow Death of the Torture Norm'. *International Relations* 23(1): 5–25. doi:10.1177/0047117808100607.

Melzer, Nils. 2008. *Targeted Killing in International Law.* New York: Oxford University Press.

Mérand, Frédéric, and Vincent Pouliot. 2013. 'Bourdieu's Concepts'. In *Bourdieu in International Relations: Rethinking Key Concepts in IR*, edited by Rebecca Adler-Nissen, pp. 24–44. Oxford: Routledge.

Meyer, Jane. 2009. 'The Predator War'. *New York Times*, October 26. www.newyorker.com/reporting/2009/10/26/091026fa_fact_mayer.

Miles, Anne Daugherty. 2016. 'Perspectives on Enhanced Interrogation Techniques'. Washington, DC. https://fas.org/sgp/crs/intel/R43906.pdf.

Miller, Greg. 2012. 'Plan for Hunting Terrorists Signals U.S. Intends to Keep Adding Names to Kill Lists'. *Washington Post*, 23 October.

Miller, Greg, Julie Tate, and Barton Gellman. 2013. 'Documents Reveal NSA's Extensive Involvement in Targeted Killing Program'. *Washington Post*, October 26. www.washingtonpost.com/world/national-security/documents-reveal-nsas-extensive-involvement-in-targeted-killing-program/2013/10/16/29775278-3674-11e3-8a0e-4e2cf80831fc_story.html.

Miller, Stuart Creighton. 1982. *'Benevolent Assimilation': The American Conquest of the Philippines.* New Haven, CT: Yale University Press.

Mitchell, Melanie. 2009. *Complexity: A Guided Tour.* New York: Oxford University Press.

Mitzen, Jennifer. 2006a. 'Anchoring Europe's Civilizing Identity: Habits, Capabilities and Ontological Security'. *Journal of European Public Policy* 13(March): 270–85. doi:10.1080/13501760500451709.

2006b. 'Ontological Security in World Politics: State Identity and the Security Dilemma'. *European Journal of International Relations* 12 (3): 341–70. doi:10.1177/1354066106067346.

Mitzen, Jennifer, and Randall L. Schweller. 2011. 'Knowing the Unknown Unknowns: Misplaced Certainty and the Onset of War'. *Security Studies* 20(1): 2–35.

'The Montreaux Document: On Pertinent International Legal Obligations and Good Practices for States Related to Operations of Private Military and Security Companies during Armed Conflict'. 2008. Geneva: International Committee of the Red Cross (ICRC). www.icrc.org/eng/ assets/files/other/icrc_002_0996.pdf.

Moore, George Edward. 1993. *Principia Ethica*. Cambridge: Cambridge University Press.

Morgenthau, Hans. 1967. *Politics among Nations*. New York: Knopf.

Morrow, James D. 2014. *Order within Anarchy: The Laws of War as an International Institution*. Cambridge: Cambridge University Press.

Moughty, Sarah. 2015. 'John Rizzo: The Legal Case for "Enhanced Interrogation"'. *PBS Frontline*, 19 May. www.pbs.org/wgbh/frontline/ article/john-rizzo-the-legal-case-for-enhanced-interrogation/.

Musah, Abdel-Fatau, Kayode Fayemi, and J'Kayode Fayemi. 2000. *Mercenaries: An African Security Dilemma*. London: Pluto Press.

Musgrave, Paul, and Daniel H. Nexon. 2018. 'Defending Hierarchy from the Moon to the Indian Ocean: Symbolic Capital and Political Dominance in Early Modern China and the Cold War'. *International Organization* 72(3): 591–626.

Nadelmann, Ethan A. 1990. 'Global Prohibition Regimes: The Evolution of Norms in International Society'. *International Organization* 44(4): 479–526.

National Commission on Terrorist Attacks upon the United States. 2004a. 'Intelligence Policy: Staff Statement No. 7'. Washington, DC. doi:10.1080/02684529008432037.

2004b. 'The 9/11 Commission Report: Final Report of the National Commission on Terrorist Attacks upon the United States'. Washington, DC. Available at https://books.google.ca/books?id=juJxMFmJCEMC&pr intsec=frontcover#v=onepage&q&f=false.

Nexon, Daniel H. 2009. *The Struggle for Power in Early Modern Europe: Religious Conflict, Dynastic Empires, and International Change*. Princeton, NJ: Princeton University Press.

Nexon, Daniel H., and Iver B. Neumann. 2018. 'Hegemonic-Order Theory: A Field-Theoretic Account'. *European Journal of International Relations* 24(3): 662–86. doi: 10.1177/1354066117716524.

Nexon, Daniel H., and Vincent Pouliot. 2013. '"Things of Networks": Situating ANT in International Relations'. *International Political Sociology* 7(3): 342–5. doi:10.1111/ips.12026_4.

O'Brien, Kevin A. 2007. 'What Should and What Should Not Be Regulated?' In *From Mercenaries to Market: The Rise and Regulation of Private Military Companies*, edited by Simon Chesterman and Chia Lehnardt, pp. 29–48. Oxford: Oxford University Press.

Olson, Mancur. 1965. *The Logic of Collective Action*. Cambridge, MA: Harvard University Press.

Onuf, Nicholas. 1989. *World of Our Making: Rules and Rule in Social Theory and International Relations*. Columbia: University of South Carolina Press.

Opp, Karl-Dieter. 1982. 'The Evolutionary Emergence of Norms'. *British Journal of Social Psychology* 21(2): 139–49.

Orford, Anne. 1999. 'Muscular Humanitarianism: Reading the Narratives of the New Interventionism'. *European Journal of International Law* 10 (4): 679–711.

Ortiz, Carlos. 2007. 'The Private Military Company: An Entity at the Center of Overlapping Spheres of Commercial Activity and Responsibility'. In *Private Military and Security Companies: Chances, Problems, Pitfalls and Prospects*, edited by Thomas Jäger and Gerhard Kümmel, pp. 11–22. Wiesbaden: VS Verlag für Sozialwissenschaften.

Panke, Diana, and Ulrich Petersohn. 2011. 'Why International Norms Disappear Sometimes'. *European Journal of International Relations* 18(4): 719–42. doi:10.1177/1354066111407690.

Parsons, Talcott. 1937. *The Structure of Social Action*. New York: Free Press.

Payne, Rodger A. 2001. 'Persuasion, Frames, and Norm Construction'. *European Journal of International Relations* 7(1): 37–61.

Percy, Sarah. 2007a. 'Mercenaries: Strong Norm, Weak Law'. *International Organization* 61: 367–97.

  2007b. *Mercenaries: The History of a Norm in International Relations*. Oxford: Oxford University Press.

Petersohn, Ulrich. 2011. 'The Other Side of the COIN: Private Security Companies and Counterinsurgency Operations'. *Studies in Conflict and Terrorism* 34(10): 782–801. doi:10.1080/1057610X.2011.604832.

  2014. 'Reframing the Anti-Mercenary Norm: Private Military and Security Companies and Mercenarism'. *International Journal: Canada's Journal of Global Policy Analysis* 69(4): 475–93.

Petraeus, David. 2007. 'Address from Headquarters, 10 May 2007'. Baghdad: Multi-National Force – Iraq. www.washingtonpost.com/wp-srv/nation/documents/petraeus_values_051007.pdf.

Pickard, Daniel B. 2001. 'Legalizing Assassination-Terrorism, the Central Intelligence Agency, and International Law'. *Georgia Journal of International & Comparative Law* 30: 1.

Plaw, Avery. 2006. *Targeting Terrorists: A License to Kill?* Farnham, UK: Ashgate Publishing.

Posen, Barry R. 1993. 'Nationalism, the Mass Army, and Military Power'. *International Security* 18(2): 80–124.

Pouliot, Vincent. 2007. '"Sobjectivism": Toward a Constructivist Methodology'. *International Studies Quarterly* 51: 359–84.

2008. 'The Logic of Practicality: A Theory of Practice of Security Communities'. *International Organization* 62(2): 257–88.

2010. *International Security in Practice*. Cambridge: Cambridge University Press.

2016. *International Pecking Orders*. Cambridge: Cambridge University Press.

Powell, Christopher, and François Dépelteau. 2013. 'Introduction'. In *Conceptualizing Relational Sociology*. New York: Palgrave Macmillan. doi:10.1057/9781137342652.

Pratt, Simon Frankel. 2013. '"Anyone Who Hurts Us": How the Logic of Israel's "Assassination Policy" Developed During the Aqsa Intifada'. *Terrorism and Political Violence* 25(2): 224–45. doi:10.1080/09546553.2012.657280.

2015. 'Crossing off Names: The Logic of Military Assassination'. *Small Wars & Insurgencies* 26(1): 3–24. doi:10.1080/09592318.2014.959769.

2016. 'Pragmatism as Ontology, Not (Just) Epistemology: Exploring the Full Horizon of Pragmatism as an Approach to IR Theory'. *International Studies Review* 18(3): 508–27.

2017. 'A Relational View of Ontological Security in International Relations'. *International Studies Quarterly* 61(1): 78–85.

Price, Bryan C. 2012. 'Targeting Top Terrorists'. *International Security* 36 (4): 9–46.

Price, Richard. 1995. 'A Genealogy of the Chemical Weapons Taboo'. *International Organization* 49(1): 73–103.

1997. *The Chemical Weapons Taboo*. Ithaca, NY: Cornell University Press.

2008. 'Moral Limit and Possibility in World Politics'. *International Organization* 62(2): 191–220.

'Protocol Additional to the Geneva Conventions of 12 August 1949, and Relating to the Protection of Victims of International Armed Conflicts (Protocol I), June 1977'. 1977. Geneva: International Committee of the Red Cross (ICRC).

Pugliese, Joseph. 2013. *State Violence and the Execution of Law: Biopolitical Caesurae of Torture, Black Sites, Drones.* Oxford: Routledge.

Ragazzi, Franceso. 2009. 'Governing Diasporas'. *International Political Sociology* 3(4): 378–97.

Razack, Sherene. 2008. *Casting Out: The Eviction of Muslims from Western Law and Politics.* Toronto: University of Toronto Press.

Reichertz, Jo. 2007. 'Abduction: The Logic of Discovery of Grounded Theory'. In *The Sage Handbook of Grounded Theory*, edited by A. Bryant and K. Charmaz, pp. 214–18. London: Sage.

Rejali, Darius M. 2007. *Torture and Democracy.* Princeton, NJ: Princeton University Press.

Rescher, Nicholas. 1996. *Process Metaphysics: An Introduction to Process Philosophy.* Albany: SUNY Press.

Ricoeur, Paul. 1970. *Freud and Philosophy.* New Haven, CT: Yale University Press.

Rid, Thomas. 2013. *Cyber War Will Not Take Place.* New York: Oxford University Press.

Risse, Thomas. 2000. '"Let's Argue!" Communicative Action in World Politics'. *International Organization* 54(1): 1–39. doi:10.1162/002081800551109.

    2006. 'Transnational Governance and Legitimacy'. In *Governance and Democracy: Comparing National, European and International Experiences*, edited by Arthur Benz and Yannis Papadopoulos, pp. 179–99. London: Routledge.

Risse, Thomas, Stephen C. Ropp, and Kathryn Sikkink. 1999. *The Power of Human Rights: International Norms and Domestic Change.* Cambridge: Cambridge University Press.

Rodriguez, Jose A. 2014. 'Today's CIA Critics Once Urged the Agency to Do Anything to Fight al-Qaeda'. *Washington Post*, 5 December. www.washingtonpost.com/opinions/todays-cia-critics-once-urged-the-agency-to-do-anything-to-fight-al-qaeda/2014/12/05/ac418da2-7bda-11e4-84d4-7c896b90abdc_story.html.

'Rome Statute of the International Criminal Court'. 1998. UN General Assembly.

Rosenau, William, and Austin Long. 2009. 'The Phoenix Program and Contemporary Counterinsurgency'. Santa Monica, CA: Rand Corporation. www.rand.org/pubs/occasional_papers/OP258.html.

Rosenberg, Carol. 2020. 'He Waterboarded a Detainee. Then He Had to Get the C.I.A. to Let Him Stop'. *New York Times*, 22 January. www.nytimes.com/2020/01/22/us/politics/cia-torture-interrogation-guantanamo.html.

Ruggie, John Gerard. 1975. 'International Responses to Technology: Concepts and Trends'. *International Organization* 29(3): 557–83.

1998. 'What Makes the World Hang Together? Neo-Utilitarianism and the Social Constructivist Challenge'. *International Organization* 52(4): 855–85.

Rumelili, Bahar. 2015. 'Identity and Desecuritisation: The Pitfalls of Conflating Ontological and Physical Security'. *Journal of International Relations and Development* 18(1): 52–74.

Sandholtz, Wayne. 2008. 'Dynamics of International Norm Change: Rules against Wartime Plunder'. *European Journal of International Relations* 14(1): 101–31. doi:10.1177/1354066107087766.

SASC (Committee on Armed Services, United States Senate). 2010. 'Inquiry into the Role and Oversight of Private Security Contractors in Afghanistan'. https://fas.org/irp/congress/2010_rpt/sasc-psc.pdf.

Scahill, Jeremy. 2007. *Blackwater: The Rise of the World's Most Powerful Mercenary Army*. New York: Nation Books.

2013. *Dirty Wars: The World Is a Battlefield*. New York: Nation Books.

Schatzki, Theodore R. 1996. *Social Practices: A Wittgensteinian Approach to Human Activity and the Social*. Cambridge: Cambridge University Press.

Schatzki, Theodore R., Karin Knorr Cetina, and Eike von Savingy, eds. 2001. *The Practice Turn in Contemporary Theory*. London: Routledge. doi:10.1016/S0956-5221(03)00029-0.

Schimmelfennig, Frank. 2001. 'The Community Trap: Liberal Norms, Rhetorical Action, and the Eastern Enlargement of the European Union'. *International Organization* 55(1): 47–80.

Schmidt, Sebastian. 2014. 'Foreign Military Presence and the Changing Practice of Sovereignty: A Pragmatist Explanation of Norm Change'. *American Political Science Review* 108(4): 817–29.

Schmitt, Michael N. 1992. 'State-Sponsored Assassination in International and Domestic Law'. *Yale Journal of International Law* 17: 609.

Scott, James C. 1985. *Weapons of the Weak: Everyday Forms of Peasant Resistance*. New Haven, CT: Yale University Press.

Searle, John R. 1995. *The Construction of Social Reality*. New York: Free Press.

Shain, Yossi, and Aharon Barth. 2003. 'Diasporas and International Relations Theory'. *International Organization* 57(3): 449–79. doi:10.1017/S0020818303573015.

Shannon, Vaughn P. 2000. 'Norms Are What States Make of Them: The Political Psychology of Norm Violation'. *International Studies Quarterly* 44(2): 293–316.

Shaw, Ian G. R. 2013. 'Predator Empire: The Geopolitics of US Drone Warfare'. *Geopolitics* 18(3): 536–59.

Shlomo, Avineri. 1981. *The Making of Modern Zionism: Intellectual Origins of the Jewish State*. London: Weidenfeld and Nicolson.

Shoemaker, David P. 2008. 'Unveiling Charlie: U.S. Interrogators' Creative Successes against Insurgents'. In *Interrogation: World War II, Vietnam, and Iraq*, pp. 77–146. Washington, DC: National Defense Intelligence College.

SIGIR. 2009. '*Field Commanders See Improvements in Controlling and Coordinating Private Security Contractor Missions in Iraq*.' Arlington, VA.

Singer, Peter Warren. 2008. *Corporate Warriors: The Rise of the Privatized Military Industry*. Updated edition. Ithaca, NY: Cornell University Press.

Soldz, Stephen. 2011. 'Fighting Torture and Psychologist Complicity'. *Peace Review* 23(1): 12–20. doi:10.1080/10402659.2011.548240.

Solis, Gary D. 2010. *The Law of Armed Conflict*. Cambridge: Cambridge University Press.

Solomon, Ty. 2013. 'Attachment, Tautology, and Ontological Security'. *Critical Studies on Security* 1(1): 130–2.

   2014. 'The Affective Underpinnings of Soft Power'. *European Journal of International Relations* 20(3): 720–41.

Soufan, Ali H. 2011. *The Black Banners*. New York: W. W. Norton.

Spracher, William, ed. 2008. *Interrogation: World War II, Vietnam, and Iraq*. Washington, DC: National Defense Intelligence College Press.

SSCI. 2014. 'Committee Study of the Central Intelligence Agency's Detention and Interrogation Program, Findings and Conclusions'. Washington, DC.

Steele, Brent J. 2005. 'Ontological Security and the Power of Self-Identity: British Neutrality and the American Civil War'. *Review of International Studies* 31: 519–40. doi:10.1017/S0260210505006613.

   2008. *Ontological Security in International Relations: Self-Identity and the IR State*. Oxford: Routledge. doi:10.4324/9780203018200.

   2010. *Defacing Power*. Ann Arbor: University of Michigan Press.

   2017. 'Organizational Processes and Ontological (in)Security: Torture, the CIA and the United States'. *Cooperation and Conflict* 52(1): 69–89. doi: https://doi.org/10.1177/0010836716653156.

Steinmetz, George. 2013. 'Toward Socioanalysis: The "Traumatic Kernel" of Psychoanalysis and Neo-Bourdieusian Theory'. In *Bourdieu and Historical Analysis*, edited by Philip S. Gorski, pp. 108–30. Durham, NC: Duke University Press.

Steinmo, Sven. 2008. 'Historical Institutionalism'. In *Approaches and Methodologies in the Social Sciences*, edited by Donatella Della Porta and Michael Keating, pp. 118–38. Cambridge: Cambridge University Press.

Subotic, Jelena. 2015. 'Narrative, Ontological Security, and Foreign Policy Change'. *Foreign Policy Analysis* 12(4): 610–27. doi:10.1111/fpa.12089.

Subotic, Jelena, and Ayse Zarakol. 2013. 'Cultural Intimacy in International Relations'. *European Journal of International Relations* 19(4): 915–38.

Tannenwald, Nina. 1999. 'The Nuclear Taboo: The United States and the Normative Basis of Nuclear Non-Use'. *International Organization* 53 (3): 433–68. doi:10.1162/002081899550959.

2007. *The Nuclear Taboo: The United States and the Non-Use of Nuclear Weapons since 1945*. Vol. 87. Cambridge: Cambridge University Press.

Tarrow, S. 2010. 'The Strategy of Paired Comparison: Toward a Theory of Practice'. *Comparative Political Studies* 43(2): 230–59. doi:10.1177/0010414009350044.

Tenet, George. 2007. *At the Center of the Storm: My Years at the CIA*. New York: Harper Collins.

Tenet, George, Porter Goss, John McLaughlin, Albert Calland, and Stephen Kappes. 2014. 'Ex-CIA Directors: Interrogations Saved Lives'. *Wall Street Journal*, 10 December. www.wsj.com/articles/cia-interrogations-saved-lives-1418142644.

Thelen, Kathleen, and Sven Steinmo. 1992. 'Historic Institutionalism in Comparative Politics'. In *Structuring Politics: Historical Institutionalism in Comparative Analysis*, edited by Sven Steinmo, Kathleen Thelen, and Frank Longsreth, 1–32. Cambridge: Cambridge University Press.

Thomas, Gary. 2010. 'Doing Case Study: Abduction Not Induction, Phronesis Not Theory'. *Qualitative Inquiry* 16(7): 575–82.

Thomas, Ward. 2000. 'The Case of International Assassination'. *International Security* 25(1): 105–33.

2001. *The Ethics of Destruction*. Ithaca, NY: Cornell University Press.

Thomson, Janice E. 1994. *Mercenaries, Pirates, and Sovereigns: State-Building and Extra-Territorial Violence in Early Modern Europe*. Princeton, NJ: Princeton University Press.

Tilly, Charles. 1999. 'The Trouble with Stories'. In *The Social Worlds of Higher Education: Handbook for Teaching in a New Century*, edited by Bernice Pescosolido and Ronald Aminzade, 256–70. Thousand Oaks, CA: Pine Forge Press.

Timmermans, Stefan, and Iddo Tavory. 2012. 'Theory Construction in Qualitative Research: From Grounded Theory to Abductive Analysis'. *Sociological Theory* 30(3): 167–86.

Towns, Ann E. 2012. 'Norms and Social Hierarchies: Understanding International Policy Diffusion "from Below"'. *International Organization* 66(2): 179–209.

United States Senate Select Committee on Intelligence. 2014. 'The Committee Study of the Central Intelligence Agency's Detention and Interrogation Program'. Washington, DC.

'Universal Declaration of Human Rights'. 1948. UN General Assembly.

US Department of Justice. 2012. Department of Justice White Paper.

Van Krieken, Robert. 1998. *Norbert Elias*. London: Routledge.

Van Munster, Rens. 2007. 'Review Essay: Security on a Shoestring: A Hitchhiker's Guide to Critical Schools of Security in Europe'. *Cooperation and Conflict* 42(2): 235–43.

Von Wright, Georg Henrik. 1963. *Norm and Action*. London: Routledge and Keegan Paul.

1971. *Explanation and Understanding*. Ithaca, NY: Cornell University Press.

Wahlbeck, Osten. 2002. 'The Concept of Diaspora as an Analytical Tool in the Study of Refugee Communities'. *Journal of Ethnic and Migration Studies* 28(2): 221–38. doi:10.1080/1369183022012430.

Walker, Jeremy, and Melinda Cooper. 2011. 'Genealogies of Resilience from Systems Ecology to the Political Economy of Crisis Adaptation'. *Security Dialogue* 42(2): 143–60.

Walldorf, C. William. 2010. 'Argument, Institutional Process, and Human Rights Sanctions in Democratic Foreign Policy'. *European Journal of International Relations* 16(4): 639–62. doi:10.1177/1354066109344015.

Weber, Martin. 2014. 'Between "Isses" and "Oughts": IR Constructivism, Critical Theory, and the Challenge of Political Philosophy'. *European Journal of International Relations* 20(2): 516–43.

Weber, Max. 1997. *The Methodology of the Social Sciences*. Edited by Edward A. Shils and Harry A. Finch. New York: Free Press.

Weiner, Tim. 2007. *Legacy of Ashes: The History of the CIA*. New York: Doubleday.

Wendt, Alexander. 1987. 'The Agent-Structure Problem in International Relations Theory'. *International Organization* 41(3): 335–70.

1999. *Social Theory of International Politics*. Cambridge: Cambridge University Press.

Whittle, Richard. 2014. *Predator: The Secret Origins of the Drone Revolution*. New York: Henry Holt.

Widmaier, Wesley W., Mark Blyth, and Leonard Seabrooke. 2007. 'Exogenous Shocks or Endogenous Constructions? The Meanings of Wars and Crises'. *International Studies Quarterly* 51(4): 747–59.

Widmaier, Wesley W., and Susan Park. 'Differences beyond Theory: Structural, Strategic, and Sentimental Approaches to Normative Change'. *International Studies Perspectives* 13(3): 123–34.

Wiener, Antje. 2004. 'Contested Compliance: Interventions on the Normative Structure of World Politics'. *European Journal of International Relations* 10(2): 189–234. doi:10.1177/1354066104042934.

2007. 'The Dual Quality of Norms and Governance beyond the State: Sociological and Normative Approaches to "Interaction"'. *Critical Review of International Social and Political Philosophy* 10(1): 47–69.

2008. *The Invisible Constitution of Politics: Contested Norms and International Encounters*. Cambridge: Cambridge University Press. doi:10.1017/CBO9781107415324.004.

2009. 'Enacting Meaning-in-use: Qualitative Research on Norms and International Relations'. *Review of International Studies* 35(1): 175–93.

2014. *A Theory of Contestation*. Heidelberg: Springer.

Wight, Colin. 2006. *Agents, Structures, and International Relations: Politics as Ontology*. Cambridge and New York: Cambridge University Press.

Wilcox, Lauren. 2017. 'Embodying Algorithmic War: Gender, Race, and the Posthuman in Drone Warfare'. *Security Dialogue* 48(1): 11–28. https://doi.org/10.1177/0967010616657947.

Winch, Peter. 1958. *The Idea of a Social Science and Its Relation to Philosophy*. 3rd edition. London: Routledge and Kegan Paul.

Winston, Carla. 2018. 'Norm Structure, Diffusion, and Evolution: A Conceptual Approach'. *European Journal of International Relations* 24(3): 638–61. https://doi.org/10.1177/1354066117720794.

Wittgenstein, Ludwig. 1958. *Philosophical Investigations*. Oxford: Basil Blackwell.

Yoo, John. 2014. 'Yoo: The Feinstein Report Cannot Deny a Clear Record of Success'. *Time Magazine*, 9 December. https://time.com/3626957/yoo-senate-torture-report-feinstein/.

Youngs, Gillian. 2006. 'Feminist International Relations in the Age of the War on Terror: Ideologies, Religions and Conflict'. *International Feminist Journal of Politics* 8(1): 3–18.

Zanotti, Laura. 2014. 'Questioning Universalism, Devising an Ethics without Foundations: An Exploration of International Relations Ontologies and Epistemologies'. *Journal of International Political Theory* 11(3): 277–95. doi:10.1177/1755088214555044.

Zarakol, Ayse. 2010. 'Ontological (In)Security and State Denial of Historical Crimes: Turkey and Japan'. *International Relations* 24(1): 3–23. doi:10.1177/0047117809359040.

Zarate, Juan Carlos. 1998. 'The Emergence of a New Dog of War: Private International Security Companies, International Law, and the New World Disorder'. *Stanford Journal of International Law* 34: 75–162.

Zellman, Ariel. 2015. 'Framing Consensus: Evaluating the Narrative Specificity of Territorial Indivisibility'. *Journal of Peace Research* 52 (4): 492–507.

Zengel, Patricia. 1991. 'Assassination and the Law of Armed Conflict'. *Military Law Review* 134: 123–65.

1992. 'Assassination and the Law of Armed Conflict'. *Mercer Law Review* 43(2): 615–44.

Zenko, Micah. 2012. 'The Seven Deadly Sins of John Brennan'. *Foreign Policy*, 19 September.

2013. *Reforming U.S. Drone Strike Policies – Council of Foreign Relations, Special Report No. 65*. Washington, DC: Council of Foreign Relations.

Index

Milton Keynes UK
Ingram Content Group UK Ltd.
UKHW020612291023
431526UK00015B/62